SOLIAH: THE SARA JANE OLSON STORY

SoLiAh

THE SARA JANE OLSON STORY

Sharon Darby Hendry

Cable Publishing, Inc.

BLOOMINGTON, MINNESOTA

Cable Publishing
Post Office Box 20328
Bloomington, MN 55420 U.S.A.

Printed in the United States of America

Library of Congress Cataloging-in-Publication Data
Hendry, Sharon Darby
    SoLiAh, The Sara Jane Olson Story
    By Sharon Darby Hendry—1st edition

Includes photographs and references.
ISBN 1-893088-35-9

Library of Congress Control Number: 2002090093

Cover Design by Axon Garside Hill
Text Design and Composition by Stanton Publication Services
Printed by Bang Printing
Photographs courtesy of family members; AP/World Wide Photos;
San Gabriel Valley newspaper; *Sacramento Bee* newspaper; Jon Opsahl;
Barnesville Record Review; FBI; Bruce Hendry; and author's personal
collection.

For my first granddaughter,
Olivia Darby Parish

Contents

Cast of Supporting Characters

✎ Family

Kathleen Soliah (Kathy, Jessica Henderson, Kathleen Anger, Nancy Bennett, Linda Bernasconi, Catherine Beggs, Michal Ann Mora, Sara Jane Olson): Symbionese Liberation Army (SLA) fugitive from Los Angeles police and the FBI for 23 years. She was arrested in St. Paul, Minnesota, in June 1999.

Gerald (Fred) Peterson: Sara Jane Olson's husband, a physician she married in 1980 who claims to know nothing about his wife's past.

Martin Soliah: Kathy's father.

Elsie Engstrom Soliah: Kathy's mother.

Steven Soliah: Kathy's brother. Helped to support the SLA and his lover Patty Hearst when they hid from authorities. He was accused, tried, and acquitted of robbing the Crocker National Bank in Carmichael, California, where a woman, Myrna Opsahl, was murdered.

Josephine Soliah: Kathy's sister. Helped support the SLA and Patty Hearst. She marries alleged bombing expert and bank robber Michael Bortin.

Michael Bortin: Josephine's husband, Kathy's brother-in-law. In 1972, he was arrested and charged with possession of explosives. He spent eighteen months in jail. A leader of the SDS on the Berkeley campus, he was a friend of Steven, Josephine, and Kathy before Patricia Hearst's kidnapping. Later, he joined the SLA/New World Liberation Front.

James Kilgore (Jim): He was Kathy Soliah's boyfriend in the seventies. Along with Soliah, he was also indicted for planting bombs under police cars in 1975. As of this publication he is still a fugitive from authorities.

⮩ SDS (Students for a Democratic Society)

Rennie Davis: Cofounder of Students for a Democratic Society with Tom Hayden. Responsible for May Day riots in Washington, D.C. in 1971.

Tom Hayden: Cofounder of SDS with Rennie Davis. Hayden was active in the American Civil Rights movement, and an avid anti-war protester. He was a member of the New Left—that generation's conviction that they could re-create a new socialist vision without "Stalin's stigma."

Abbie Hoffman: With cofounder Jerry Rubin, Hoffman formed a group called the Yippies (Youth International Party) in 1967.

Bernardine Dohrn: She believed that the SDS was not violent enough and became the leader of the Weathermen, a terrorist group that planted bombs all over the United States in the early 1970s. Dohrn was on the FBI's most wanted list for eleven years before turning herself in. She came to a rally in Minnesota in 2000 to defend Sara Jane Olson.

⮩ SLA (Symbionese Liberation Army)

Donald DeFreeze (Cinque): An escaped convict from Soledad prison near Monterey, California, DeFreeze conceived of the SLA. Its mission was to free all "oppressed people from United States Imperialism." The SLA was responsible for the murder of Oakland School Superintendent Marcus Foster and for the kidnapping of publishing heiress Patricia Hearst. Donald DeFreeze would be one of six SLA members to be killed in a Los Angeles police shootout in 1974.

Angela Atwood (Gelina): A core member of the SLA, she was Kathy Soliah's best friend in the early 1970s. Atwood was also killed in the 1974 police shootout.

Camilla Hall (Gabi): An artist and poet from St. Peter, Minnesota. Hall was killed in the shootout.

Emily Schwartz Harris (Yolanda): Along with her husband, Bill Harris, and Patty Hearst, the only remaining members of the SLA after the shootout until the Soliahs, Jim Kilgore and Michael Bortin agreed to help them. She was jailed for eight years for kidnapping Patty Hearst.

William Harris (Bill, Teko): Emily's husband, he was the new leader of the SLA—now called the New World Liberation Front—after the shootout, in which six of his comrades were killed. With help from his new "Second Team," he, Emily, and Patty Hearst would be able to elude authorities for seventeen months. He was later jailed for eight years for kidnapping Patty Hearst.

Patricia Campbell Hearst (Patty, Tania): Publishing heiress kidnapped by the SLA in February 1974 when she was nineteen years old. Allegedly tortured and brainwashed, she would later participate in group activities that included the Hibernia Bank robbery. She would spend one and a half years in prison before President Carter commuted her sentence in 1979. She was pardoned by President Bill Clinton in 2001.

Russell Little (Osi): Convicted of killing Marcus Foster. The SLA hoped they could trade Patty Hearst for Little.

Joe Remiro (Bo): Convicted of killing Marcus Foster. The SLA hoped they could trade Patty Hearst for Remiro.

Nancy Ling Perry (Fahizah): Killed in the 1974 police shootout.

Patricia Mizmoon Soltysik (Zoya): Camilla Hall's lover. Killed in the 1974 police shootout.

Willie Wolfe (Cujo): Killed in the 1974 police shootout.

⌐ Defense

Lawyers: Shawn Chapman: Other clients include O.J. Simpson.

Stuart Hanlon: Former clients include William and Emily Harris, Joe Remiro, and Geronimo Pratt. He quit Sara Jane Olson's case early on for personal reasons, but continues to vocally support her.

Tony Serra: Her last attorney (presumably). Along with Chapman, he would represent her in court in the bombing trial. Former clients include William and Emily Harris and the Black Panthers.

⌐ LAPD (Los Angeles Police Department)

Captain Mervin King: On the scene at the Los Angeles shootout. He also investigated the pipe bombs underneath the Los Angeles police cars in 1975.

Officer Tom King: Mervin's son, who followed through with the pipe bombing case to find closure for his retired father.

Detective David Reyes: Assigned the case by Tom King. Discovered that Kathleen Soliah was Sara Jane Olson living in Minnesota. He was one of the authorities who arrested her.

Detective Mike Fanning: David Reyes' partner. He was one of the authorities that arrested her.

⌐ FBI (Federal Bureau of Investigation)

Agent Mary Hogan: Arrested Kathleen Soliah.

⌐ Websites for additional references:
   www.soliah-sla.com
   www.glensheensdaughter.com
links to these websites:
   www.saraolsondefense.com
   www.soliah.com
   www.lektrik.com/sinc/
   www.myrnaopsahl.com

Pertinent Political and Radical Players

⌐ SDS

Students for a Democratic Society was founded in 1960 by Tom Hayden, a civil rights activist and an avid war protester. The SDS began as a nonviolent organization of young people who were against America's "imperialist aggression" in regards to the Vietnam War.

⌐ Weathermen

After the 1968 Democratic convention, Bernardine Dohrn was elected president of the SDS, which soon died out to evolve into a more militant and violent group of revolutionaries. They called themselves the Weathermen.

⌐ Venceremos

The name came from Fidel Castro's rallying cry during the Cuban Revolution: "Patria o muerte, venceremos!" or, "Nation or death, we shall triumph!" A committed revolutionary group, which was in the forefront of Bay Area demonstrations against the Vietnam War in 1971. The Venceremos described themselves as a "disciplined fighting organization guided by Marxism–Leninism–Mao-Tse-tung thought." Members were mostly prison inmates. The SLA would evolve from this group.

⌐ SLA

Symbionese Liberation Army was founded in 1973 by Donald DeFreeze (Cinque), an escaped convict from California's Soledad Prison. The SLA murdered Oakland School Superintendent

Marcus Foster, but the kidnapping of publishing heiress Patty Hearst is the crime that put them on the map.

⌐ *NWLF*

New World Liberation Front was conceived by Eldridge Cleaver in 1969. In 1975, the SLA attached itself to this group, which had a thirst for action and no time for political discussion. The NWLF randomly planted bombs all over California in the mid-1970s to protest "corporations that exploit the people." They sent communiqués claiming responsibility for more than seven bombs. In fact, in 1975, one bomb went off in California every sixteen days. Kathleen Soliah allegedly supported this group.

Setting the Scene

Los Angeles Times
Thursday, August 22, 1975

2 Bombs Aimed at L.A. Police Cars Defused

Bomb squad experts this morning defused two pipe bombs apparently intended to blow up police cars, authorities reported. The devices, both placed on the ground at locations in East Los Angeles and Hollywood, were similar, but no connection has yet been established between the two. The discovery of the bombs here followed explosions in San Rafael Wednesday night that destroyed two Marin County sheriff's cars outside the county's Civic Center. The cars were unoccupied and no one was hurt.

The New World Liberation Front claimed responsibility for the San Rafael blasts that went off five minutes apart in front of the courthouse where six San Quentin Prison inmates are on trial for a bloody attempted escape four years ago. The radical group also said it bombed a police car in an Oakland suburb August 13. No one was hurt in that explosion.

The first device defused in Los Angeles this morning was found shortly after midnight in a restaurant parking lot at Sunset Blvd. and Orange Ave. by patrons leaving the establishment. The bomb, wrapped in plastic that was sealed with a metal clothespin, was found on the ground where a police car had been parked minutes before. The restaurant was evacuated and a four-block area was sealed off while the bomb squad defused the device.

Hollywood Captain Mervin King then put out the alert to the other police divisions to check under all vehicles for explosives. That search turned up the second bomb at about 2:30 a.m. under a police car outside the Hollenbeck Division at 2111 E. 1st St. It was also wrapped in plastic and was defused by the bomb squad. No group has yet claimed responsibility for the placing of the bombs.

St. Paul Pioneer Press
Friday, June 18, 1999

Suspected Fugitive Held Without Bail

When authorities began hunting Kathleen Ann Soliah 23 years ago, she was a radical who allegedly planted bombs in police cars. By the time they tracked her down, she was a pacifist and mother behind the wheel of a minivan.

In the two decades between, investigators say she transformed from a radical fugitive into an upper-middle-class mother whose life was remarkable mainly for her social activism. She renamed herself Sara Jane Olson, married a Harvard-educated physician, raised three daughters, pursued an acting career and showed little apparent fear of appearing in public.

Now, the woman known as Sara Jane Olson has been arrested and faces extradition to California to answer for the crimes of Kathleen Soliah. Meanwhile, even friends who have known her for decades struggle to reconcile the image of the radical fugitive with the woman they knew.

Soliah, a former member of the Symbionese Liberation Army, disappeared in 1976 after being indicted on charges of conspiracy to murder police officers in Los Angeles. Authorities believe the bombs were planted in retaliation for a fiery shootout in 1974 that killed six SLA members, including one of Soliah's best friends.

Prologue

On May 15, 1999, the Symbionese Liberation Army (SLA) terrorist group of the 1970s was featured on the "America's Most Wanted" (AMW) national television show to commemorate the twenty-fifth anniversary of the shootout in Los Angeles between LA cops and six members of the SLA—the group that had kidnapped heiress Patricia Hearst.

The show aired an edited version of actual TV news footage that had been broadcast live, in its entirety, on the evening news on May 17, 1974. On that day, a shabby neighborhood of Victorian-style houses, stucco bungalows, and small apartments in the Compton neighborhood of South Central Los Angeles filled television screens. Inside one of the houses were the most wanted fugitives in America, six members of the SLA armed with shotguns, hand grenades, and jugs of gasoline.

As viewers watched in horror, Flak-jacketed police officers wearing black jumpsuits and helmets ducked behind cars, trees, and power poles with their rifles poised for battle. One Los Angeles policeman yelled into a bullhorn, "Come out with your hands up. The house is surrounded." After two minutes, another policeman dropped to his knees and fired a tear-gas canister into the window of a small, yellow, stucco house, which signaled the opening of a furious battle that would last for almost two hours.

At one point, about six members of a family scampered out of the window of a neighboring house while a policeman with an M16 rifle guarded their retreat.

Terrified women darted from nearby houses screaming, arms flailing, as they begged SWAT teams not to shoot them. Children jumped off porch railings and ran every which way to get out of the line of fire.

As cameras panned the area, a crowd of about 200 people gathered about a half a block away and cheered until more tear-gas shells were lobbed into the yellow house and a cloud of eye-searing gas wafted into their midst. With shouts of anguish, they fled to the nearest source of water to rinse their eyes.

The house started to burn at 6:30 P.M. Viewers watched as flames gutted a house and an apartment building on either side of the besieged structure. Four police helicopters circled overhead, often swooping low through the billows of black smoke. The neighborhood looked like a scene from a war, with constant shooting. There was the pop-pop-pop of the lawmen's semiautomatic weapons, interrupted at times by the staccato bursts of machine-gun fire coming from windows and vents in the house. Abruptly, at 6:45 P.M., the shooting stopped, but the fire burned on.

The first two bodies to be discovered, one white and one black, had cartridge bandoliers strapped to their bodies. The flames had caused the ammunition in the bandoliers to fire. At the end of the siege, 9,000 rounds of ammunition had been used and the six members of the SLA who were in the house were dead. Most of them were burned beyond recognition. One of the six who died was Angela Atwood.

The AMW narrative continued: Fifteen months after the shootout, in August 1975, pipe bombs were found beneath two Los Angeles police cars. Authorities believed that the pipe bombs had been placed under the police cars in retaliation for (Kathleen's friend) Angela Atwood's death. The AMW segment also showed a re-enactment of a police car being blown to bits by a pipe bomb similar to the one allegedly planted in 1975 by Kathleen Soliah, whom the FBI had been seeking for 23 years. Then AMW displayed Wanted Posters for Kathleen Soliah with digitalized, age-enhanced photographs of how she would look today. After the story aired, nineteen people called in to identify her. Those calls led authorities to St. Paul, Minnesota.

/// Sara Jane Olson lived in Highland Park, one of St. Paul's most upscale neighborhoods, with stucco and brick homes, professional landscaping, and manicured lawns. Her five-bedroom, four-bath, Tudor-style home was one of the most impressive that lined Hillcrest Avenue, with red trimmed window frames and ivy that climbed up the chimney, sprawled out over the outside walls, and wrapped around the space over the front door. Zinnias and a massive maple tree adorned her front yard. Her neighbors included a diplomat, lawyers, accountants, bankers, authors, and doctors like her husband, Gerald (Fred) Peterson.

Sara Jane Olson's friends regarded her as an intelligent woman, a doer, who was generous with her time and her spirit. She performed many social services in her community. She read regularly to the blind and prepared meals for the homeless. She acted in local theater plays and narrated the Christmas pageant at Minnehaha United Methodist Church, where she was a member. She was an avid jogger and had completed a marathon. In her neighborhood, she had a reputation for being a gourmet cook and wowed the neighbors every time they held a potluck neighborhood dinner. She was noted for her "foot-thick" cheesecake. She hosted Democratic fundraisers for all of her favorite candidates. She was also the mother of three teenage daughters.

On June 16, 1999, a month after the AMW airing, at 8:15 A.M., Sara Jane backed her family's 1998, gold Plymouth minivan out of her garage. It was a cool day for June, with scattered showers predicted. (A local forecaster had described the day as "unsettled.") On this morning, she was on her way to teach citizenship and English as a second language to a class of immigrants. She took her usual route, heading east on Hillcrest and north on Snelling to Niles Avenue. Three law enforcement agencies—the LAPD, the FBI, and the St. Paul Police—were watching her. Her house had been under surveillance for twenty-four hours.

As she approached Niles Avenue, flashing lights of a police car signaled her to pull over. All at once, a group of plainclothes men approached her van while police cruisers blocked the front and back of her car. At 8:21 A.M., FBI Agent Mary Hogan approached the minivan and Sara Jane rolled down the window. She looked calm at first.

"What's wrong, officer?" she asked. Then she looked in the rearview mirror and saw the other police cars pull up.

Agent Hogan showed her credentials to Sara Jane Olson. "FBI, Kathleen," she said. *"It's over."*

Act One

"Nothing in the world is more dangerous than a sincere ignorance and conscientious stupidity."

— MARTIN LUTHER KING JR.

Growing Up

Even as a child, Kathleen Ann Soliah (pronounced: SOH-lee-ah, accent on the first syllable) had a flair for the dramatic, the unusual, for leading her own show. At the age of three, she was organizing other kids in neighborhood performances. Though she was a tomboy, preferring the monkey bars to the swings, she could play the part of the little lady as well. One cousin remembers Kathy visiting, dressed up and wearing gloves. She was polite and proper. Even after being offered some lemonade, she never took off her gloves.

By eight, Kathy was using her imagination and leadership qualities to run the school playground. A classmate remembers her making up games and plays and assigning the roles: "You be the mom, you be the little brother." "She was smart as a whip," said her great-aunt Alvara, "too smart for her own good."

Kathy was born in Fargo, North Dakota, on January 16, 1947, but she spent the first years of her life in a town twenty miles to the east, in a two-story corner house in Barnesville, Minnesota. Barnesville is hardly the place one associates with bomb plots or terrorism, secret lives or famous crime cases. The town would rather be known for its annual Potato Days Festival, with potato picking and peeling contests. It's a peaceful town with community-minded people and events. In the late 1940s and early 1950s, Barnesville's population hovered near 1,600. On the edge of a North Dakota prairie, farming was the biggest industry, and St. Paul, Minnesota's state capital, was 250 miles to the southeast.

Kathy's father, Martin (Marty) Soliah had grown up in a similar farming community—Hatton, North Dakota, on a farm about an hour northwest of Fargo, but he'd left that town to earn his fortune. He became a soldier during World War II, serving in the American ski troops for a year, after which he transferred to the Air Corps. As a fighter pilot, he flew P-38s. He used to brag that he'd flown his plane underneath the Golden Gate Bridge.

After the war, he sold toothbrushes in Chicago for a year before using the GI Bill to get more education. He married a young woman named Elsie Engstrom, and took some graduate courses in 1946 in physical education at the University of Minnesota. He said that his dream was not to hold a big-time coaching position but to someday coach at a "medium-sized college close to a trout stream."

To attain that dream, he had to work his way up. He was hired by Barnesville High School as both a teacher and athletic coach. Marty and Elsie moved to Barnesville, where Marty taught boys' Physical Education and served as assistant football coach, track coach, and head basketball coach. That year (1947), the Soliahs' first child, Kathleen, was born.

Elsie Soliah was tall and slender, described by some as nervous, on edge, and high-strung. Her husband was the man in the limelight. She stayed behind him, or at home, rarely coming to faculty parties or events, but she was busy—nearly two years later, in August 1948, Steven was born. Three years later, Josephine arrived, Kathy's new baby sister. Lance arrived two years after that.

Kathy grew up long and lanky, with strawberry blond hair, usually tied up in braids. She loved to cook and would follow the actions of both her mother and her father around the kitchen. Her mother taught her to bake, but she called her father "a great cook." He could concoct recipes without the benefit of a cookbook, as well as manage to dirty every pot and pan in the house.

At her grandmother Soliah's Norwegian kitchen, all meals were served with coffee. Kathy began drinking the brew at five. Grandma Soliah's luscious meals were all homemade with fresh ingredients, chickens from the coop and milk from the cow barn pail. Kathy came to associate good times and community with food.

The Soliahs were Lutheran, so Kathy grew up used to the rhythms and teachings of the conservative Lutheran church. Marty's politics were just as conservative; he was a tried and true Republican.

Throughout Kathy's early years, Marty was becoming more visible in the community, known by all the junior high and high school athletes. The boys with athletic ability found him inspirational and looked to him as a mentor.

Other former students remembered him giving them piggyback rides in the gym at a seventh grade party. He drove a '41 Ford back then. "It wasn't much of a car," Marty remembered. "I like fishing and hunting, and it was a good car for that. One of its doors was knocked off when it rolled down a hill while I was fishing. I welded the door back, and it was always difficult getting in the car." The students fondly recalled Mr. Soliah's jalopy, and how he'd drive up to a full-service gas station and command in his famed one-liner fashion: "Fill it up with oil and check the gas!"

One Barnesville resident philosophized about Marty: "I don't know if Marty is a great coach, or a good coach. A lot depends on the material a coach has to work with. But Marty sure gets the most from his material. Marty is just the kind of man a boy will play his heart out for."

Track was Marty's favorite sport because, he said, "you can see a boy without too much ability work hard, and really obtain something. That gives me a lot of satisfaction. Also I think boys have more fun at track. They have time to meet the players on the opposing teams, get to know them, joke around. At other sports, you just play the game and then go right home. I think track often helps heal the frictions that other sports establish."

In March 1955, the *Barnesville Record Review* hailed Marty for his coaching successes. The headline read, "Electric Toothbrushes and Winning Basketball Teams Are Soliah Traditions." Marty talked to the reporter about his triumphs and his disappointments. He said that his biggest thrill was when one of his students broke the Region 880 (track record) for Barnesville in 1954. The race he ran was beautiful, Marty observed, everything "just right." The article stated that Soliah had suffered his biggest disappointment in 1953: "I lost half of my ball club for infractions of training rules. That could have been a good ball club, but now we'll never know how good."

Those who liked Soliah remembered him fondly; others merely stayed silent. Gerald Parker was a thirteen-year-old son of the superintendent of schools in Barnesville, Minnesota, when Marty was a teacher and coach. These were his words:

"Martin Soliah may have been a winning football coach but he was a loser when it came to being a teacher in charge of young boys.

"Soliah's father was an abusive, sneering, law-breaking school teacher who left a trail of damaged psyches in his wake. He was my junior high school physical education teacher and I was one of many overweight and uncoordinated kids who he delighted in abusing and humiliating in public. He was not above walking through the locker room during shower time and commenting upon the physical development of the thirteen-year-old boys in his charge. This man's influence made me fearful of any participation in any organized sports during my entire high school experience. After we moved from Barnesville, I still would become physically ill before any phy-ed class and still have flashbacks to the humiliation that I experienced from this man. I later went on to become a military officer and proved myself equal to all of the physical demands that that experience entailed."

In his interview, when Soliah was asked about the key to his success, he wouldn't answer, but smiled briefly, looked at the ground and muttered, "I don't know."

A classmate who sat in the desk next to Kathy remembered her as quiet and moody. That's why the class was shocked one day when she broke out singing, "There's no business like show business. . . ." Kathy's love for acting was obvious early on.

In third grade at Florence Atkinson Elementary School, she was cast as an angel in a Christmas play, one of the few times she wore her hair down. It was her first memorable performance. Around the time that she was discovering her talents and realizing her first taste of fame, her father accepted a job in Lompoc, California.

Gerald Parker recalled an incident that occurred on the day the Soliahs were leaving Barnesville: "My father got a call from some astute neighbors or school officials telling him that Marty had loaded hundreds of dollars of school property, chairs, tables, and a desk, into a yellow school bus, which he drove home. I rode along with my dad to the Soliah house. We picked up the school janitor and the local constable on the way. When we got there, the policeman stood aside as my dad informed Marty that the school property would have to be unloaded. The presence of the police officer must have intimidated Marty Soliah because he didn't argue." The boy's father and the janitor unloaded all of the school property and it was returned to the school. Nothing came of the incident, and the Soliahs departed for California to begin a new life.

They stayed in Lompoc only a year, and then it was on to Palmdale, California where the Soliahs would finally settle. Marty had been offered a job as a teacher and coach at Palmdale High School.

Palmdale is located in the southern region of the Antelope Valley, about sixty miles northeast of downtown Los Angeles, off Highway 14, the Antelope Valley Freeway. Nearly six times larger than Barnesville with a population of about 12,000 people, Palmdale was more cosmopolitan. It would earn the label the "Aerospace Capital of the World" in the early eighties. Temperatures range from around ninety-eight degrees in the summer to fifty-six degrees in the winter, averaging only four inches of snow—a far cry from Barnesville, Minnesota. If Marty still had the dream to fish in a trout stream, he was hard-pressed to find it in the desert. Kathy's trips to see her grandparents and cousins in North Dakota were now few and far between.

Kathy Soliah, though, held on to her dream. "I'm going to be a famous actress," she told her friend in junior high, "and everyone will know me." A track star and student actress, Kathy dreamed of fame.

She turned thirteen in 1960, when John F. Kennedy, at forty-three years of age, became the youngest man ever elected president of the United States. His youth, his good looks, his charisma, and his attractive family made good press—Americans young and old felt proud of their first family.

During JFK's presidency, Cold War tensions between Communist and Western nations increased considerably. During the 1800s and early 1900s, many foreign countries, especially France, had colonized parts of Vietnam. After World War II, a bloody seven-and-a-half year struggle had raged between the Communist Vietnamese and the French for control of the land. In 1954, the French essentially lost the war and gave up their attempt to control northern Vietnam. As a result, the country was divided into North and South Vietnam.

The United States entered the war supporting South Vietnam, which had a Republican government and was run by Nho Dinh Diem. North Vietnam was backed by the U.S.S.R. and was under Communist rule led by Ho Chi Minh. His name meant "he who enlightens." Ho Chi Minh pledged to "liberate" South Vietnam (viewcomptons: Internet).

The United States feared the expansion of Soviet-style Communism. Beginning in 1957, then president Dwight D. Eisenhower sent troops for a "police action" to keep the Communists at bay. The Kennedy administration continued the build-up of United States troops in Vietnam. The cold war in Vietnam became a hot war as terrorist attacks upon American installations in South Vietnam became frequent.

Kathy was still in the eighth grade when Tom Hayden and Rennie Davis—intelligent, idealistic college students—founded a group called the Students for a Democratic Society (SDS). The SDS protested against America's "imperialist aggression" in Vietnam.

The SDS was part of what came to be known as the New Left, a radical and political social movement in America that demanded equal rights for all members of the society, despite race or gender. It opposed capitalism, claiming that the desire for profits led to imperialism, a national policy that favored extending influence over another country. The New Left thought of themselves as "Marxist revolutionaries." Many New Left proponents were "red diaper babies," children of the "Old Left," Communists who had immigrated to America. After the horrors of Stalin had been revealed in the Khrushchev Report in the 1950s this new generation wanted to separate themselves from the Old Left and free themselves from the taint of Stalin. The movement included many college students and others who demanded fundamental changes in American society. Activists, mostly students, became vocal in support of peace, women's liberation, civil rights, and racial equality. In his biography, *Radical Son,* David Horowitz, a red-diaper baby himself, quoted a contributor to the SDS publication, *New Left Notes*: "The issues were never the issues. Anything that undermined the system contributed to the revolution and was therefore good."

Since World War II, the United States' selective service system had registered males over the age of eighteen for the draft. Also called conscription, this system determined how long a man would serve and to what branch of the service he would be assigned. It had been a way to guarantee manpower in case there were not enough volunteers to serve. The SDS felt that Vietnam was "not our war," and encouraged draft resistance. All over the country, students demonstrated and burned their draft cards in protest. The United States had not seen this much rebellion since the American Civil War.

Most men of Marty Soliah's generation had fought in World War II and were proud of it. They believed that the government knew what it was doing, and when their children told them that this was not their war, their parents considered it a sign of disrespect—not only for the country but for them as well.

Young people grew angry at their parents, teachers, and politicians about their country's involvement in Vietnam, a country far from home. The war was a catalyst for their anger, and it spread to other areas of their lives. Civil rights problems had escalated throughout the United States. During this time of growing confusion and tension, Kathy Soliah became a teenager.

In 1960 four unknown black students staged a sit-in at a segregated lunch counter in Greensboro, North Carolina. This unprecedented event began what was called "The Movement." Students across the country demonstrated for social change. The Student Nonviolent Coordinating Committee (SNCC) was also founded this year. This group organized peaceful protests to speed desegregation in the South.

One year later, in 1961, when Kathy was fourteen years old, her youngest sister, Martha Jane, was born. She would only be four years old when Kathy would leave home for good.

Kathy had entered high school in Palmdale when President Kennedy stepped up American aid to South Vietnam. There were demonstrations and protests all over the nation against the war and discrimination against blacks.

In spite of these conflicts, Kennedy looked forward to the next presidential election, and in spite of warnings, he decided to campaign in Dallas, Texas, with his wife, Jacqueline. While the president's motorcade rolled through Dallas on November 22, 1963, three shots rang out. At 1:00 P.M., President John F. Kennedy was pronounced dead.

Americans were devastated. Ask anyone over fifty years old what he or she was doing nearly forty years earlier when they heard that President JFK had been assassinated, and they will be able to tell you. Kathy Soliah was only sixteen years old in 1963.

Within hours of John F. Kennedy's death, Lyndon B. Johnson was sworn in as President and just two days later, he signed a national security memorandum that restated that the United States' goal in Vietnam was helping the Saigon government to a military "victory." The war escalated.

Kathy was a sophomore at Palmdale High School at the time of Kennedy's assassination. Intelligent and lively, she was pep chairman for the football team and very popular. Her algebra teacher said that Kathy was "very well liked. She was a great, great student. She was just wonderful to everyone and a very smart girl, too."

A teacher remembered, "All I had to do was point at her, and she would blush. She would wear those big, scoop necklines, and she would pull that over her head and hide." He recalled how Kathy would construct creative bulletin boards for him. "She was a great artist and very creative."

Kathy's younger brother, Steve, was a star in high school as well. Their father was teaching and coaching at Palmdale High School and later on, Marty Soliah would boast, "Steve was the best athlete I ever coached. I coached him in track and football until he was a senior. He was a gutsy ball player and fast. . . . And he was a good student, a B student. Never missed school—maybe one day in twelve years—even with a broken leg." Marty was so proud of him, he quit coaching during Steve's senior year in order to avoid accusations of favoritism.

While Steve excelled on the athletic field, Kathy starred in her classes and on the stage. Her English teacher and her high-school yearbook advisor, Herb Helton, directed student stage productions. He said she was a student who was a pleasure to teach and an actress who was a pleasure to direct. "She was one of my all-time great students—so full of life and energy," he said. "She was my best Lady Macbeth ever."

Macbeth is a tale of murder, deception, guilt, and finally atonement. One lead character's line is: "False face must hide what the false head doth know." In Shakespeare's play, Lady Macbeth cries, "Out damned spot! Out I say! Here's the smell of the blood still. All the perfumes of Arabia will not sweeten this little hand." Mr. Helton noted, "I still remember when she did that 'out damn spot' speech."

Like her teachers, Kathy Soliah's fellow classmates liked and admired her. A hard-core Beatles fan, she was proud of her Alma Mater, which in part pledged, "We're the future of our land; honesty must be our stand."

During this time, America was rapidly changing, and Kathy's years of innocence and naiveté were about to end. The nation had evolved from agriculture to consumption in a short time, and Kathy and her friends were part of one of the most affluent generations the world had known—the baby-boomers. Television had become a daily part of life for the first time, and kids were inundated by the mass media. The birth control pill had been introduced to the United States in 1960, giving young people a new sexual freedom. The controversial musical "Hair," about flower children and draftees, introduced live frontal nudity to large audiences. Arlo Guthrie sang "Alice's Restaurant" ("you could get anything you wanted there"), when just thirty years before, his father, Woody Guthrie sang about "Pastures of Plenty." Music reflected the impatience of youth, while clothing and hairstyles reflected the mood.

Todd Gitlin wrote in his book *The Sixties, Years of Hope, Days of Rage,* "Boys grew their hair long and wore ponytails, beards, and sideburns." Girls wanted to look 'natural, organic,' and wore long, stringy hair, stopped shaving their legs and underarms, wore no bras, and shunned makeup. "They preferred boots, long dresses, granny glasses, and army jackets. Fabrics were tie-dyed and earthy colors of blues, grays, greens, and browns prevailed. Boys and girls wore beads from India and headbands. Masculinity and femininity blended together. At times, it was hard to tell one gender from another. Ironically this need to be different from everyone else created a culture, or counterculture as they were called, of people who all looked alike."

In Palmdale, California, most of this rebellion was witnessed only on television. It was a smaller town, where authority was still respected. Although the residents of this community shook their heads in amazement when they turned on their televisions for the six-o'clock news, for the most part, life went on as usual with work and church and school. But Kathy was heading to a larger world that would introduce her to new, socialistic ideas that would contradict everything she had been raised to believe.

In 1965, the year that Kathy graduated from Palmdale High School, John Kennedy's younger brother Robert F. Kennedy became the U.S. senator from New York. Like his brother before him, Robert Kennedy was able to relate to the youth of America. He fervently opposed the continuing escalation of the war in Vietnam, and he also solidified his position as one of Congress' most vocal supporters of the civil rights movement.

Bart Weitzel of the *Antelope Valley Press* wrote that during the sixties, Antelope Valley was "a rural island, isolated from the political strife of protests and the still emerging counterculture movement. Woodstock was yet to come," he said, "and so was Charles Manson and the Weather Underground." It was home to Kathy and she entered Antelope Valley College where she studied acting. The two years she spent there were in some ways an extension of high school. She was sheltered in a small town and not involved in the conflicts that were disrupting college life on larger American campuses.

Nonetheless, Kathy was being introduced to new, liberal views. According to a high school friend, Sande Gordon, Kathy's political views began to form during her two years at this community college. She became romantically involved with a young philosophy teacher who introduced her to a wide range of political literature. Gordon said, "She used to read a lot of Marx—and she understood it." Marty, who had raised his children to be Republicans, probably would not have approved if he had known that his daughter was reading and enjoying the works of Marx.

Marty was proud of his stint as a fighter pilot in World War II.

In those days, men and women had enlisted in the military, not avoided it. In order to provide war materials, Americans rationed things such as food, nylons and gas.

However, many Americans did not feel threatened by Vietnam, as they had by World War II, and therefore were unwilling to sacrifice goods or give up their lives for a war they thought did not concern them. While their parents had been afraid that Hitler and his Nazis would take over the world, the sixties generation had no such fear about Vietnam. This abstract war lacked the depth of feeling engendered by World War II and did not have broad citizen support.

The war continued to escalate during Kathy's college years. Classmates of Kathy's from Palmdale High School had died in Vietnam. Like thousands of people in her generation, Kathy mourned the loss of these young men and vowed that this war "is not our war." She believed her father was wrong and the government that his generation had fought and died for was wrong. Marty's daughter, who had been a top student, who had graduated from Palmdale High School with a Spirit and Service Award, who had been apolitical, had gained a new perspective that would dramatically change her life.

Perhaps if she had transferred to a more conservative college, she would have remained on the sidelines, watched the war on television, observed the protests from a distance, and gone on with her life, as thousands of people of her generation did. Instead, Kathy Soliah chose to continue her education at the University of California Santa Barbara (UCSB). The Centennial Year for the UCSB was 1967. It was an exciting year with parades, celebrations, and college rituals, unlike anything Kathy had ever seen at Antelope Valley College. Enrollment was about 12,000, the same as the population of all of Palmdale, and the entire community was caught up in the spirit of the times.

In contrast to the UCSB celebrations, however, there was also an undercurrent, a dark tension that permeated the campus.

Ronald Reagan had been governor of California since 1966. He and the legislature were slashing budgets. As the Vietnam War escalated, draft quotas were initiated and antiwar groups formed, including a Student Peace Committee on the UCSB campus, which opposed the Reserve Officer's Training Corps (ROTC), the draft, and on-campus recruitment by war-connected contractors.

Kathy moved to an apartment on El Colegio Road in a community called Isla Vista, known affectionately as "IV" by its residents. Just a few miles north of Santa Barbara, Isla Vista had been developed in the early 1960s to provide housing for the rapidly growing university. Most of the housing, which consisted mainly of apartments, duplexes, and older homes, stretched along the coastline and was rented to university students.

The UCSB campus was considered a fun-loving party school, and because it was built along the cliffs next to the Pacific Ocean, with miles of isolated beaches, it was sometimes referred to as the University by the Sea. UCSB seemed to be as much a resort area as it was an institution of higher learning. Students could surf, lie on the beach, or play volleyball between classes. But at about the time Kathy arrived on campus eager for the college experience, the community's carefree attitude underwent a rapid transformation.

Ironically, Isla Vista was also known as a "ghetto for young people." The apartment houses were fairly new, side-by-side, with 13,000 people in less than a square mile—one of the most densely populated cities in California. Kathy's apartment was just on the edge of Isla Vista. Life was friendly and communal. Sometimes young men and women lived together, their doors open to each other, and people drifting in and out. It was a loose arrangement; often neighbors didn't know who was living with whom. The "street people" of Isla Vista, the non-students, or transients, on route from Los Angeles to Berkeley, often "crashed" with the students, staying in their apartments.

The tension felt at UCSB in 1967 was being felt at campuses all over the country. Antiwar groups had sprung up everywhere. Students were angry with the Vietnam War, and they were afraid. Why should they be asked to die for a war that had nothing to do with them? To Kathy Soliah's generation, the Vietnam War had become intensely personal.

A Step Back

Kathy was a twenty-year-old sophomore when she entered the University of California, Santa Barbara (UCSB) in 1967. This had been dubbed the year of the Yippies (Youth International Party), after a radical group formed by Abbie Hoffman (he told his brother that the term meant "Jewish hippies") and Jerry Rubin, two young graduates out of the University of California, Berkeley (UC Berkeley). The caption under Hoffman's baby photo, written by his father, was "Hell Unleashed," and Abbie would live up to the title. He had earned his Master's Degree in psychology at UC Berkeley before he got into political activism. Jerry Rubin had been a part of Berkeley's Free Speech Movement in 1964 to protest a ban on political propagandizing and recruitment on campus property.

In the summer of 1967, these two men joined up with Tom Hayden's SDS with a plan to "confront the warmakers" at the Pentagon, which they announced they were going to "levitate." Dave Dellinger, a longtime pacifist who was twenty years older than Hoffman or Rubin, joined in the effort. Dellinger, a Yale graduate and a seminary student in the 1940s, could have had a deferment for service in World War II but instead refused to register for the draft and, as a result, had been sentenced to three years in prison. Jerry Rubin and the Yippies' March on the Pentagon was carried out in October 1967. Students at college campuses around the country took notice.

Civil rights became an issue on Kathy's campus just as it had in the rest of the country. The majority of students at UCSB were white, and campus officials wanted to attract more minorities. On the national scale, Martin Luther King Jr. had been searching for a peaceful way to end discrimination against blacks.* Like Tom Hayden, he thought that instead of a foreign war most people did not believe in, money should be spent to fight poverty and end discrimination at home.

While King searched for peaceful solutions, other black leaders wanted changes to come about more quickly. In the early 1960s, Malcolm X had led the Black Muslims in the "Black Revolution," and stressed "liberation through the ballot of the bullet." He had been assassinated in a Harlem ballroom the year that Kathy graduated from Palmdale High School. Another black leader of the time was Stokely Carmichael, who called for "Black Power." He urged black Americans to form their own standards and reject the values of white America.

The peaceful solutions that Martin Luther King Jr. professed were much too slow according to these men. Radical groups began to lose patience. And as these groups listened to Stokely Carmichael, who was now leading the once nonviolent SNCC, and Malcolm X, racial tensions increased and a more violent civil rights movement began to form.

In Oakland, California, Huey Newton, a young, diminutive man with a high-pitched voice and a history of felonies, formed the Black Panthers along with Bobby Seale, a radical young man who was a part-time comedian, part-time sheet metal mechanic. Newton and his followers turned their backs on Martin Luther King Jr. and his nonviolent integrationist sermons. Huey Newton wrote that all blacks should be exempt from military service and that all blacks in prison were political prisoners and should be freed. He stated: "We believe that all black people should arm themselves for self-defense."

The protests were contagious. As the Panthers were organiz-

---

* In the 1960s and 1970s African Americans were referred to as blacks.

ing all over the country, H. Rap Brown (who made famous the saying "Violence is as American as cherry pie.") lauded black rioting as "dress rehearsals for revolution," urging black Americans to "wage guerrilla warfare on the Honky white man."

In October 1967, one month after Kathy had begun her fall term, Huey Newton was accused of shooting an Oakland police officer who was attempting to arrest him. The officer had been shot in the back from a distance of twelve inches. Immediately, the New Left denounced the "frame-up" of this young black leader, and organized support for his defense. Newton became a cause cèlébre, an example of America's continuing injustices to its black citizens. A giant photograph of Newton sitting on a wicker throne—spear in one hand, shotgun in the other—adorned college dorm walls across the nation. Newton had become a hero of sorts. The Panther chant of "Free Huey/Off the Pig" was taken up at movement rallies on campuses everywhere.

Kathy's first year at UCSB brought speakers during Black History Week who urged blacks to work for self-determination, self-respect, and self-defense—and to organize. One young man mounted a platform to discuss the massive urban disruptions that were going on around the country. While on the platform members from the Black Action Group yelled that it was useless to talk with whites. They stated that whites needed to admit that their problems stemmed from "white guilt."

Kathy was becoming aware of the underdogs, and the unfair treatment of minorities disturbed her greatly.

Newspapers were laden with the horrors of Vietnam. The death rate for young men serving in Vietnam was high, even among the boys from Palmdale High School. By now, hundreds of thousands of Americans were involved in antiwar protests.

Martin Luther King Jr. continued to speak out against the war's immorality and connected it with the immorality of race prejudice and oppression. The Vietnam Veterans Against the War (VVAW) was formed and those members spoke out of a sense of disillusionment and betrayal based on firsthand experience of

the war's horror. These veterans had credibility and gave a driving force to the antiwar movement.

In early 1968, during Kathy's junior year, Martin Luther King
Jr. traveled to Memphis, Tennessee, to support a strike of poorly
paid sanitation workers. There, on April 4, a sniper, James Earl
Ray, a white drifter and escaped convict, assassinated him. King's
death shocked the nation and precipitated rioting by black
Americans all over the country. All classes at UCSB were cancelled for a mass observance of national mourning.

Todd Gitlin wrote in *The Sixties, Years of Hope, Days of Rage,*
that on the night of King's assassination, a young white lawyer,
Bernardine Dohrn, who had worked with King on fair housing
issues, showed up at a friend's house with tears streaking her face,
saying that though King's politics may have been passé, she'd admired the man. Later, she excused herself to go home and change
into her "riot clothes" so she could join the mayhem on the
streets in Times Square. Still later, she became the leader of the
radical group the Weathermen.

King was buried in Atlanta under a monument inscribed with
the final words of his famous "I Have a Dream" address. Taken
from an old slave song, the inscription read: "Free at Last/Free at
Last/ Thank God Almighty/I'm Free at Last."

As the 1968 Democratic National Convention for the presidency neared, John Kennedy's brother, Robert F. Kennedy, announced his candidacy to run for president. Bobby was young,
energetic, tough-minded, and had become a fierce critic of the
Johnson Administration. Like Martin Luther King Jr., he supported civil rights and opposed the war. Young people in Kathy's
generation looked up to him just as they had his brother John
Kennedy. Johnson withdrew from the race. Liberal working-class
citizens, antiwar activists, blacks, and younger voters helped
Kennedy to win the crucial California State Primary on June 4.
Shortly after giving his victory speech in Los Angeles, Bobby
Kennedy was assassinated by Sirhan Sirhan, a Jordanian-born
immigrant who opposed the senator's strong pro-Israeli plat-

form. America mourned again. Later in the summer of 1968, the Democratic National Convention was held in Chicago. Tom Hayden, Rennie Davis, and David Dellinger planned a week of protest to confront the leaders at the center of power over issues of race and war. Jerry Rubin threatened to the media that he would put LSD in Chicago's water supply. Thousands of people rallied together at the Democratic National Convention to vent their anger over the war, the lack of civil rights, and the general state of affairs in America.

Alarmed, Chicago Mayor Richard Daley was determined to not allow riots in Chicago like the ones that had occurred after Martin Luther King Jr.'s assassination. Unruly protesters were not going to ruin his city's convention. Preparing for the worst, he amassed an army of 12,000 police officers and put them on twelve-hour shifts for the convention. He also called in 7,500 U.S. Army troops and 6,000 National Guardsmen, an overwhelming force of 25,500 armed men.

The violence began on August 25, the Saturday before the convention. Organizers of the protests were furious because they had not been granted the permits they'd requested. They gathered in Chicago's parks and authorities issued an 11:00 P.M. curfew. That night, snake dances by protesters, a Japanese paramilitary formation, provoked the armed officers. The protesters screamed "Pigs!" at the police and flaunted banners that read, "Victory for the Viet Cong." When the police tried to get them to disperse for the curfew the crowds yelled, "Hell no, we won't go." The riots took on a life of their own. Police officers wielded clubs while protesters hurled chunks of concrete, rocks, and bags of urine.

The next day, the demonstrators marched through police headquarters to protest Tom Hayden's arrest for letting the air out of a police car tire. Protesters swarmed into Grant Park, opposite the convention's headquarters hotel, the Conrad Hilton, and hoisted Viet Cong flags. The police fired tear-gas into the crowd and the protesters got the prime time media exposure they had hoped for.

Cult slogans rose out of the protest speeches: "We're gonna barbecue us some pork!" Bobby Seale (Black Panthers), referring to the "pig" cops; and Tom Hayden's, "Make sure that if blood is going to flow, let it flow all over the city." Hayden, Dellinger, Davis, and Bobby Seale addressed about 10,000 demonstrators at the bandshell in Grant Park, That evening, the Democrats nominated Hubert Humphrey as their candidate for president.

But the riots had taken their toll. Daley's police force had clubbed and used mace not only on the "unruly protesters," but also on members of the press, clergymen, women, old, young, and anyone else within swinging distance. And there was a big difference between this riot and riots that had taken place in Chicago before: This one was covered on national television.

Until enactment of the 1968 Civil Rights Act, rioting and incitement to riot had been a strictly local law enforcement issue. Even though the new law made it a federal crime to cross state lines with the intent to incite a riot, Attorney General Ramsey Clark was reluctant to enforce the new provisions and viewed the Chicago violence as a "police riot."

Mayor Daley, however, refused to accept that view, and through his connections an indictment would be handed down on March 20, 1969 to eight of the organizers: Tom Hayden, Rennie Davis, Jerry Rubin, Abbie Hoffman, Bobby Seale, David Dellinger, John Froines, and Lee Weiner. These men who would come to be known as "The Chicago Eight," were charged with inciting a riot.

In his insightful autobiography, *Deep Cover, An FBI Agent Infiltrates the Radical Underground,* Cril Payne, who worked undercover during the convention, viewed the violence from the protesters' perspective. Because he worked undercover, he had long hair and was dressed like the young people in the crowd. For no reason, policemen accosted him, beat him with nightsticks, and handcuffed him. He said that for the first time in his life, he experienced the "overwhelming anger that can cause human beings to take the life of another." When he screamed, the cops jabbed their nightsticks into his rectum, which would later require surgery. He realized that night how simply looking like a member of the counterculture could induce rage among law-enforcement officers. Millions of Americans watched the violent clash of "young" protesters against the "old" establishment. Students around the nation became even more active.

At UCSB, the Legislative Council became politically active. National-Anti-Draft week was held one month into Kathy's junior year. As written in *Transformations, University of California, Santa Barbara, 1909-1979* by Robert Kelley, professor of history, eighteen UCSB students went into the city of Santa Barbara to turn in their draft cards. Ten of their professors supported them by making a public statement that the draft was compelling young men to commit illegal and immoral acts. The protest was peaceful, and the well-mannered, well-dressed students were a contrast to the "wild ones at Berkeley." By November, student legislators had passed a resolution calling for "immediate and unilateral American de-escalation and gradual withdrawal" from the Vietnam War.

On November 5, 1968, Richard Nixon was elected the thirty-seventh president of the United States. Many people believed that Hubert H. Humphrey lost the election because of the riots in Chicago. Nixon's election was good news for Marty Soliah, a lifelong Republican. Later, even after Watergate, he would contend, "I would vote for him again." Kathy Soliah, who was in her junior year at UCSB, and her fellow classmates found Nixon as unacceptable as Humphrey or even worse. They were both "the establishment."

In April 1969, Kathy had her first run-in with the law. She stole a street sign in Oakland to decorate her room. The Oakland police called it malicious mischief and the charges were dismissed.

As Kathy continued her classes toward an English major, racial tensions on campus, as well as across the country, grew. A favored slogan among students was "Revolution Now." America was spelled with a *k*. And in the more radical groups, tactics turned toward terrorism. At San Francisco State, Columbia University, Harvard, UC Berkeley, University of Wisconsin-Madison, and hundreds of other institutions, arson and hit-and-run bombings created a steady stream of incidents that brought education nearly to a halt.

Radical Rage

Following the Democratic National Convention, the Students for a Democratic Society (SDS) had been split into two factions: The Progressive Labor Party (PLP), which believed in Marxist ideology and "class struggle," (They had no strong leaders and would therefore become irrelevant.), and the Weathermen, who considered themselves revolutionaries for "armed struggle"; they would have strong leadership in Bernardine Dohrn.

The riots in Chicago had driven the wedge between these two factions even further, so the national office of the SDS held an election for new leadership. Dohrn won the election by a land-slide once she declared, "I consider myself a revolutionary Com-munist," which meant a supporter of the New Liberation Front (NLF), the Cubans, and Third World revolutionaries in general. Now, virtually all of the national leaders of the SDS saw them-selves as "revolutionaries," and considered the Progressive Labor Party (PLP) to be "too mechanical." Dohrn called for "anti-pig self-defense movements and armed struggle." It was the end for the "conservative" Progressive Labor Party.

Dohrn's group, the Weathermen, took their name from a lyric from a Bob Dylan song, "Subterranean Homesick Blues," which declared that you don't need a weatherman to know which way the wind blows. They issued a 30,000-word manifesto inspired by the Maoist doctrine of "People's War." The doctrine predicted the coming of a global Armageddon in which the Third World would take revenge on "Amerika" by "bringing the war home." The Weathermen wanted to atone for their "white-skin privilege."

Bernardine Dohrn was a smart, stunning beauty, a far cry from the stereotype of the dour, homely, "women's libber." Poise and charm came to her naturally. Peter Collier and David Horowitz wrote in *Destructive Generation* that her mother was a Christian Scientist, her father a Jew who was the credit manager of a furniture store in suburban Whitefish Bay, Wisconsin. He had changed their family name from the Jewish *Ohrnstein* to the German *Dohrn* because people had used racial slurs, accusing him of "Jewing" them or cheating them out of their money. Dohrn had earned her law degree at the University of Chicago's Law School. Back in 1965, the year that Kathy had graduated from Palmdale High School, Dohrn had been a law student and also worked for Martin Luther King Jr.'s civil rights organization helping to organize a citywide rent strike against owners of low-income housing, sometimes referred to as "slumlords." Dohrn said that working for King had transformed her life. His opposition to the Vietnam War and his determination to align with the labor movement is what pushed her into "revolutionary consciousness."

Dohrn then worked as an organizer for the National Lawyer's Guild. The Guild challenged the legality of the Vietnam War, which they held was a violation of international law. They also supported people who were arrested in mass demonstrations against the war and the draft.

Thirty-four years later Dohrn would appear in Minneapolis at a rally to support Kathleen Soliah's (*aka* Sara Jane Olson) defense.

Once elected president of the SDS and the newly formed Weathermen, Dohrn promoted her view that the university was the key institution for social change. The Weathermen issued a position paper advocating "Student Power." They were a more charismatic group than the old guard of the SDS, with more spirit and style. It didn't hurt that they were a good-looking group, important for the press and TV attention, and many of them came from wealth. Although wealth did not apply to Bernardine, she had the looks and the guts to lead the group.

Todd Gitlin in his book *The Sixties, Years of Hope, Days of Rage,* wrote that she exuded "sexual charisma that left men dazzled."

Radicals in the sixties and seventies tended to share certain characteristics later identified by Kenneth Keniston, a Yale psychologist interviewed by the *New York Times*: "Radical youth—whether overt or underground—are very idealistic, highly intelligent, highly educated, and tend to be the best students. They attend the top three percent of the colleges and universities in the nation. They are mainly from upper-middle-class families—mostly liberal Democrats—who generally are involved in higher levels of political activity than most families."

The Weathermen's vice president, Billy Ayers, was the son of a chairman of the board of the Illinois Commonwealth Electric Company. He dubbed his parents "Ma and Pa Powerbrokers." Ayers was proud to announce that he "had not read a book in a year," which was embarrassing and disappointing to the former SDS leaders, who considered themselves intellectuals. (When LBJ had announced that he was not running for president, Ayers had stalked the streets of downtown Detroit late that night, heaving stones through windows.)

Ayers's girlfriend at the time was Diana Oughton. She was the daughter of an Illinois banker and a Republican legislator and the great-granddaughter of the founder of Boy Scouts of America. Her friends described her as elegant, gentle, and refined before she met Ayers.

Former SDS president Tom Hayden's father had been an accountant. In fact, most of the former leaders of the SDS and other radical groups had come from middle-class backgrounds in which their parents had made their living as accountants or schoolteachers. The former leaders' philosophy had been to work within the establishment; this was, according to the new leaders, idealistic and slow. Patience was not a virtue that the Weathermen valued. They wanted action now and reveled in an outlaw approach to meet their own political goals.

According to the Weathermen, America was a racist and

imperialist nation trying to impose its policies on other countries, such as Vietnam. In a short time, this group, which had sprung from the Students for a Democratic Society (SDS), became a violent, militant faction, alienating other members of the New Left. The Weathermen abandoned attempts to stage national demonstrations and instead divided the organization into various small underground cells intent on bombing symbols of white oppression in the United States.

The University of California, Santa Barbara (UCSB) campus became embroiled in these conflicts. In January 1969, Kathy's senior year, a United Front formed by the Black Students Union, the SDS, and Mexican-American Students Association (UMAS) demanded that the promised increases in minority enrollment and faculty be speedily put into effect. Although the administration tried to maintain an ongoing dialogue, the students did not trust them. Angry confrontations and accusations from both sides permeated the UCSB campus.

In February, the Santa Barbara County Sheriff's Department made an early-morning raid on the Isla Vista apartment of seven Black Students' Union leaders, alleging non-payment of rent. They searched the dwelling and then arrested the students on drug charges. This incident was the impetus for more than 1,000 UCSB students to protest before the county offices in Santa Barbara, accusing police of violating due process and using selective enforcement of the law, now known as racial profiling.

Isla Vista realtors complained that the Educational Opportunity Program students defaulted in rent payments, which heightened the tension between landowners and student renters. The students marched on the University Center and seized the building to declare it a New Free University. In March, there were reports of gunfire in Isla Vista; by April, congressmen had called for the FBI to lend a hand.

During Kathy's senior year as an English major, an ethnic uprising transformed the UCSB campus. Sixteen black students occupied North Hall, which housed the campus computer center, renaming the building "Malcolm X Hall." They issued communiqués protesting institutional racism in the form of admission requirements, courses, curricula, hiring, faculty staffing, and financial aid. They demanded more black participation in the administration of the university. The university's chancellor made a commitment to increase minority enrollment and faculty presence, and to enlarge minority studies programs.

Although there was a growing division between students in Isla Vista and the university establishment—*us against them*—a new focus of social responsibility emerged, with increased awareness on student empowerment, and a greater desire on find a peaceful end to the continuing war in Vietnam.

On April 11, 1969, Dover Sharp, a custodian at the faculty club, saw a strange object against a wall in the courtyard where faculty members had lunch. As he bent over to examine the object, it exploded, blasting him backward across the patio. The device was loaded with broken bottles and the shattered glass riddled his body. He died two days later.

Robert Kelley, a UCSB professor of history, wrote in his book *Transformations, University of California, Santa Barbara, 1909–1979,* "The broken windows, his blood on the walls and the trail of blood to the wading pool where he had painfully crawled for relief, was a terrible reminder to the faculty that there were people out there who hated the university and the faculty so much that justified their need to destroy and to kill."

Tom Hayden stated in his book "*Reunion, A Memoir,* "The Vietnam War was destroying the American idealism of an entire generation, whether in Chicago or Saigon. . . . Suddenly, it was no longer deviant but legitimate—patriotic even—to express an alternative." He explained how this became evident to the nation: "Just before the Chicago trial began, Abbie Hoffman and Jerry Rubin attended the vast gathering of Woodstock, in upstate New York, the coming of age of the youth culture. Then in mid-October, the 'Vietnam Moratorium' became perhaps the largest public protests in American history. Approximately ten million

Americans gathered in town squares and college campuses to speak out against the war. The two events together—Woodstock and the Moratorium—reflected the spirit of a generation we had dreamed of expressing in the original planning for Chicago 1968."

In March 1969, UCSB students heard that the Chicago Eight had been indicted. Abbie Hoffman, Jerry Rubin, Rennie Davis, Tom Hayden, and Bobby Seale were in this group, which also included Dave Dellinger, the pacifist, John Froines, a 1963 Berkeley graduate with a chemistry degree, and Lee Weiner, a 1967 Ph.D. from Yale. As the "Chicago Eight" trial neared, the government wanted to portray the Yippies, the Mobe (National Mobilization Against the War in Vietnam), the SDS, the Black Panthers, and the New Left as anti-American. It worked for some of mainstream America, but not for the students. The news fueled their anger even more. Along with much of the country that had observed the Chicago riots, the students, Kathy Soliah among them, believed that the police were to blame.

On September 24, 1969, thirteen months after the Chicago riots shocked America at the Democratic National Convention, the leaders of these groups, the "Chicago Eight," stood trial in the oak-paneled, twenty-third-floor courtroom of seventy-four-year-old-judge Julius Hoffman (no relation to Abbie Hoffman).

William Kunstler, who had defended H. Rap Brown, was the flamboyant lead defense attorney in the Chicago Conspiracy trial. On the Chicago Seven home page on the Internet, Kunstler wrote that he grew up in New York City and he described himself as a "terrible kid until I reached high school." He straightened himself out, became an "A" student, and finally earned degrees from Yale and Columbia Law School. A few years after law school, he turned from a small business and family law practice to civil liberties law.

During the Chicago Eight Conspiracy trial, Kunstler ate, danced, drank, and demonstrated with the defendants, causing Judge Hoffman to observe at one point, "You get awfully chummy with your clients." The prosecuting attorney, Tom Foran, said later that Kunstler wasn't defending his clients; he was one of them. Kunstler and Judge Hoffman had some bitter confrontations during the trial, which would earn Kunstler a sentence of four years in prison for contempt of court.

The defendants showed no respect for the seriousness of the trial. They came to court in blue jeans and sweatshirts, and often sat with their feet up on chairs or the table. Once Abbie Hoffman stood on his head and blew kisses to the jury, and on another occasion, he and Jerry Rubin dressed in judge's robes. Hoffman and Rubin wore headbands, buttons, beads, and colorful shirts. They munched jellybeans, cracked jokes, made faces, read newspapers, interrupted the proceedings with editorial jokes, and took naps as if they were bored. Some of the defendants refused to rise when the judge entered the courtroom. The defense table was littered with candy wrappers, clothing, and on one day, a package of marijuana.

In sharp contrast, the prosecutors wore business suits, and were neat and efficient. The table had a file of index cards, a pencil, and carefully arranged notes. Tom Foran likened the proceedings to going to the dentist for a root canal every morning.

Bobby Seale, continuously and in increasingly angry tones, insisted upon his right to represent himself because his lawyer was in the hospital. He hurled frequent and bitter attacks at Judge Hoffman, calling him a "fascist pig," and a "racist." On October 29, the outraged judge ordered Seale bound and gagged.

The picture of a black man in chains was a made-to-order image for the radical melodrama. Finally, on November 5, 1969, Judge Hoffman severed Seale from the case and sentenced him to four years in prison for contempt of court. The Chicago Eight was now the Chicago Seven.

As if the Vietnam War, Civil Rights riots, and student unrest weren't enough, the summer of 1969 also saw one of the most heinous mass murders in America's history. Charles Manson had been in and out of prison all his life. In 1967, when he was thirty-two years old, he was released from prison once again. He blended right in with the "hippie" culture in San Francisco and quickly discovered how he could use drugs to influence naïve, re-bellious, troubled young women to be his slaves.

Charles Manson had a core philosophy, his own kind of Ar-mageddon. He preached that the black man was going to rise up and start killing whites, turning cities into an inferno of racial re-venge. The black man would win this war but wouldn't be able to hang on to the power he seized because of his innate inferiority. In 1968 Manson had forecasted "racial war." It was at the same time that the Beatles released their White Album, which included the song "Helter Skelter."

On a muggy weekend beginning August 9, 1969, the horrific crime occurred in the canyons above Beverly Hills, California. The battered and stabbed bodies of actress Sharon Tate, eight months pregnant, along with her baby, and five of her guests were discovered at her home. "Pig" was scrawled in blood on the lower half of the front door.

Later that night, in the Los Angeles suburb of Silver Lake, Leno and Rosemary LaBianca's teenage son found their blood-drenched bodies in their living room. They'd been strangled, smothered, and stabbed. A carving fork protruded from Leno's stomach and the word "WAR" had been carved in his flesh. His wife had been stabbed forty-one times. Written on the living room wall in the victims' blood was "DEATH TO PIGS." "HEAL-TER SKELTER," misspelled, was smeared on the refrigerator door.

The murders of Sharon Tate and her friends, and the LaBian-cas were national front-page news, taking precedence for a short time over the country's major problems. The gory murders were detailed in the print media as well as on the television news, day after day, and it was unbelievable to most people that anyone could be sick enough or evil enough to commit such a terrible crime. Bernardine Dohrn's group proved to be the exception.

The Weathermen had prepared an event, "Days of Rage," for early October 1969 to coincide with the ongoing Chicago Seven Conspiracy trial. To signal the beginning of the Days of Rage, on October 6, they blew up the police monument in Chicago's Haymarket Square. On October 8, three days of rampage began. Thousands of protestors were expected to attend, but only a few hundred showed up.

Cril Payne wrote in *Deep Cover,* "The Weathermen had pioneered the concept of affinity groups. They were first used in October 1969 during the violent Days of Rage demonstrations on Chicago's near North Side. Four or five trusted friends would walk down the street as a unit, then suddenly run in different directions, breaking windows, hurling rocks, and attacking police. The group would be armed with clubs, chains, pipes, and rocks. The usual targets were the police, government buildings, and offices of private companies having defense contracts.

"The rioters wore motorcycle helmets to cushion blows and gloves to throw back tear-gas canisters. They carried steel pipes to use as clubs. They were scared to death until Bernardine stood up on a makeshift podium with the wind furling Vietnamese flags around her. 'Just think,' she yelled through a bullhorn, 'only this number had the courage to come. You are truly a vanguard. . . .' She pumped them up and led them off, breaking into a run and flying down the streets and into the Loop, smashing windows as they went. Sirens ripped through the city. The police closed in on them but they fought furiously, setting cars on fire and trashing the famed Chicago Gold Coast."

After three days of rioting, the Days of Rage came to an end. Seventy-five policemen had been injured during the melee and one city official was paralyzed from the neck down when he attempted to tackle a running Weatherman and struck his head on a curb. Three hundred Weather People were arrested, some of them on charges ranging up to attempted murder.

The day following the Days of Rage, Charles Manson was arrested outside of Los Angeles. The Weathermen, who preached equality and civil rights, had not seemed concerned that Charles Manson and his gang had tried to pin their murderous acts on blacks, hoping to start a race war. Jerry Rubin visited Manson in prison, and later wrote: "I fell in love with Charlie Manson the first time I saw his cherub face and sparkling eyes on national TV. . . . His words and courage inspired [me] . . . and I felt great the rest of the day, overwhelmed by the depth of the experience of touching Manson's soul. . . ." *The Los Angeles Free Press* let Manson write a column and ran free ads for a recording he made; another underground paper, *Tuesday's Child,* depicted him as a hippie on the cross.

At the Weathermen's December 1969 "National War Council" in Flint, Michigan, Bernardine Dohrn exulted Charles Manson, saying that he truly understood the inequity of white-skinned America: "Dig it! First they killed those pigs, then they ate dinner in the same room with them, and then they even shoved a fork into the victim's stomach. Wild!" The new greeting of the National War Council Convention was four slightly spread fingers— to symbolize the fork.

After years of being a prominent public voice, giving speeches, distributing literature and communiqués, planning riots and planting bombs, being feared by citizens, and hunted by the FBI, the Weathermen suddenly vanished. They would now be referred to as the "Weather Underground."

Kathy's years at UCSB were a time for noteworthy headlines. Besides the Chicago trials, there were Woodstock, the Vietnam Moratorium, the Manson murders and Days of Rage, the Beatles, Paul McCartney marrying Linda Eastman, and John Lennon marrying Yoko Ono. Kathy, a hardcore Beatles fan, took special note of this.

James Earl Ray was sentenced to ninety-nine years in prison for the murder of Martin Luther King Jr. Sirhan Sirhan was sentenced to death for murdering Robert Kennedy. Man set foot on the moon for the first time and astronaut Neil Armstrong proclaimed, "That's one small step for man, one giant leap for mankind."

Senator Edward Kennedy's car plunged into the water under the bridge on Chappaquiddick Island in New England. His passenger, twenty-seven-year-old Mary Jo Kopechne, drowned. Ho Chi Minh died. The movie "Alice's Restaurant" was released with Arlo Guthrie. And the Smothers Brothers television show was cancelled because it was deemed too controversial.

As a senior, Kathy Soliah continued to live in Isla Vista in the apartment on El Colegio Road that she had found as a junior. This is where she met and fell in love with James (Jim) Kilgore, a five-foot-ten man with light brown hair and blue eyes. He'd been born in Portland, Oregon, and grown up in San Raphael, California, just north of San Francisco, where his father had been a prosperous lumber dealer.

While in high school in northern California, Jim had been a member of a law and order club, called the Supreme Court. One of his teachers said that any parent would be proud to have Jim for a son. Jim had studied economics at UCSB from 1965 until 1969. He was a natural athlete, accomplished in basketball and golf. He was also an aspiring sportswriter and had corresponded with a man named Jack Scott, a prominent Berkeley activist.

Scott had made a name for himself with a controversial mix of politics and athletics and was perhaps the leading advocate of the "Jock Liberation" movement, which protested the authoritarian nature of coach-dominated sports and the pressure of commercialization on college and professional athletes. He and his new friend Jim Kilgore were against everything that Marty Soliah's coaching career had stood for. Perhaps that was part of Kathy's attraction to Jim, a way to rebel against her father's authority. The fact that Jack Scott would play a prominent role in her future was not known at this time. Falling in love with Jim Kilgore, associating with his friends, and living at Isla Vista would change Kathy Soliah's life forever.

Isla Vista, College by the Sea

Isla Vista was unique compared to other campus communities around the country. Two-thirds of Isla Vista's total population was between the ages of nineteen and twenty-two. Over ninety percent of the residents of the eastern half of Isla Vista were between seventeen and twenty-five. About fifty percent of Isla Vista's residents were "disenfranchised" because they could not vote in the city elections even though they were dissatisfied with the way the community was governed. In addition to that, virtually every male in the community was of draft age. Because of the ongoing Vietnam War, anxiety about the draft was extremely high.

Furthermore, in Isla Vista, there was large-scale drug use. Despite the illegality of marijuana possession, smoking pot was an integral part of the Isla Vista lifestyle. A survey conducted indicated that at least seventy percent of the students used marijuana. One student explained, "The make-up of Isla Vista was not like the rest of society. The people didn't have to work and for the most part depended on their parents or the university. There was no reason for the residents to commit themselves to make Isla Vista a better place to live."

When the idealistic aspiring, young actress from Antelope College entered the stage of Isla Vista, she began to shed all of the costumes and trappings of everyday American life—a life that had come to represent "the establishment," against which one needed to rebel. The Isla Vista lifestyle—beatings, fires, and explosions—had become normal. Kathy's days as an innocent youth were over.

During Kathy Soliah's last term at UCSB, in 1969, the Chicago Seven trial finally came to an end. The jury acquitted all the defendants on the conspiracy charge. On February 20, 1970, Judge Julius Hoffman sentenced the other five defendants, Tom Hayden, Rennie Davis, Jerry Rubin, Dave Dellinger, and Abbie Hoffman, to five years imprisonment plus a $5,000 fine. (Two years later, on November 21, 1972, the Seventh Circuit Court of Appeals would reverse all convictions.)

Although Kathy graduated from UCSB in December 1969 with an English degree, she stayed on in Isla Vista with Jim. It is unknown if her family attended her graduation ceremony. It is believed that Kathy taught school that fall of 1970. It would be one of her few attempts as Kathleen Soliah to develop a "normal" profession and lifestyle.

On February 24, 1970, William Kunstler, who was free until being sentenced for his part in the Chicago Seven Conspiracy case, spoke to 5,000 students at the UCSB football stadium. He told his audience that he did not consider sporadic violence "a good tactic" but sympathized with what he called the "bitter and deep" frustration of students. Despite his admonition, the students who gathered after his talk pelted passing patrol cars with rocks and bottles and broke into an Isla Vista real estate office, overturning furniture.

Following Kunstler's speech, a group that called itself "The Conspiracy" staged a rally at Perfect Park, a grassy area near Isla Vista's Bank of America. Campus activists were angry over the Chicago Seven sentences. They also felt that they were being harassed by police and exploited by landlords. When a controversial faculty member, fired for failure to meet standards for tenure, claimed that he was being dismissed because of his outspoken anti-establishment views, students rallied in his favor. Student leaders said that Kunstler had nothing to do with their protests, but that their complaints stemmed from "long-standing problems."

On February 25, 1970, the day after Kunstler's speech, the

Bank of America in Isla Vista was burned to the ground by pro-testers who claimed that the bank was a symbol of "the establish-ment." An estimated 1,000 people set fires and broke windows in the business district. The Bank of America would continue to be assaulted by angry protesters until the middle of June.

As the bank burned, police were called in full-force, complete with riot-control gear. They were pelted with bricks and rocks that were picked up from rock gardens that decorated the lawns of nearby apartment buildings. Activists threw Molotov cock-tails, and the police fired tear-gas. Isla Vista was like a war zone. There were between 1,000 and 2,000 demonstrators chanting, "Burn baby, burn," throwing cardboard onto the blaze. They shouted, "The Bank of America breaks human laws. Death to corporations!" El Colegio was not far from there and it is un-likely that Kathy and Jim missed the excitement.

That was the first of many fires. Another one occurred on April 18, 1970. During this fire, some of the onlookers tried to extinguish the flames. They thought that their goals could be met without the destruction. Three of the students went into the bank through a broken glass door to try to douse the fire. As they were leaving the bank, a convoy of dump trucks filled with riot police turned the corner and saw them and assumed that they were the arsonists. One of the students, Kevin Moran, was shot and killed by a Santa Barbara city police officer as he stood at the broken door.

One of Kathy's fellow English majors at UCSB exclaimed, "I thought it was a crime that that kid [Moran] got killed. So what if a bank burns? Nobody has to be killed because a bank burns down. Everything that happened afterward was just too much and for what? I remember guys with guns and it infuriated me."

Cril Payne wrote about the climate in the student commu-nity at Isla Vista in *Deep Cover*: "Weapons replaced the beer and marijuana, once stockpiled in IV residences. Dynamite, blasting caps and automatic weapons became fashionable. The entire spectrum of the university began to look and dress the part of revolutionaries."

The campus as a "war zone" was not a mere metaphor; the battlefield environment had spread to colleges and universities across the country. Kent State was a public university in Ohio and the antiwar movement had been slower to build at such campuses than at some of the elite schools. But now these students joined the protests.

The ROTC building was set on fire three times; windows were smashed in the downtown area. The governor of Ohio called the protesters, who were mostly college students, "the scum of America" and warned, "We can stop them with gunfire if necessary." That is just what happened. On May 4, 1970, the Ohio National Guard fired over sixty rounds of ammunition across lawns and a parking lot, killing two student protesters and two bystanders. The front-page picture of a young girl bent over a dying young boy reminded students and parents across the country, "There but for the grace of God. . . ." The next day, Isla Vistans and other students held a rally on campus and confronted the campus police at the ROTC building. The war at home was galvanized.

On May 6, 1970, two days after the Kent State Riots, a group of the Weather Underground were manufacturing pipe bombs in a New York townhouse that belonged to the father of one of the young women. The bombs were studded with roofing nails— makeshift copies of antipersonnel bombs like those the United States was dropping in Vietnam. Someone connected the wrong wire and the house blew up, igniting the gas mains. Three Weather Underground members were killed in the explosion, including Diana Oughton, Billy Ayers's former girlfriend. In a communiqué, Bernardine Dohrn called the explosion a "military error."

The police thought that the roofing-nail bombs had been intended for use at Columbia University. The Weather Underground denied it. There was another claim that they were planning to bomb an army noncommissioned officers' dance at Fort Dix, New Jersey. The group never admitted what the target was supposed to be. But they did issue a self-critical communiqué, which concluded with a phrase made popular by Eldridge

Cleaver: "Death to the Fascist Insect that Preys Upon the Life of the People," a phrase that would later be capitalized on by the Symbionese Liberation Army. During the first two weeks of June, seventeen people were indicted for the February bank burning. Students responded in fury because a few people had been singled out and used as scapegoats when hundreds had been at the arson fire. More riots broke out. Fires were started in trash bins all over Isla Vista, rocks were thrown through windows, and a car was overturned behind the Bank of America's new temporary, prefab structure. In addition, real estate offices were attacked to protest high rents.

Governor Ronald Reagan and the Santa Barbara Board of Supervisors declared a state of extreme emergency to curb the violence. The supervisors ordered a curfew from 6:00 P.M. to 6:00 A.M. Isla Vista was put virtually under martial law. Students were arrested and booked on the spot, their pictures taken and fingerprints recorded by an officer using the hood of a patrol car for a desk. (Twenty-five years later, the records of those charged with misdemeanors had been lost, purged, or destroyed.)

On June 6, 1970, six months after Kathy's graduation, Tom Hayden came to speak to an audience at the stadium. Authorities were concerned that he might incite more rioting, but instead he spoke of solidarity, of "a decentralization of the establishment," and said that "attacking the Isla Vista Bank is not where it's at."

The next night, about thirty policemen fired tear-gas into a crowd of about one hundred students and other protesters who were throwing bottles and rocks. One student and his roommates lived just two blocks from the Isla Vista Loop, close to Kathy's apartment, where the embattled Bank of America was located. This nineteen-year-old English major watched the confrontation from his second-floor apartment. He told a reporter from the *Los Angeles Times* that he wasn't in on the action, but he could "hear it, see it, and smell it."

Later, officers returned to the intersection of Sabado Tarde Road and Camino Pescadera when a tear-gas canister exploded in the street. Wind filled the apartment rooms with tear-gas and the student observer and his roommates choked on the fumes. He said that the smell permeated everything, and it took weeks to get it out of the furniture. Rocks hit the side of the apartment building. Students were prisoners in their own homes.

Cril Payne, the FBI undercover agent, was on assignment in Isla Vista to locate members of the Weather Underground, which had become a real embarrassment to J. Edgar Hoover's FBI. He said that the walls of almost every commercial building in town were covered with brightly colored psychedelic murals and revolutionary slogans. The streets were painted with replicas of Viet Cong flags and antiwar graffiti. The stop signs were altered to say, "STOP the War," or "STOP the Pigs." The hundreds of protestors who had appeared in 1967 when Kathy had first arrived at UCSB had now grown into thousands who were united in their hatred for the "Pigs."

Undercover agents observed a Berkeley group who had arrived in Isla Vista in a converted school bus to celebrate the Tenth Anniversary Celebration of the National Liberation Front (NLF). Viet Cong flags flew everywhere in the streets and in Isla Vista's People's Park, where the celebration rally was being held. One individual stood out in particular. He was dressed to look like Cuban revolutionary Che Guevara. As the agents crossed the street, they heard a tremendous explosion, followed by cheers from the crowd. The Guevara look-alike had lofted a military hand grenade on top of the new Bank of America, blowing a large hole in the roof.

By June 10, hundreds of protestors had been arrested, most of them for violating the curfew. The get-tough policy by police made the students even angrier. Police randomly kicked in the doors of their apartments, seizing people they thought were violating the curfew, which was a problem for students who had final examinations between 7:00 P.M. and 10 P.M. They could be arrested on their way home.

One student claimed that he was sitting in his own apartment when a kid he had never seen before burst in his door and flopped down on the floor. Seconds later the door was kicked in, and a cop hit the student with his club and told him he was under arrest for harboring a fugitive. Most of the students were released, but the "street people," or college-age drifters who used Isla Vista as a crash pad—a stopping place between San Francisco and Los Angeles—remained in jail as bad bail risks.

One young, red-haired woman wearing green was arrested on her way home from surfing. It was past curfew. She was one of many students who were wrongly arrested. Few were hard-core street "rads." But the arrest process, which was frequently unjustified, was turning innocent kids into radicals. They no longer trusted the justice system. Almost everyone was involved somehow—there was no way to escape. One Isla Vista resident said that many students "had been apolitical, but they'd just been watching what was going on all year long and by the end of the year, they were ready to stand up with the radicals."

That was how Kathy Soliah was described before she moved to Isla Vista—apolitical. Now she had lived through a virtual war in her own neighborhood. Her father's influence was long forgotten and she was in love with an angry young man. She was not only going to stand up with the radicals, she was going to become one of them.

Riots, arrests, and alleged police brutality filled the front pages of the *Los Angeles Times* until June 14, when a judge dismissed 305 cases in Isla Vista. It was only then that the town began to return to normal. The riots left a stain on this college community and became a sad part of the town's history. Campus historian Bob Kelley wrote, "A pervasive mood of exhaustion and despair" had settled upon the campus by the sea.

Josef Anderson, a screenwriter who knew Kathy during her years at UCSB, later explained: "We had seen the Kennedy assassinations, Martin Luther King Jr.'s assassination, and people wanted to start a revolution." He said that someone idealistic and bright like Kathy Soliah was "ripe for the plucking. At that age," he stated, "kids are full of passion, which perhaps causes them to make decisions that are not very smart in the long run."

It was clear to the FBI that the Weathermen had a stronghold in Isla Vista. On October 8, 1970, predawn explosions ripped an armory in Santa Barbara and a courthouse in San Rafael, the hometown of Jim Kilgore, Kathy's boyfriend. About thirty minutes after the San Rafael explosion, the *Seattle Times* received a call from a young woman warning that a bomb was about to go off in the basement locker room of Navy and Air Force ROTC facilities on the University of Washington campus. Two bombs placed about thirty-five feet apart exploded at about 2:35 A.M. causing $150,000 worth of damage. They were homemade bombs, and the acts were attributed to left-wing terrorists. (The Weather Underground were suspected, of course.) Governor Reagan termed the bombings a "cowardly and despicable terror tactic by radical factions." He also said at a news conference, "I think there's going to be more of this."

Nearly twelve hours after the blast in Santa Barbara, the manager of the UCSB radio station, KCSB, received a special delivery letter signed by the "Perfect Park Home Grown Garden Society," claiming responsibility for the explosion of the National Guard Armory. The letter was postmarked "Isla Vista" and said that the bombing was timed to coincide with the third anniversary of the death of Cuban revolutionary Ernesto (Che) Guevara, who had been shot to death in Bolivia on October 8, 1967. The letter said, "To commemorate the third anniversary of Che's death, we have bombed the Santa Barbara National Guard Armory. We dedicate the attack on the domestic arm of the U.S. Military to all revolutionary people throughout the world."

In honor of the occasion, the Yippies held a news conference in New York City where they played a tape that they claimed was the voice of Bernardine Dohrn. She warned that a "fall offensive of youth resistance" was about to begin that "will spread from Santa Barbara to Boston, back to Kent and Kansas."

This date was significant because it also marked the first anniversary of the Weathermen's Days of Rage, the bombing of a statue depicting a policeman in Haymarket Square and the violent demonstrations that had engulfed Chicago, and resulted in over two hundred arrests. As the "fall offensive" began, a letter from the Weathermen (now the Weather Underground) boasted: "A year ago we blew away the Haymarket pig statue at the start of a youth riot in Chicago. Last night we destroyed the pig again."

J. Edgar Hoover had been under intense pressure from the Nixon administration to find these people and restore law and order. First the FBI used a Special Investigative Division in hopes of finding them, and when that didn't work, the FBI pronounced the Weather Underground a national security threat and posted some of them on the Ten Most Wanted list.

Whenever the FBI thought they had a lead, the fugitives would move and their false identifications would change again. When the FBI identified the vehicles they were driving and their phony registration information, the cars would be resold to another Weatherman. It was like grasping for clouds. The Weathermen had no respect for authority and no fear of being harassed, and therefore, they could not be intimidated.

The Weather Underground were masters at obtaining false IDs. One method was to assume the identity of a dead infant. They would visit local cemeteries or search through county records for an infant born in about the same year they were born who was no longer living. At that time, birth and death records were not commonly cross-referenced. The fugitive had only to fill out an application for a duplicate birth certificate in the name of the dead child. Once they got that certificate, it was easy to obtain other forms of identification, such as library cards, voter registration, Social Security cards, and drivers' licenses. The Weathermen had much to teach their members and any supporters on how to hide, change one's identity, and elude the authorities—for years, and decades, if need be.

Transitions

Since the 1960s, Berkeley, just north of Oakland and Emeryville and across the bay from San Francisco, had been a mecca for the white counterculture, the New Left movement. The Free Speech movement of 1964 originated at UC Berkeley. It was known as a hotbed of communism, Marxism, and socialism and a haven for young revolutionaries. Tom Hayden, Jerry Rubin, and Bernardine Dohrn all lived there at one time or another.

Early in 1971, Kathy and Jim decided to leave Isla Vista and try out a commune in Monterey. Plans changed, however, when Jack Scott, Jim's sportswriter friend, invited them to stay with him and his girlfriend, Micki, at their apartment in Oakland. Kathy had wanted to get into theater and the San Francisco Bay Area had more opportunities than Monterey. And Jim hoped for a career in freelance photography or perhaps as a sportswriter like his friend. So they took Jack up on his offer. They stayed with him and Micki for three weeks before moving to their own place on Shattuck Avenue in Berkeley. Paul Rubenstein, twenty-two, a Lawrence, Kansas, SDS-Weatherman roomed with them.

Perhaps money was tight after the move or perhaps Kathy was looking for a quick thrill. In July 1971, she was shopping at the Little Daisy, an upscale store in Oakland, and she went into a dressing room with a size fourteen pair of brown pants. A clerk saw her rapidly exiting the store as a special detection device went off. After the clerk approached her, Kathy admitted stealing the $7.00 pair of pants. The Oakland police arrested, fingerprinted, photographed, and booked Kathleen Soliah for shoplifting. She was

convicted of theft and fined $35.00 with thirty days jail sus-
pended, and one-year probation. Her second run-in with the law
was minor compared to other events that year.

On April 19, 1971, the judge pronounced that Charles Manson, Patricia Krenwinkel, Susan Atkins, and Leslie Van Houten were each
guilty of murder and conspiracy to commit murder, and sentenced them to the death penalty. (In the following year, though,
the California Supreme Court abolished the death penalty in that
state, and all of the defendants are still serving life sentences.)

That summer of 1971, highly sensitive and politically damaging Pentagon documents regarding America's involvement in
Vietnam were leaked to the *New York Times*. Nixon quickly established a White House special investigations unit to trace and
stop any further leaks to the press. This "unit" investigated the
private lives of Nixon's enemies and critics. They didn't stop
there. They also broke into the Democratic National Headquarters in the Watergate office building in Washington, D.C., to tap
the phones. They were caught. Bob Woodward and Carl Bern-
stein from the *Washington Post* were the first reporters to reveal
this scandal to the public.

Once the defendants revealed during their trial that they had
been pressured politically to keep quiet, and had been paid hush
money that had personally been approved of by Nixon, impeach-
ment was inevitable. On August 9, 1974, Richard Nixon would become the first, thus far, and only president of the United States to
resign from office.

The nation, like Kathy and Jim, was in transition, and the war
effort in Vietnam was beginning to wane.

Kathy and her brother Steve had always been close. Steve was
now twenty-three years old and still a star athlete—a record-
breaking runner at Humboldt State College in Northern California. He was born on August 21, 1948, a significant date because
most boys that age were eligible for the draft, a system of selecting men for required military service.

Steve had been classified 1-A, available for induction in the draft, but because he had registered for college, he had not been drafted and sent to Vietnam. As soon as he got his deferment in his junior year though, Steve dropped out of college and at Kathy's invitation, joined her and Jim in Berkeley.

They were compatible roommates. Steve was an easygoing young man who could get along with anybody. He and Jim Kilgore were both sports enthusiasts, so they had a natural bond. However, Steve only lived with Kathy and Jim for one month. He had been introduced to some friends of theirs, Michael Bortin and his girlfriend, who lived in a Berkeley Way commune. (Bortin had been an SDS officer at Berkeley in 1969.) Steve also had a girlfriend, Emily Toback, so the two of them decided to join Bortin at Berkeley Way, not far from his sister's house.

Michael Bortin was a twenty-three-year-old San Francisco native who had graduated from UC Berkeley the previous June. He was about five-feet-nine, muscular and tough looking, with wild red hair, two chipped front teeth, and a tattoo of a large dragon on his arm. While he was a student, he had started his own private house-painting contracting firm. Now that he had become friends with Steve Soliah and Jim Kilgore, he hired both of them to work with him as painters. They called their company Able Painting. It was a no-pressure job, a job well suited to Steve and Jim. The three men would find that they had more in common than painting houses.

On March 30, 1972, just a few months after Steve arrived in Berkeley and about six months after Kathy and Jim settled on Shattuck Avenue, someone in their neighborhood called the police because they smelled gas fumes in a nearby garage. When the police arrived, they discovered what was described as a "massive bomb factory." The garage had been rented by an "Anne Wong"— later identified as Wendy Yoshimura, a twenty-nine-year-old Japanese-American woman.

After the police evacuated the area, they found several hundred pounds of various chemical explosives, gunpowder, fuses, blasting caps, a large quantity of ammunition, and a small arsenal of rifles and pistols (including an AK-47 machine gun, probably of Vietnam War origin) in the garage. They also found a fused pipe bomb, a partially completed beer-can grenade (particularly vicious: gunpowder and heavy carpet tacks—a deadly crowd bomb), and a three-gallon oil–ammonium nitrate chemical bomb.

Police staked out the garage, and that night, at about 3:00 A.M., three men in a small blue Volkswagen drove up, unlocked the garage, and went in. All three men were armed, dressed in dark clothing, and carried flashlights and glasscutters. Police burst into the garage and the men were trapped, surrendering without a fight. When the police searched their car, they found a ready-to-mail communiqué from "The Revolutionary Army," claiming credit for an arson bombing of the UC Berkeley Naval Architecture Building, apparently scheduled for that night. They also found notes with plans to bomb the U of C Berkeley Space Science Laboratory and a detailed multi-page plan for the kidnapping or assassination of former Secretary of Defense Robert McNamara.

Vin McLellan and Paul Avery, journalists and investigative reporters, wrote in their meticulously detailed history of the SLA, *Voices of Guns*, that the men trapped in the garage were twenty-three-year-old Michael Bortin, of Able Painting, twenty-four-year-old Willie Brandt, and twenty-two-year-old Paul Rubenstein, Kathy and Jim's roommate.

The next day, police went to the home on Shattuck Avenue, and Kathy answered the door. Steve was there too. They were very polite and invited the police in when they were shown the search warrant. All that the officers found was a gas receipt, signed by Jim Kilgore, so they thanked the Soliahs and left with no charges against them being filed. Later they would discover that additional evidence from Steve Soliah's home that he shared with Michael Bortin had been removed overnight and destroyed, as well as from Willie Brandt's apartment, which he shared with Wendy Yoshimura (alias Anne Wong).

Wendy Yoshimura was one of a generation of Japanese-Americans who had been born in U.S. concentration camps in California during World War II. Although both her parents were American-born, they had been imprisoned in the infamous Manzanar detention camp in Southern California as part of the national program to jail Japanese-Americans during the war.

After the war, her parents fled the United States and went to Japan—her mother's first time there—where Wendy was brought up in the A-bombed city of Hiroshima. In 1957, when Wendy was eleven, the family moved back to California. Her parents were returning home, but their daughter was a native-born foreigner; unable to speak English, she was dropped from the seventh to the second grade. She was seventeen when she entered high school, but she won a prize for her art while still a student and later at Fresno State College. In 1965, she transferred to the California College of Arts and Crafts in Oakland. She was apolitical, socializing largely within the Bay Area Japanese community for the first three years she was in the Oakland-Berkeley area. But then she met Willie Brandt. In her journal, she described Willie as the man who helped her understand about social injustice, about the Vietnam War, capitalism, colonialism, imperialism, racism, classism, and sexism. She fell in love with him.

A Marxist-Leninist-Maoist organization had been formed at Stanford University in Palo Alto in 1971. They called themselves "Venceremos." The Venceremos handbook stressed that members "must learn to operate and service weapons correctly, must have arms available, and must teach the oppressed people the importance and methods of armed and organized self-defense." Like other New Left groups at the time, their goal was to crush U.S. imperialism.

Unlike Wendy, most of their members were young and white but their creed demanded that the white and student Left submit to dominant black leadership. The members of Venceremos were guilt-ridden by their own white-middle-class domination of op-pressed people. They were angry with the establishment that had imprisoned some of their fellow students for drug use. It was through this connection that Wendy came to rent the garage for the Berkeley Bomb Factory.

When the police came to the apartment she shared with Willie Brandt, Wendy was not to be found. Police believed that Kathy Soliah had called Wendy and warned her that the police might show up. On that night of the arrests, Micki Scott, Jack's wife, went to the Brandt-Yoshimura apartment and "helped clean it out." Then Jack arranged for Wendy's transportation to the East Coast where she would live as a fugitive for the next two years.

All three men pled guilty in a plea bargain to charges of pos-session of materials for the manufacture of explosives. Later, Rubenstein provided information that associated the three, par-ticularly Brandt, with a long series of Bay Area bombings—ten during 1971 and one in late January 1972. Most of the targets were banks. Bortin and Rubenstein were each sentenced to one-year county jail terms. Rubenstein got out in eight months. Bortin served a full year, until he was released in the spring of 1973 with three more years of probation. Brandt got a one-to-fifteen-year state prison sentence.

Kathy Soliah and Jim Kilgore, along with their sportswriter friend, Jack Scott, were among Willie Brandt's visitors at Soledad prison near Monterey. Kathy Soliah had been Brandt's most fre-quent visitor in 1973, usually making the hundred-mile drive south to Soledad once a month. When she missed a month, Jim filled in.

After his release from prison, Michael Bortin went back to work painting houses with Jim Kilgore and Steve Soliah. Bortin said later that the Soliahs and Kilgore were "intellectually radical but not practically." Kathy Soliah had watched as Bortin, Brandt, and Rubenstein committed themselves by direct violent actions to "the revolution" and even went to jail for their beliefs. Though it seems Kathy aided and abetted, she had not as yet instigated any acts of revolution of her own. Had she not met Angela Atwood, perhaps she would have remained merely a supporter.

Angela was the daughter of an upwardly mobile, Italian-Catholic family in North Haledon, New Jersey, where her father was an official of the Teamster's Union. Her mother had died in 1965. A straight-A student and one of the most popular girls in high school, her friends called her Angel. When she signed her name, she would insert a halo over the "g." Like Kathy Soliah, Angela had also been the captain of her high-school cheerleaders. They both were aspiring actresses, and in the next few years they would find that they shared many more interests.

In 1969, the year that Kathy graduated from UCSB, Angela was attending the University of Indiana, where she met Gary Atwood, a fellow drama student and antiwar activist. Gary introduced her to leftist politics. Angela's father was just as opposed to her "radical" views as Marty had been to Kathy's. Once she had been close with her father, and now she didn't want to fight with him. Because of many heated disagreements over politics, Angela rarely visited home. Gary was the man in her life, a fact her father would have to accept. Through the University of Indiana's drama Department, Angela and Gary met Bill Harris and Emily Schwartz (later Emily Harris).

Bill Harris, one of three children, had grown up in Carmel, Indiana, a suburb of Indianapolis. Harris was an acolyte in his family church and a good student in high school, known as the class wit. Though short, he was athletic, like Steve Soliah and Jim Kilgore, played golf, and competed on his school's cross-country track team. He loved other sports, but he was too small to compete.

Bill hated his father, a building equipment salesman, who seemed to Bill insensitive about his son's height. Bill's father told him he would never amount to anything and Bill was determined to prove him wrong. In 1965, after one year at the University of Indiana, Harris enlisted in the Marines. Just before he went overseas, his father died of a heart attack, and it hurt Bill that he would never be able to win his approval. Bill held a grudge, one he couldn't shake. Enlisting in the Marines may have been the worst decision he ever made. The Vietnam experience radicalized him, and he came home a different person.

Appalled at the war and the prejudice against blacks in the service, he joined the Vietnam Veterans Against the War (VVAW) when he returned to the university in 1967. He attended Jerry Rubin's "March on the Pentagon." And he began dating a pretty coed named Emily Schwartz.

Emily was one of four children in a family from Clarenden Hills, Illinois, near Chicago. Her father, Frederick Schwartz, was a consulting engineer. She had entered the University of Indiana in 1965 with straight "A"s, pledged Chi Omega Sorority, and was very popular. A co-worker at the Disneyland Hotel in Anaheim, California, where she worked during the summer of 1967, described Emily as a sweet, smiling, nonpolitical sorority sister. However, during the next two years, through her association with Bill, she became involved in radical politics.

Sharing a love for the stage and the same political views, Angela, Gary, Bill, and Emily became good friends. At first, Angela was the quietest of the group, seemingly with few opinions of her own, but soon she began speaking her mind on political issues, particularly Women's Liberation. She and Emily became active in women's groups on the University of Indiana campus.

Both couples got married in 1970, and their friendship continued. They were next-door neighbors in Bloomington, Indiana, until 1971, when the Atwoods decided to head for the West Coast. They moved to the Bay Area, where Gary performed his alternative service as a conscientious objector to the war. Angela worked in the Bank of America, while taking courses in Marxism at the Free University. Gary also read the works of Marx, Gorky, and Trotsky, which greatly influenced his life.

The Harrises missed their good friends and decided that they too would move from Indiana to the Bay Area. When they got there, they were disappointed to learn that Angela and Gary were having problems, both political and personal. The dynamics of the foursome would not be the same.

Marty Soliah always said that Kathy had great influence over her siblings. Steve had followed her to Berkeley and now, two years later in 1973, her twenty-two-year-old sister, Josephine, opted to join them. Jo had dropped out of the California State University at Long Beach during her senior year, deciding that she no longer wanted to be a teacher. She wanted to be a nurse, but she couldn't get into a training program at that time.

Kathy's new feminist beliefs had caused a rift between her and Jim Kilgore, and they separated. When Jo arrived, the sisters moved into an Oakland commune. The painting business with Jim, Steve, and Michael Bortin was still going strong, and Kathy and Jo often helped them with the bigger projects. They were all close friends.

At this time, Angela and Gary called an end to their marriage, and Gary went back to Indiana to resume school, not realizing that he would never see his ex-wife again. Angela moved in with the Harrises. She worked as a waitress, Bill drove a mail truck, and Emily was a clerk-typist at the UC Berkeley.

Now that Gary was gone, Angela dated Russell Little, who lived in a commune on Channing Way. His best friends were Joe Remiro and Willie Wolfe. She introduced her new friends to her best friend, Kathy Soliah.

In 1972, Willie Wolfe went to the prison medical facility in Berkeley to gather material he was writing for a black studies course. He attended meetings of the Black Cultural Association (BCA), a group of inmates dedicated to forging black identity and unity. The meetings were designed to help relieve tensions that had been building within the facility and prison. Authorities allowed visitors, such as Wolfe, to attend meetings and work with the inmates. One of the more active members, Donald DeFreeze, was serving a term of five years to life for robbery and a shootout with police.

Impressed by what he heard at the meetings, Wolfe brought his friend Russell Little and other young radicals from Berkeley. After leaving the prison the students would sometimes gather at a commune residence in Oakland dubbed the "Peking House." There, they would spend hours debating the fine points of Maoist politics and radical theories on race, poverty, and the war in Vietnam.

The war had been winding down since 1970 and the anti-draft movement had disintegrated. In 1969 America began to pull out its troops. But this wasn't the end of the war in the United States. In some ways, it was another beginning. David Horowitz wrote in his autobiography, *Radical Son,* "The real importance of Vietnam to the radical cause was not ultimately about Vietnam but about our own antagonism to America, our desire for revolution. Vietnam served to justify the desire; we needed the war and its violent images to vindicate our destructive intentions. That was why the victory of our 'antiwar' movement seemed so hollow when it came. The peace killed the very energies that gave our movement life. When it was ratified, there was no dancing in the streets by massive crowds of antiwar activists, no celebrations to match the protests that had made the communists' triumph possible. Long before, our revolution had failed—and the marchers had all gone home."

Angela, Russell, Joe, and Willie were young and idealistic, and they were lost souls in a way. Like the war protesters before them, they were angry and shook their collective fist at authority, but the war was over. They needed a cause. Soon they would meet their new leader, who would give them what they were looking for.

Act Two

> "It is often easier to fight for principles than to live up to them."
>
> ↗ ADLAIS STEVENSON SPEECH,
> NEW YORK CITY, AUGUST 27, 1952

Birth of the SLA

> *In a matter of months the Symbionese Liberation*
> *Army achieved a notoriety and visibility unparalleled*
> *among the extremist minisects, dominating the politi-*
> *cal extreme, imprinting the whole of the fringe with*
> *their own quixotic image. It was they, finally, who*
> *gave a wholly American root to the word "terrorist,"*
> *succeeding where so many others had failed.*
>
> ✎ VOICES OF GUNS

Donald DeFreeze (Cinque, Cin)

No one would have expected Donald DeFreeze—a lonely young man, only five feet, nine inches tall, with slender build, a narrow face, and brooding eyes—to become a leader of anything. His voice could have an alien quality as if he were speaking from a distance, and within the same breath he could switch to a tone of passion and caring.

In his childhood, Donald was sensitive and moody, and for good reason. While his mother was a gentle woman, his father was an out-of-work alcoholic, full of rage, which he directed at Donald, the oldest of eight children. Sometimes he beat his son with his bare fists, or if he was really out of control, a hammer or baseball bat was his weapon of choice. Donald was fourteen years old the first time he ran away from home. He spent much of his teen years shuttling between his parents in Cleveland and relatives in Buffalo, New York. By the time he entered high school, his father had broken one of Donald's arms three separate times. It was hardly surprising that Donald DeFreeze became an angry teenager.

In 1963, when only nineteen years old, he moved to New Jersey and married an older woman of twenty-three, who already had three small children. To earn a living, he painted houses and repaired furniture. Together they had three more children. There was never enough money, and they fought constantly. Donald would disappear for weeks at a time, often ending up in a seedy apartment that he rented in New York City. Here, alone and away from his family, he developed an interest in guns and firearms.

In March 1965, one month after Malcolm X's assassination, neighbors called the police when they heard a gun go off in Donald's New York apartment. When the police arrived, they discovered that the apartment was full of guns, ammunition, and a homemade bomb. He was arrested but released on $500 bail. The community was on edge and the neighbors afraid of him. Unable to get work, he hauled his wife and six children to Los Angeles to make a new start. There was still no money, and his wife had had enough. She took the kids and moved back to Cleveland, leaving Donald to pursue his own interests.

At the age of twenty-seven, Donald, alone and destitute, spent his time reading weapons manuals and rifle magazines. Later his lifelong interest in guns and bombs would read like a resumé on his arrest record—possession of weapons and bombs, gun-shop burglary, sale of unauthorized weapons, discharging firearms within city limits, and more.

In 1968 while he was doing time in California's Chino prison, the guidance staff referred to him as "an emotionally confused and conflicted young man with deep-rooted feelings of inadequacy." They also noted his problems with his father and stated that his "fascination with firearms made him dangerous."

Donald was in and out of prison, getting lost in the system and paroled before he should have been released. In 1969 he was sent to Vacaville prison in the Sacramento Valley.

The town of Vacaville is fifty-five miles north of San Francisco and forty-one miles from Berkeley. The prison was a mental facility designed to handle inmates whose problems required treatment less intense than that offered at maximum-security prisons. Inmates considered Vacaville an "easy hitch," and the prisoners' goal was usually simply to earn an early probation.

Donald was considered a model prisoner, and he began to educate himself, reading the works of Frantz Fanon, Malcolm X, and other black writers who commented on the oppression of the Third World. George Jackson, a former prisoner and revolutionary writer, became Donald's inspiration. Jackson's books, *Soledad Brother* and *Blood in My Eye*, had detailed his life as a convict in California prisons.

Marx, Lenin, and Trotsky's writings also appealed to Donald, but he thought that their methods of revolution were too slow. Comparing them with Fidel Castro and Che Guevara's guerrilla techniques, Donald preferred the latter in that their methods were fast, violent, and effective. Like Bernardine Dohrn, Donald DeFreeze had no patience. One of his favorite passages from George Jackson's books was, "We're going to have to fight to win. The logic of procrastination has been destroyed."

Donald DeFreeze had been fighting all of his life. He had fought with his father, he had fought with his wife, and he had fought to survive. There had never been a cause other than himself before he began his self-education. Through Jackson's writings, Donald learned the meaning of bourgeois (middle-class with materialistic values) and of the New Left. Being black and bourgeois became the worst imaginable sin for DeFreeze. When George Jackson was killed in a 1971 San Quentin prison shootout, Donald was devastated that blacks had lost their true leader.

Even before Donald entered Vacaville prison, a group called the Black Cultural Association (BCA) had been founded at the prison to heighten black awareness, address inmate social concerns, and recruit tutors to come to the prison to educate inmates. Some of the tutors were black and some of them were white, which would ultimately cause dissension between some of the white inmates and their black tutors. Some inmates used the white tutors to smuggle things into the prison or get them to communicate with someone on the outside, which was strictly forbidden. Finally, the black tutors stopped coming.

Members of the BCA took on "reborn" African names. Inspired by this, Donald DeFreeze rechristened himself "Cinque M'tume," a combination of a number given a captive Mendi chief by Portuguese slave traders in the 1830s and the Swahili word for profit. "Cinque" was the name that stuck, but people sometimes called him "Cin" (pronounced Sin). Cinque, still the model prisoner, was allowed to teach a class, which he named "Unisight." White tutors assisted him. In his class, he professed Kawaida's seven principles—self-determination, production, co-operation, collective work and responsibility, faith, unity, and creativity— the code of conduct for members of the Los Angeles–based black nationalist group, United Slaves (US). These principles would carry over to his preachings to the Symbionese Liberation Army (SLA).

Being a model prisoner was good as far as the guards were concerned, but it didn't sit well with the other black prisoners. They didn't trust Cinque. That didn't bother him too much, because by now he had his own agenda: parole, or at the very least, be assigned to a low-security job. Once he was on the outside again, he was going to put a group together, a group of people who shared his new philosophies. Cinque spent a lot of time in the prison library, searching for a name that would be appropriate for his group. He found what he was looking for. "Symbiosis"—the living together of two or more dissimilar organisms— appealed to him. The concept of this group would be the "coming together of black, white, brown, and yellow people in symbiosis of armed struggle in urban America." Thus the Symbionese Liberation Army (SLA) was conceived.

Cinque would strive to combine people from all political parties, a wide array of organizations and a broad spectrum of races. He especially sought the most oppressed people of what he called "this fascist nation," with the goal of "thereby forming unity and the full representation of the interest of all the people." Cinque drafted a document for his new organization, which in part demanded that the New Left be set aside for the Symbionese Liberation Army. The officers of the SLA would fight for the freedom of "our people and our children."

In December 1972, Cinque gained the "trusty" status for an inmate and was transferred from Vacaville to Soledad prison, which was the same facility as that of Willie Brandt, located in the middle of the Salinas Valley, about 100 miles from Berkeley. As Cinque had hoped, he had been reclassified as a minimum-security prisoner, determined to be unlikely to attempt escape.

Kathy Soliah had first met Angela Atwood in September 1972 when they auditioned for a production of Ibsen's *Hedda Gabler*. Both of them won lead roles. Kathy confided to Angela that she needed a job, and Angela got her hired as a waitress at a downtown restaurant-lounge, the Great Electric Underground in San Francisco. Their friends said that the two women soon became inseparable. They could spend hours discussing their disappointing relationships with their fathers, and also shared disdain for their boss.

Kathy and Angela wrote a one-act play called *Edward the Dyke*. Kathy played Edward, a lesbian; Angela played a psychiatrist who tried to convince Kathy that a soft bed and a sexy man would solve her problems. Angela was shedding her wifely image and replacing it with a tough stance on feminism. Together, she and Kathy took a night course in radical feminism.

At the restaurant, they tried to organize a waitresses' union, but other employees weren't interested in joining. Friends found Angela's tough feminist stance offensive. She had become an evangelist on the subject of women's liberation, and the subject wore thin with her coworkers. She also became consumed with "social classes." Kathy agreed with Angela but didn't preach as much. Both women were unhappy with their jobs. Their boss insisted that they wear brief, ruffled skirts with V tops to titillate the bored afternoon clientele of bankers and brokers. This did not sit well with these emerging feminists and they let him know it.

In *Voices of Guns*, the authors reported: "Just a few days before Christmas in 1973, Kathy and Angela, frustrated that their efforts were not appreciated, wrote a four-page denunciation of management and their co-workers: 'We consider our employment situation a microcosm of the working world at large. Our actions here are a reflection of our beliefs in the radical political spectrum. At Great Electric Underground we have gone as far as we can. We have no support from our peers. No one is willing to take chances . . . we leave to find areas in which our concerns and actions are productive.'"

On March 5, 1973, at 12:15 A.M., Cinque began his first night on the job as an automatic-boiler attendant at Soledad prison. His "conformity" had paid off. Although he had spent an extra three years behind bars and had been denied parole, he had been treated with leniency and granted an unsupervised job. He planned his escape.

A guard had dropped him off at the minimum-security compound and would check back later. As soon as the guard's truck was out of sight, Cinque spied the twelve-foot wire fence that separated him from the valley, the mountains, and the Pacific Ocean. Within minutes, he climbed the barbed-wire fence and jumped to freedom. The guard showed up twenty-five minutes later at 12:40 A.M.; Cinque was gone.

Cinque had confided in one fellow prisoner, Thero Wheeler, a black revolutionary who had been in and out of prison since 1962 with offenses ranging from second-degree armed robbery to attacking a police officer. Through his Venceremos contacts, Wheeler arranged for Cinque to be taken care of after his escape. And Wheeler himself would escape from Vacaville prison just five months after Cinque escaped from Soledad. It would be Wheeler's idea to kidnap Patricia Hearst. It would also be his idea to put the ransom money towards "PIN," People in Need. Asking money for someone other than themselves would make them look legitimate, he thought.

In preparation for his early departure, Cinque had stopped corresponding to his friends on the outside and burned all of his personal letters. Then he bided his time until the right moment. All that he took with him were the clothes on his back. Fourteen hours after his escape, Cinque found himself in Berkeley.

Peking House

In Berkeley, a loose and disorganized group of white radicals ruled, whereas the Black Panthers reigned in Oakland with militaristic organization and pride. The contrast between the two groups was stark.

Cinque arrived in Berkeley in March 1973 at the height of the tension between the New Left and the Black Panthers. He fit in both camps and neither. His path would integrate the most violent elements of both groups. To his new Berkeley contacts who had helped him escape, he explained the plan he'd formed in Soledad: whoever escaped first would organize the revolution. Since he was the first to go, the revolution would belong to him. Cinque gave himself the title, "General Field Marshal."

By the time he arrived in Berkeley, the Movement of the sixties was about over. The flower children had children of their own. According to Les Payne and Tim Findley in their book *Life and Death of the SLA,* the mood then and there was reflected in the motto "The political is personal and the personal is political." That motto belonged to Channing Way, a street stretching south of the Berkeley campus. Adherents of that motto helped establish the Berkeley Free Clinic, the Women's Health Collective, and the Women's Union. Others eventually joined Cinque's SLA. When residents referred to Channing Way, they usually meant a three-block strip between Shattuck and Milvia that was lined with Victorian houses. This area was a haven of counterculture consciousness. Usually the houses had names such as the "Red Family," or the "Rainbow Tribe." Cinque spent his first night of freedom in the Peking House on Chabot Road, approximately two miles from Channing Way.

Willie Wolfe and Joe Remiro introduced him to other Berkeley radicals from various communes who would become the core of his dream: Russell Little, Angela Atwood, William and Emily Harris, Patricia Soltysik, Camilla Hall, and Nancy Ling Perry. His new friends were ripe for revolution.

Many of the Peking House residents (some students, some non-students) were regularly involved in Venceremos-sponsored activities, such as the BCA tutoring to inmates. The tutors became the Venceremos liaison with militant convicts. Bill and Emily Harris didn't live at the Peking House, but they became friends with the residents there. The Harrises played a key role in facilitating communication between the prisoners and the outside world of Venceremos. They opened up a post-office box, in Berkeley, under phony identifications, to use as a drop box and then spent long hours writing and forwarding inmates' letters.

Peking House residents shared daily chores—cooking and maintaining the house's business, which was a small sidewalk stand or kiosk on Bancroft, in front of the campus. Chinese food was sold at the stand, and they called it the "Peking Man," which is how the house got its name. David Gunnell, a fellow inmate at Vacaville when Cinque was there, who claimed to be one of Chairman Mao's political disciples, was the landlord, and leader of the commune.

The Peking House shared responsibilities with other houses in the neighborhood. Earlier, in 1972, the residents of these houses had formed a cooperative, or "Food Conspiracy," as they called it. Russ Little bought huge blocks of cheese wholesale for the cooperative, and they bought meat and vegetables from farmers. On weekends, they'd have a spaghetti dinner and the residents filled their plates and sat on the floor under posters of Mao and the People's Army.

Twenty-five years later, Kathy Soliah, who had by then changed her name to Sara Jane Olson, wrote in an introduction to her cookbook, *Serving Time, America's Most Wanted Recipes*: "In the 1970s, I learned about organic food when I moved to the Bay Area in California. I belonged to the "Food Conspiracy," an umbrella group of neighborhood food-buying clubs that bought organic food from rural farms and local distributors. The Conspiracy was large enough to purchase food at wholesale prices and pass the savings on to individual members. So I guess, I do admit to once being a member of a conspiracy."

Peking House became the home office of Cinque's organization, the Symbionese Liberation Party. Other founding members of the SLA set up camp in their Berkeley and Oakland apartments. Through these communes, Cinque's prison dreams were about to come to fruition. These bright, frustrated young people, who gathered in Berkeley by the chance of fate, all at vulnerable times in their lives, were now going to find a way to vent their anger. But first they had to prepare themselves for armed battle.

Russell Little had grown up in Florida, graduating from high school in 1967 with the distinction of being ninth in a class of 600. His parents were very proud of him. After a year in junior college, with a partial scholarship, he attended the University at Gainesville, Florida, where he studied electrical engineering and philosophy. Even though he was raised in the segregated South, Little was oblivious to the Civil Rights movement until he started college. Then, in the fall of 1968, he took a course in philosophy with a young Marxist professor who introduced him to Marx, Lenin, Mao, and Eldridge Cleaver. This is the course that changed his life forever.

Little attended rallies, demonstrations, and marches. He was furious over the Kent State catastrophe, and that summer, he went home an angry radical with long hair and an attitude, which his parents didn't know how to handle. The next year he was organizing campus demonstrations. He and his friends attended the 1971 May Day demonstrations in Washington, D.C.

Russell Little had come to Berkeley from Florida with his

girlfriend, Robyn Steiner. He had become disillusioned with what he called Berkeley's "legal revolutionaries," and was looking for some action. He met Angela Atwood at the Peking House, and they began dating. He also met and became friends with Joseph Remiro, who had come from a middle-class family in San Francisco.

Remiro, of Mexican and Italian descent, was called "cruelly handsome," with his thin face, light olive complexion, and knitted brow. He was raised Catholic and was always a high achiever. He had graduated from high school in 1964 and enrolled at San Francisco City College. Instead, though, he volunteered to go to Vietnam. He was there for eighteen months—two tours—where he served as a rifleman in active combat on reconnaissance missions with the 101st Airborne Division. He was only nineteen years old when he became a squad leader for a six-man commando team and dropped behind enemy lines to scout and locate concentrations of Viet Cong forces.

The day before he'd shipped back to the States, the camp he was in came under attack. There was a huge explosion and he stood "stone-still" watching shrapnel and debris shower around him like rain. He was not hurt, but friends thought that this experience permanently changed his life. When his tour of duty was over he developed Post-Traumatic Vietnam Syndrome, a sense of disorientation and dislocation. He was consumed with guilt and bitterness when he returned to the Bay Area. He was shocked and disillusioned that during the year and a half that he'd been gone, nothing had changed at home. But he had.

When Remiro returned home to the Bay Area in 1969 he became an immediate pacifist, a vegetarian, a habitual dope-smoker, and an LSD addict. He suffered from anger, bitterness, and disillusionment as well as Post-Traumatic Vietnam Syndrome. . . . Guilt-ridden, he tried to relate his war stories to his father, who didn't believe him. World War II veterans in his dad's generation could not relate to the horrors of Vietnam. When the World War II veterans learned of the civilian bombings in Laos, they thought it was a one-time incident. They couldn't believe the common-place nature of it in Vietnam. Remiro's friends at home didn't understand either. Remiro couldn't relate to anyone he'd known before his Vietnam experience.

He became involved in revolutionary politics and joined Venceremos. Later he became one of the founding organizers of the Oakland chapter of the Vietnam Veterans Against the War (VVAW). Remiro's pacifist views, however, soon turned violent. He pushed a doctrine of maximum militancy and revolutionary activism, which now alienated him from the other vets who were into VVAW. By 1973, he had given up drugs, which friends said made him even more "wired." Joseph Remiro wanted to bring the war home.

Remiro entered the College of Alameda and made the dean's list while studying auto mechanics. At the same time, he worked for the Black Panther's Bobby Seale, who was running for office in Oakland. Remiro was a doer, not one to take a back seat.

Camilla Hall, who lived on Channing Way, had been in Berkeley since 1971. Camilla, an overweight, sometimes obese girl, had spent her life enduring painful rejection by males and had committed herself to being a lesbian. In Patty Hearst's memoir, *Every Secret Thing,* which she wrote with author Alvin Moscow, she described Camilla as "the cheese that stands alone at the end of the children's game, 'The Farmer in the Dell.' Nobody wanted her. I considered her the most sensitive person in the group."

At home in Minnesota, Camilla had been known as "Candy," the daughter of a Lutheran minister and missionary, the only surviving child of four. The others had died of congenital kidney failure. Camilla had been a sociology student at the University of Minnesota and, in the mid-1960s, was an open campus advocate of Gay Liberation. This was her first commitment to a radical cause. She would say later, "I never do anything half-assed."

After college, she worked two years as a social worker in Minneapolis. Before landing in Berkeley, she had traveled around the country, forming militant feminist groups at out-of-the-way communes in Arkansas and Colorado, as well as in the larger cities such as Los Angeles. When she arrived on the Berkeley scene, settling in an old apartment building on Channing Way, the blond, blue-eyed twenty-five year old with thick frameless glasses was ready for a new life. In the beginning, she lived on her savings from the job in Minneapolis, but finally, she was able to earn some money by selling her poetry and line drawings to small art publications and Berkeley galleries. Her upstairs neighbor was Patricia Soltysik.

Patricia was one of seven children. Her father, a pharmacist, was a brooder and his children could never please him. Her mother, who had seen Nazi horrors in Belgium during the war, worked as a practical nurse, striving to keep the family together. Both parents demanded hard work and a commitment to education from their children.

At Dos Pueblos High School in Los Angeles, Patricia Soltysik was attractive and well liked. She earned good grades and was president of the status-conscious "Usherettes." She was active in 4H, training guide dogs for the blind. She also liked to cook and sew. Patricia hung out with surfers and thought one day she would marry an "intellectual surfer."

Patricia graduated from high school in 1968 and went to Berkeley on three scholarships, majoring in French and Spanish. Patricia soon drifted into the periphery of Berkeley's radical community, her grades falling to mediocrity. She had become a nonconformist during her sophomore year, ready for a revolution.

In 1970, there was a protest in Berkeley for "the people" to claim a vacant, barren lot on the campus. The land belonged to the university and it was believed that they were going to turn it into a mall, leaving no place for the homeless to hang out. According to Tom Hayden, the hippies, teenage runaways, jewelers, and tarot card readers, who inhabited the area, began their own beautification project, planting grass, placing benches in the park, and building swings for the children. Politicians were distressed with these actions, and eventually Berkeley police were called in. A major demonstration ensued, which escalated into days of street battles, rioting, and tear-gas. The National Guard was called in. A sheriff's deputy killed one demonstrator. This event became known as the People's Park demonstration, and Patricia had been an eager participant.

She was angry at women instructors, actually sneering at them for their "visceral consciousness." She was militant and fought for the Women's Union, which was strongly influenced by lesbian and bisexual women. Patricia worked as a janitor at a center for the radical feminist movement in Berkeley and lived with her boyfriend on Channing Way when Camilla Hall moved into her building.

By the end of Patricia's sophomore year, her parents had divorced; she dropped out of college, broke up with her boyfriend, and became Camilla's lover. They shared a bond of pain— Patricia, over her brooding father and her parents' divorce, Camilla over the loss of her siblings and also the despair she witnessed during her job as a social worker in Minneapolis. Camilla would re-christen Patricia as "Mizmoon" in a love poem, and Patricia eventually went to court to make the name change legal.

In his book *Deep Cover,* Cril Payne said that he was unprepared for the number of antiwar activists who were openly bisexual. He said that the number of men who "swung both ways," astounded him. The women's movement was in full swing and Payne thought that there was peer group pressure to prove that women were "liberated."

"You couldn't be a true revolutionary if you had to depend on men," he wrote. He surmised that this female commitment and dedication to each other made them more dangerous as urban terrorists. They undertook more brazenly illegal acts than their male counterparts would even consider. He believed that the "female activists were the moving force behind the fundamental changes that occurred during those years of protest."

Despite the name change, Mizmoon and Camilla were not able to sustain their relationship. Mizmoon also wanted to be with men and this eventually drove a wedge between them. After they broke up in 1973, Mizmoon (hereafter referred to as Patricia) stayed involved in the Women's Union, her personal choice of radical movement. As early as 1972, she had corresponded with inmates and written letters to prison officials on behalf of convicts in California. Through these associations, she met the other boarders at the Peking House. They told her of their work at the BCA at Vacaville prison. Here she met Russ Little, Robyn Steiner, Willie Wolfe, and Cinque, who was not like any man she had ever met.

He was confident, poised, romantic, and he liked to cook! His political views appealed to her the same way that George Jackson and Eldridge Cleaver had appealed to other white radicals. Patricia had viewed men as the enemy, but, in her mind, black men were victims of society, so she could separate them from the white men she had previously known.

Patricia experienced a sexual joy with Cinque that had not been present in her relationship with Camilla. Soon, they became partners in drafting and writing the plans for the Symbionese Liberation Army. One of Patricia's drawings of a gossamer-winged, fairy-gypsy figure shooting a termite-like cop illustrated the SLA's future slogan: "Death to the Fascist Insect That Preys on the Life of the People."

Willie Wolfe was nineteen years old when he arrived in Berkeley in 1971. By now, he had developed into a radical trying to sort out his life. He enrolled at UC Berkeley, lived two months in a dorm, and then moved into the Peking House commune. He became caught up in the East Bay subculture and declared himself a Maoist and a revolutionary.

Willie Wolfe had been raised in Connecticut and New York. His father was a wealthy anesthesiologist who divorced from Willie's mother when his son was fifteen years old. Even with re-marriages and a large extensive family, Willie managed to stay close to both parents. He attended an exclusive Massachusetts prep school and was sports editor of the paper as well as a varsity swimmer.

A lanky six-footer, Willie was a quiet, unassuming boy, who didn't drink or smoke and believed in following the rules. His friends nicknamed him "Wee Willie." He graduated from high school in 1969 as a National Merit Scholar finalist, but like the other Berkeley radicals, including Kathy Soliah, Willie suffered from despair over the Vietnam War and guilt regarding his own good fortune.

Instead of going to Yale, like the rest of his family, he moved to Harlem for a year. He bought secondhand clothes while working as an insurance-company clerk. He borrowed some money from his father and traveled in Europe for almost a year. This is when he noticed the contrasts to American affluence.

In 1972, Nancy Ling was working at a small food and beverage stand, called Fruity-Rudy's, along the southern boundary of the Berkeley campus. Fruity Rudy's was located near the Peking Man in front of the Peking House. Nancy was experimenting with drugs, using and selling, and performing odd jobs to pay for her habit. Through her job at Fruity-Rudy's, she eventually met Willie Wolfe and Russ Little and other boarders at the Peking House.

Born on September 19, 1947, Nancy Ling was a middle child, the same age as Kathy Soliah. Her family owned a furniture store in Oakland and the Lings were prominent in the business community.

Nancy was a "curious girl," always asking questions and never satisfied with the answers. Her friends affectionately called her

"Ling." In junior high school, her life seemed to parallel other teenagers' lives. She worked on the Pep Club, as Kathy did in Palmdale, and although popular, Nancy's peers remembered her as being quiet and introspective. If she had any political views at this time, she kept them to herself.

When Nancy graduated from high school, she attended Richard Nixon's alma mater, Whittier College, for a short time, but she found the rules too stringent and could not conform to policy. Eventually, she transferred to Berkeley, but they had rules too. Nancy didn't like them. She hung out on Telegraph Avenue with other free-spirited souls, listened to Bob Dylan music, and tuned in to jazz, particularly Miles Davis. She was looking for work at an Oakland Opportunities Center when she met a twenty-three-year-old black musician, Gilbert Perry. Her parents were against their daughter's biracial relationship, but in spite of their disapproval, Nancy secretly married Gilbert the day after Christmas in 1967 and became Nancy Ling Perry.

Nancy graduated from Berkeley in 1970 and did her student teaching to get her certificate. But once again, rules got in the way and she quit. Her marriage was also on the rocks. Gilbert came and went, carrying on affairs with other women. They were always short of money. They loved French wine, and when they couldn't afford it, Nancy stole it.

Nancy was also an active participant in the People's Park demonstration. She was among the 400 people who were detained by authorities. Because she was petite and feminine, she was able to convince a Guardsman to let her go through the lines so that she could get home to take care of her one-month-old baby, which did not exist. He let her go, and she enjoyed telling the story to friends later on.

Nancy Ling Perry would become Cinque's most trustworthy comrade. After his vision of a *black* revolutionary army faded, it was she who came to personify for him the Berkeley white radical ready for battle. She was the first to declare, herself publicly a soldier in the Symbionese Liberation Army. She became its earliest symbol, the group's nurse, chemist, editor, and vigilant astrologer.

Cinque adopted a seven-headed cobra as the symbol for the SLA. Each head represented one of the seven principles of Kawaida—the same principles that he taught in his Unisight class when he was in Vacaville prison. He and his comrades created a flyer that read, "We have chosen the Seven-Headed Cobra as the emblem of the SLA because our forces are from every walk of life, from every religion, and of every race, and by our unity does our strength and our common goal for freedom from the chains of capitalism make true the meaning of our seven principles of unity."

By the spring of 1973, the Symbionese Liberation Army, firmly ensconced in Berkeley, had formally withdrawn from the mere theoretical pursuit of a Marxist revolution. They wanted immediate action to end U.S. imperialism and to "aid all oppressed people." Their intense, action-oriented agenda was not compatible with other Berkeley radicals, who moved too slowly for their taste. They wrote a "Declaration of War." They would stage a "People's War." Their declaration stated that they would "mobilize and initiate guerrilla warfare in the United States in order to start a revolutionary war and the total annihilation of the capitalist ruling class."

By the end of 1973, in place of rank, his soldiers in arms would have code names similar to the Latin American revolutionaries they admired.

(Mizmoon)* Patricia, making the final name change of her life, now became *Zoya*. Nancy Ling, for her spirit and drive, became *Fahizah*. Russ Little, in deference to his Floridian background, took the name of the great Seminole leader Osceola, *Osi*. Though not yet part of the army, Joe Remiro was designated *Bo*, and

---

* In most cases, members of the SLA will be referred to by their birth names.

Angela Atwood was renamed *Gelina.* Later, Emily Harris would become *Yolanda,* and Bill Harris, *Teko.* It is not known how Camilla came to be called Gabi.

There were a dozen more associates, who had been or were being recruited, tested, and observed before being considered for membership in the SLA. It is not known whether Kathy Soliah was being recruited at that time, but it is important to note that members were not required to fill out applications. They didn't need to produce resumés. There would be no way to prove who "joined" and who didn't.

The members' regimen was similar to Marine boot camp. At times members would practice surveillance, randomly selecting cars and people to watch and follow. They were secretive and did not want visitors or possible new recruits to see where they were living, so when the SLA members escorted them to wherever they were staying, the newcomers were warned to keep their eyes closed.

In the evening, SLA members drank Acadama plum wine and had endless discussions about the oppression of fascists and the cowardice of the inactive leftist movement. By the fall of 1973, the group was holding regular political education classes during which they would engage in "Criticism-Self-Criticism," a discipline handed down by Chairman Mao. They began to train their "army." They practiced urban guerrilla warfare and had regular drills. They practiced hand-to-hand combat, wrestling, martial arts, and even ear-biting. They shot BB's into a shower curtain so that they could retrieve them and do it again. They performed this drill so often they actually wore out their pistols.

Cinque also required the members to read Bay Area newspapers, compile information, and cut out pictures of the executives of major U.S. companies. They documented the addresses of their homes and businesses. They tailed them for days at a time, learning their routes to and from work. They observed the habits of their children, their pets, even the types of birds and trees in their neighborhoods, noting possible places to hide or avenues of escape. Joseph Remiro taught the group these tactics, which he had learned in Vietnam. Cinque supervised the training and chose the targets. In the end, they targeted fourteen business executives for either execution or kidnap for ransom.

It is not known if Kathy Soliah was aware of her best friend Angela's extracurricular activities. When the two of them auditioned and won parts for a production of Ibsen's *Hedda Gabler* with the Theater Company of Oakland, the producer said that Angela was "a nonentity, and not very bright either." But he called Kathy "an excellent actress. She had emotions, could feel love, hate, and anger. Kathy was able to balance and discipline her energies."

Marcus Foster

Thanks to reports in the media, Cinque was able to narrow down his search for someone to execute: Marcus Foster. Foster had just begun his third year as the Oakland schools superintendent.

Oakland schools were riddled by violence and crime, mostly black-on-black, and parents were demanding something be done. Foster was in the news because he was wavering on whether or not to support student identification cards and bring policemen into the schools to reduce crime. The sixties were over, and Foster thought it was time to cultivate a good relationship with the law-enforcement establishment. He hoped that students and police-men could attain some respect for each other. Fighting city hall was always a battle, and he wanted acceptance for his programs. Like many politicians, he realized that compromises had to be made. Unfortunately, he vacillated about what he thought was the right thing to do. Some Oakland leftists were calling him an Oreo cookie, black on the outside, white on the inside, but most people, black parents especially, were relieved at his insistence on doing something and advocating community involvement.

Cinque had been following the newspaper stories about Marcus Foster and the Oakland school crisis. What he didn't read was that Foster had actually withdrawn his support of student IDs. From the news reports, the SLA derived that Foster was linked to the police, and they thought it was horrible that he would actually promote the "pigs" in black schools. Cinque came to the conclusion that Foster was the "people's enemy."

One day in mid-October, Cinque and his army were gathered

in their Oakland safehouse, drinking plum wine. They had just finished their Criticism-Self-Criticism drill, which they performed daily. Together, they watched the evening news, which reported on Foster's police plan and opposition from some in the community. Cinque was furious. He vowed, "We're gonna off that nigger."

Marcus Foster was a bit overweight. He looked dignified with his thin-rimmed glasses and small mustache. He had a high-pitched voice that could be husky when he was enthused, and with his gesturing hands and piercing eyes, he might have been a Baptist preacher.

Before his stint as Oakland Schools Superintendent, Foster had had an illustrious career in education. In the mid-1960s, student bodies of public schools in Philadelphia's black communities were almost 100 percent black, while teachers and administrators were white. Foster had earned his master's and doctorate degree from the predominantly white University of Pennsylvania.

He went on to become principal of Catto Disciplinary School in Philadelphia where he managed to interest street kids and potential delinquents in reading books. When his tenure was up, so was the waiting list to get into Catto—a huge accomplishment for a school that had been reputed to be a steppingstone to prison.

Foster then became the first black man to become principal of a regular high school in Philadelphia's history. Before Foster appeared on the scene, students called Simon Gratzs High School, "Gratz for Rats." Foster won a fight against city hall to raze fourteen homes in the white community that bordered the school in order to allow for the construction of a gymnasium and sixteen new classrooms. Foster and his teachers persuaded dropouts to re-enroll, and during a three-day recruiting period, reclaimed 105 students. By 1969, the school's new motto was "Gratz is Great." That same year, Foster was honored with the Philadelphia Award for his leadership and for reversing the descending quality of education at Gratz.

A thirty-four-year-old white man, Robert Blackburn, appointed Foster director of the Office of Community Affairs in 1969. They had known each other at Gratz, where Blackburn had been on the board of education. Foster took the job, but he felt like a buffer between whites and blacks, and he missed working with children. So in 1970, when he was offered the job as Oakland school superintendent, he was ready for the change.

He accepted the job on two conditions: he insisted on a complete management review system, which would increase parent participation, and he wanted Robert Blackburn to be part of "the salt and pepper team" as his deputy superintendent. Blackburn had a good sense of humor; but his tough demeanor would earn him the reputation in Oakland as "Foster's hatchet man." Foster's no-nonsense attitude, his sincerity, and his approachability helped to ensure his popularity. Many who met him compared him to Martin Luther King Jr.

Foster's popularity probably made him even more of a target for the SLA. According to Payne and Findley (*The Life and Death of the SLA*), members of the SLA used surveillance techniques to locate Foster's home in the Oakland Hills area, follow him to work, and record his daily habits. They drew maps of the administration building of Oakland schools, including the auditorium, and they learned the assigned parking spaces for Foster and for his assistant, Blackburn. They all carried photographs of Foster. There would not be a mistake.

Nancy Ling Perry rented an apartment near Foster's office. She and Russ Little also rented another safehouse in suburban Concord, under the names of Mr. and Mrs. DeVoto, where they planned to retreat after the attack.

At this point, the army's daily BB pistol exercise became more personal. They placed a sketch of Foster over the cardboard human figure they had attached to the shower curtain. They stood at the end of the hall and used his sketch for their target practice. They took meticulous notes on all of the school crisis news, which would later be confiscated by authorities.

Some believed that Cinque targeted Marcus Foster because, like Cinque's own father, Foster was a strong, aggressive, black man. However, unlike Louis DeFreeze, Foster had not been defeated in life. To Cinque, though, Foster represented the black bourgeois, which was even worse than being a drunk or a child beater. Foster personified the establishment. Cinque's targeting a black man to kill confused the other members of his army. He even wanted to kill Huey Newton, the Black Panther leader, because Cinque believed Newton had morphed from a true revolutionary into a bourgeois capitalist.

It was Election Day, November 6, 1973. Cinque had been a fugitive from prison for eight months. The Fosters awakened early, as was their routine. Mrs. Albertine Foster made breakfast while her husband dressed before heading to his fourteen-hour workday at his office on Second Avenue.

From early morning until 4:30 P.M., Foster was at city hall trying to convince the Oakland City Council that they needed more money for recreational facilities in the city's ninety schools so that the kids would have someplace to go when school was out. He pleaded that cutting back such activities would lead to desperation and trouble. "I shudder to think about all the violence we'll see," he warned. After his lecture, he drove to the board of education meeting, back at district headquarters, for a debate on student ID cards and armed cops in the hallways. The SLA would not know that Foster tentatively withdrew his support at this meeting.

The three-story poured concrete headquarters of the Oakland school system was near Lake Merritt—only two blocks from the city's jail and also near the luxury apartment house where Huey Newton had rented a penthouse suite and had hired a four-hundred-pound bodyguard and a personal tailor.

John Bryan sets the scene in *This Soldier Still at War*: It was raining that evening after the meeting. Foster carried an umbrella as he and Blackburn made their way to Blackburn's car. One parking stall was marked "Superintendent" and the other

"Deputy Superintendent." To get to this dimly lit parking space, they had to pass through a narrow, boxed-in courtyard, and then through a narrower aisle between the main building and a small, wooden, temporary structure that was between the administration center and the annex. It was an ideal spot for an ambush.

As Foster and Blackburn headed for Blackburn's car, they were discussing the day's events and noticed two slight figures standing out in the rain between the big administration building and the old, wooden, portable structure. Blackburn and Foster almost brushed up against them, as they turned left into the parking area. Blackburn said later that although the two figures did look out of place, he thought they were probably stragglers from the board of education meeting, waiting for a ride.

As Blackburn and Foster entered the narrow space where Blackburn's 1971 Chevy Vega was parked on the wet pavement, Blackburn headed to the passenger side of the car to open the door for Foster, who was right behind him. The shooting happened without warning.

Blackburn described the ambush in *This Soldier Still at War*:

"'I saw the muzzle flashes of the guns. I had my briefcase in one hand, my keys in the other. They seemed to be repeated shots in very fast sequence. A split second later I saw Dr. Foster. He seemed to stumble forward.'

"Eight bullets popped out of the barrels of two pistols blazing away in the steady hands of the two long-haired youths who had followed Foster and Blackburn onto the parking lot. The first seven slugs hit Foster in the back. He whirled to face his assassins, and the last shot tore through the front of his body. The hollow-pointed slugs simply ripped him apart. They chewed up his entire torso."

When Blackburn tried to go to the aid of Dr. Foster, Cinque, crouching low in some wet shrubbery, cocked the hammer of his 12-gauge shotgun and aimed. The first shot missed Blackburn and hit the car's right fender. But on the second shot, ten to twelve hard, steel balls cut into Blackburn's flesh. They entered his liver and spleen, his left kidney, abdomen, and left arm. He screamed in surprise but managed to run more than two hundred feet from the parking lot to the administration building where he fell into the arms of an employee who was working late. "Marc's been shot!" he yelled.

The police arrived at the scene quickly. They noticed a strange, sharp odor around Foster's body. It smelled like almonds. Later, they discovered that the tips of the bullets had been hollowed and the cavities filled with cyanide. The SLA would become known for its cyanide-tipped bullets. When the poison entered any part of the body, even the hands, it would get into the bloodstream and the victim would die.

At 6:30 P.M., Mrs. Albertine Foster was just going out to vote when the phone rang. The voice told her that her husband had been shot, and they were sending a security car to take her to the hospital. She didn't know if he was dead or alive but Marcus Foster had died en route to the hospital. Blackburn, who was seriously injured, was hospitalized for ten days. Apparently cyanide was not a sure thing.

There were dozens of memorial services for Marcus Foster who was called among other things, "A man's man, a people's man." Thousands of people attended, and among the mourners was Black Panther Bobby Seale. At the last memorial service, Albertine Foster urged the multitude of mourners to "Pray for Dr. Foster's assassins."

(After Robert Blackburn recovered, he became the new superintendent for the Oakland school district, carrying on Foster's legacy.)

Marcus Foster's murder caused outrage in the community and the SLA found the fame it was looking for. That Saturday they were on the front page of every newspaper in the Bay Area. The group studied these articles, cut them out, stapled them together, and reviewed them in their Criticism-Self-Criticism sessions. Three days after Foster's execution, the SLA sent its first communiqué to Bay Area newspapers. In it, they bragged about using cyanide, a fact that only the police knew about.

David Horowitz later wrote this about the incident in an unsigned editorial for *Ramparts* under the title "Terrorism and the Left":

"In executing Marcus Foster and in making no effort to justify that execution by any doctrine of specific guilt, the SLA assumes the power of life and death over everyone.... It recognizes no authority except its own will, which it identifies with the will of the people in much the same manner that many psychopathic killers claim to be instructed by God. It has killed a defenseless individual whose guilt is not only not proved, but is mainly a fantasy of his executioners. It has committed a crime not only against the individual in question, but against the entire black, brown and Asian communities of Oakland."

Not all of the attention the SLA received was what they had hoped for. Other members of the New Left condemned them for their violence; they now wanted to distance themselves from the Symbionese Liberation Army. Some people in the revolutionary movement feared the SLA, and their small donations to the terrorist group ceased. The dozen or so core members who were left—Angela (Gelina), Patricia (Mizmoon, Zoya), Nancy (Fahizah), Camilla (Gabi), Bill (Teko), and Emily (Yolanda)—didn't make enough money in their minimum wage jobs to pay their rent, let alone support their cause.

On January 10, 1974, two months after Marcus Foster's execution, a van going too slowly in the Concord area caught a patrolman's attention. It was 1:20 A.M. He flashed his headlights and turned on his red light to signal the van to pull over to the curb. Before he got out of his car, he radioed the van's license number to his dispatcher and also asked for a backup. He got out of his car, approached the van, and asked the driver, Russell Little, for his license. Little's license read "Robert James Scalise," a name he had taken from a child who had died of leukemia in 1953 at the age of six. The patrolman asked for the license of the van's passenger. The name on that license was Joe Remiro.

Little explained to the officer that he and Remiro were looking for the "DeVoto" residence, but he didn't bother to ask the officer to help with directions, which raised the officer's suspicions even further. He went back to his patrol car and learned that there were no warrants out for these men's arrests but he also found out that there were no DeVoto's living in that neighborhood.

He went back to the van and asked Remiro and Little to get out of the van and submit to a search. Remiro got out, closed the door, and opened his jacket. The officer noticed his pistol. Knowing what was next, the officer ran to the rear of his patrol car and crouched behind the trunk. He saw the muzzle blast of the two shots being fired at him. They missed. He described it as "being similar to flashbulbs going off in your face in the dark." The officer shot back. As Remiro ran for cover, Little sped off in the van. The officer radioed for help. Two more patrol cars screeched on to the scene and blockaded the streets. One of the officer's bullets had gone through the van's back windshield and had hit Little in the shoulder. He was bleeding heavily, and now he was trapped. When ordered to do so, Russell Little got out of the van with his arms raised and said, "I give up."

When the officers searched the van, they found a loaded .38-caliber pistol and a 9-mm rifle that had been purchased in Los Angeles. They also found over 2,000 leaflets titled "Goals" with covers emblazoned with the seven-headed cobra and titled "Symbionese Liberation Army." They had their first break in the Marcus Foster murder.

Remiro, dodging between houses and through back yards, made his way to the safehouse at 1560 Sutherland Court. He blurted out the events of the night's disaster to Cinque, Nancy, and Patricia. They all heard the police outside, stalking in and out of bushes searching for Remiro. They knew that they couldn't take a chance on the police finding more evidence in the house. Collectively, they decided that Remiro would have to steal out of the house and turn himself in. That would give the rest of them time to escape.

For some reason, Remiro agreed. He was going to be the sacrifice. He walked out of the safehouse and hid behind a car across the intersection. According to *Voices of Guns*, Remiro gave himself up to the police at 5:32 A.M. "I'm coming out," he called with his hands raised. When he was searched, the officers found his .380 PP Walther automatic pistol, the same gun that had fired the cyanide shots into Marcus Foster two months earlier.

At 6:00 P.M., the police got a call informing them that a house in Concord on Sutherland Court was on fire. It was Nancy Ling Perry's botched attempt to extinguish evidence. Neighbors saw Nancy and another man speed out of the driveway in what would turn out to be Willie Wolfe's car. The fire was a dud, and the first firemen to arrive were able to douse it with just one hose before it could destroy documents, clothes, and ammunition boxes. Among the evidence found were two pipe bombs, fire bombs, bullets with their tips drilled out and packed with cyanide, revolutionary how-to books, two BB pistols, typewriters, maps, radical posters, and more.

There was also a handwritten diagram labeled "Ambush," showing the exact layout of the Oakland schools administration building parking lot where Foster and Blackburn had been shot. Police also found a long hit list of high-powered executives including the presidents of Wells Fargo Bank, Bank of America, Standard Oil, Kaiser Corporation, and more.

The closets were full of middle-class clothing, an assortment of women's wigs, a theatrical make-up kit laden with tones for African-American complexions, and a book on creating false faces for TV and movies.

Little and Remiro were jailed for a time at San Quentin. Remiro was star-struck by the other inmates, past and present. George Jackson had been gunned down there, and according to John Bryan in *This Soldier Still at War*, Jackson's books, *Soledad Brother* and *Blood in My Eye* were the bibles of San Quentin.

Later, Remiro said of his fellow inmates, "These are the guerrillas of the prisons. These are the combat veterans. . . . We had a chance to talk to a lot of really fine comrades in San Quentin. . . . Fine comrades . . . fine comrades."

Remiro's father was devastated over the news of Joe's arrest: "He wouldn't have harmed anyone. He wouldn't even hurt a bird. But ever since he came back from the Army, he's never been the same." His father had thrown Joe out of the house when Joe had tried to tell him about the massacres he had participated in during the Vietnam War. Now, it was too late for empathy. He did not visit Joe in jail.

One week after the house fire, Nancy (Fahizah) wrote an open "Letter to the People" explaining why she started the blaze: "The house in Concord, California, was a Symbionese Liberation Army information/intelligence headquarters, nothing more. The house was set afire by me only to melt away any fingerprints that may have been overlooked.

"The report that mass armaments were found in that house is a lie. It is an attempt to frame my two comrade brothers. . . . We can easily verify that the ballistics on the .380 now in the hands of pig agents do not match those of the weapon used in the attack on the Oakland Board of Education." Nancy claimed that Little and Remiro were members of the intelligence unit and thus not involved in the group's violent action. Little and Remiro were charged with the murder of Marcus Foster and would end up in San Quentin prison.

The day after the arrests, police raided the Peking House on Chabot Road. Investigators discovered trunk loads of books, posters, and typewriters, an M-1 carbine, boots that belonged to Little, and an electric drill with many bits that they surmised may have been used to hollow out the bullets for the cyanide. The press was there to observe the raid, as was David Gunnell, the landlord who served the press tea while the six-hour search went on.

Other radical groups and people working in the prison move- ment were angry about Foster's murder. It brought unwanted attention to them. Angela Davis and Jerry Rubin were openly critical of the murder. The Black Panthers said that they had no time for the SLA. Remiro later said that was no surprise since Huey Newton was at the top of every revolutionary's hit list.

Willie Wolfe was visiting his father in Pennsylvania the night Remiro and Little were arrested. He had hitchhiked there, leaving his car with Nancy (Fahizah). (Wolfe was not an official SLA member yet because Cinque felt he was too young to be trusted.) Willie's father, Dr. Wolfe, had planned a special dinner for Willie for the night of January 11, but that morning, Willie got a call from the Bay Area telling him what had happened. He didn't tell his father that he had to leave, but instead told his mother he was taking a bus to New York. His parents would never see him again.

Following the arrests of Russell Little and Joe Remiro, Nancy Ling Perry and Cinque dropped out of sight. Patricia Soltysik quit her job as a janitor at the Berkeley library and also disappeared. Emily Harris called in sick at the Survey Research Center in Berkeley where she was working as a clerk-typist and resigned several days later for "personal reasons." Bill Harris quit his job as a mail carrier. Angela Atwood quit her job as a waitress.

Over the Christmas holidays in 1973, Kathy Soliah went to Mexico for an "extended vacation." According to *Voices of Guns*, Kathy's parents later said that Kathy's traveling companion was an "overly masculine" woman. By mid-January, Angela had become a fugitive, Gelina, of the SLA, and Kathy reportedly lost touch with her. Kathy took on several odd jobs, working in a bookstore and, for a while, house painting with Jim and Steve. Then she got another acting job with the Emeryville Shakespeare Company.

Through the evidence that was found, police learned that the SLA was connected with the Vietnam Veterans Against the War (VVAW). They deduced that there were about twenty-five members of the SLA and that they were well educated, with some members involved in the lesbian movement. But they missed one important piece of evidence.

They had confiscated a little green notebook in the Concord house with the name "Patricia Campbell Hearst." It contained personal information about her. The notes said, "At UC—daughter of Hearst—Junior—Art student" and "on the night of the full moon of January 7. . . ." Apparently, the authorities didn't think it was important. Randolph Hearst would not learn of that notebook until twelve weeks after his daughter's kidnapping.

Patricia Hearst was now going to be the trade-off for Remiro and Little. After a few months, Emily, Bill, and Angela came out of hiding and rejoined their friends. Willie Wolfe also returned to the Bay Area. He had told his sister in Pennsylvania that he was afraid for his friends' lives. Camilla Hall came back because of her love for Patricia Soltysik. Although they were small in numbers, Cinque believed his army was strong enough to perform a political kidnapping—so now they could finally get the respect and publicity they deserved.

Patricia Hearst: Kidnapped

Randolph Hearst was chairman of the board of the Hearst Corporation, which owned a chain of newspapers, magazines, and television and radio stations nationwide. As always, Cinque and his group had done their homework.

Patty Hearst was only nineteen years old when the SLA changed her life forever. Born in San Francisco in 1954, she had grown up with her parents and four sisters in a mansion in Hillsborough, about twenty miles south of San Francisco. Her mother, Catherine, was a devout Catholic. On the board of regents at the University of California, Catherine Hearst was a staunch conservative and had been an outspoken critic of student demonstrations in the sixties. The Hearsts were a tight, loving family, and most people would say that Patty had led a charmed life.

February 4, 1974, began as a day like any other. Patty was a student at UC Berkeley, living with her fiancé, Steven Weed. After a day at classes and the library, she looked forward to making dinner for Steve. After dinner, she began to clean up the kitchen so they could both settle down and study. Patty Hearst describes her abduction in *Every Secret Thing,* her memoirs, published eight years later, in 1982. (Much of Hearst's version of the events was corroborated by FBI reports, and testimonies at Wendy Yoshimura's and Steve Soliah's trial. Newspaper accounts also corroborated her story.)

At about 9:00 P.M., the doorbell rang and Steve answered it. From the kitchen, Patty heard a girl's nervous voice exclaiming that she had hit a car outside and needed to use the phone.

Patty's first thought was that the girl might have hit her MG, which was in the carport. But she didn't have time for second thoughts because the next thing she knew, two men burst into their apartment. The first man knocked Steve to the floor, and the second man rushed over to Patty and clamped a hand over her mouth just as she screamed. As Steve tried to get up, one of the men kicked him in the side of his face, and then the girl with the nervous voice who had followed them in kicked him again. She produced a nylon rope and they tied Steve's hands behind his back.

The girl then shoved Patty against the stove and pointed a black automatic pistol at her face. She clamped her hand over Patty's mouth and warned her to be quiet so no one would get hurt. Patty noticed that the girl was about her size, small, with a pale face. She had frizzy blond hair, which she would later find out was a wig. Next, one of the men came into the kitchen and pushed Patty to the floor. He sat on her back and warned her to keep her head down. He tied her hands behind her back and then thrust a rag with knots into her mouth and tied it behind her head. Next, he blindfolded her and tied that behind her head as well. The girl was shouting for them all to get out of there.

As Steve lay on the floor, yelling for them to take "anything you want," Patty was being dragged out of the house, down the concrete steps to the carport below, to be thrown into the trunk of a car. In the trunk, she managed to get the ropes off her wrists and remove her blindfold. Within several minutes, the car stopped, and she was yanked out of the trunk. Next, she was shoved into a waiting station wagon on the floor in front of the back seat, and the three people who had abducted her piled in over her. Later, she would learn that those three people were Donald DeFreeze (Cinque), Bill Harris (Teko), and Angela At-wood (Gelina), Kathy Soliah's best friend.

Two others were waiting in the car: Emily Harris and, report-edly, Thero Wheeler, another escaped convict who had helped Cinque, through Venceremos contacts, to escape from prison. It had been Wheeler's idea to kidnap Hearst. A blanket was thrown over Patty's head, and as she cried, the black man yelled, "Shut your mouth, bitch, or I'm going to blow your fucking head off!"

They retied her hands and blindfolded her again. She had seen their faces. They drove for several hours before parking in a garage. Patty Hearst was led up some stairs and down hallways and finally stuffed into a closet that reeked of body odor. Her captors guided her into a sitting position and warned her not to touch her gag or her blindfold or the ties around her wrists. They put a radio on the floor, which further assaulted her senses with loud, raucous soul music. Patty was very sensitive to sound and at home had played her radio so softly that her sisters, Anne and Vicki, wondered how she could hear it. The door was slammed shut. Patty Hearst would remain a prisoner in that tiny closet for the next fifty-seven days, a total of 1,368 hours.

After several hours, General Field Marshal Cinque entered the closet and introduced himself as the leader of the SLA. He told her that his army had kidnapped her because her father was a "corporate enemy of the people." He told her the SLA had declared "War on Amerikkka," and explained that the three *K*s symbolized Klu Klux Klan, to represent racism in the capitalist system. Soon, Angela Atwood (Gelina) came in and told her how lucky she was to be in that closet rather than in a pig's prison like their comrades Russ Little (Osi) and Joe Remiro (Bo), who were being beaten and tortured in prison. Once they were released, she said, Patty would be freed.

During those fifty-seven days, her captors constantly re-minded her of her "bourgeois life" and of her "capitalist narcissism." Through that closed door they recited their favorite Marxist readings and read her news clippings about events in Third World countries.

Every day she heard them perform calisthenics and military drills. They ran from room to room, clicking their rifles and jamming their ammunition into place. They would sneak up to the closet door and simulate rapid fire. They cut her long hair to one inch from her scalp. Cinque told her that she would be treated the same way that Russ Little and Joe Remiro were being treated.

Cinque wanted the world to know that the SLA was responsible for Patty Hearst's kidnapping. He decided that they would tape messages, which they called "communiqués," and send them to the media. Just to make sure that the public knew that Patty was still alive, Cinque had her talk into the tape recorder. Eventually he removed Patty's gag and the ties around her wrists so that she could tape the communiqués, which they rehearsed over and over again. However, the blindfold stayed on—while Cinque and Willie Wolfe (Cujo) repeatedly raped her. (Cinque had finally let Willie Wolfe in as a full SLA member.)

The first communiqué was sent that week. The SLA ordered the media to reprint all their materials including the SLA symbol: the seven-headed cobra and its slogan, "Death to the Fascist Insect that Preys upon the Life of the People."

The next week, Cinque sent a letter and tape to Berkeley's radio station, KPFA, to remind the Hearsts that their daughter had been "arrested by the SLA for their sins." He charged Randolph Hearst with being the head of "the fascist media empire of the ultra-right Hearst Corporation, which is one of the largest propaganda institutions of this present military dictatorship of the armed corporate state that we now live under in this nation."

The tape went on: "It is therefore the direction of this court that before any term of negotiations for the release of subject prisoner be initiated, that an action of good faith be shown on the part of the Hearst family to allow the court and the oppressed people of the world and this nation to ascertain as to the real interest and co-operative attitude of the Hearst family, and, in so doing, show some form of repentance for the murdering and suffering they have aided and profited from. And this good faith gesture is to be in the form of a token gesture to the oppressed people that they aid the corporate state in robbing, and removing their rights to freedom and liberty. This gesture is to be in the form of food for the needy and unemployed and to which the following instructions are directed to be followed to the letter."

This "gesture" was to be carried out over a four-week period each Tuesday, Thursday, and Saturday beginning on February 19. The distributions were expected to occur in large supermarkets in poor communities all over the Bay Area. In closing, the document read, "If this gesture of good faith is not met, then we will assume that there is no basis for negotiations and we will no longer take and maintain in good health and spirits prisoners of war."

Patty Hearst was also on this tape. She first explained to her parents that she was okay and then tried to tell them something about her captors: "These people aren't just a bunch of nuts. They've been really honest with me, but they're perfectly willing to die for what they're doing. I'm here because I'm a member of a ruling-class family." She asked them to try to understand why she was kidnapped. She begged them to "get the food thing organized before the nineteenth" to speed up her release.

It didn't work. On live television, Randolph Hearst told his daughter and the SLA that their demand was impossible to meet. (According to the California State Department of Social Welfare, the cost for such a demand would have been approximately $400 million.) Hearst promised that he would make a counter offer that was acceptable. On February 16, Cinque responded to Hearst's broadcast with another tape: "We will accept a sincere offer on your part."

Patty Hearst spoke on that tape as well. In part, she said, "Whatever you come up with basically is okay. Just do it as fast as you can, and everything will be fine."

After much negotiating with the board of Hearst Corporations, Randolph Hearst finally came up with what he thought was an acceptable ransom figure. On February 19, he announced that he would set up a $2 million charitable organization to "benefit the poor and needy." The distribution would begin that Friday on February 22 at the sites the SLA had demanded. Thousands of people lined up on that cold, foggy morning. It was a disaster.

People were frustrated from waiting in the long lines and fights broke out at the distribution centers. Food was thrown from the trucks, actually hitting some people. More than twenty people ended up in hospitals. Some of them filed lawsuits against the Hearst Corporation and against the program, which had been named "People in Need" (PIN). Thousands of dollars of food was stolen daily from the warehouses and the distribution centers. Some of the food that was purchased from various companies was inferior, and some was never even distributed.

Now the SLA's demands were upped an additional $4 million. Randolph Hearst's response was one of defeat. He told the press that the demand was far beyond his financial capabilities. "The matter is now out of my hands," he stated. And then he cried.

A spokesman told the press that the Hearst Corporation would give $2 million in 1974 and another $2 million in 1975 to PIN if Patty Hearst were returned to her family unharmed. Using this information, members of the SLA tried to convince their prisoner, who was still in the closet, that her father was not interested in helping her.

During her days in the closet, she was forced to rehearse the scripts for the communiqués. It was important to the SLA that she sound believable. She knew that her life depended on it. She was hungry and weak. The group now included her in their sessions of Criticism-Self-Criticism. They went over her taped messages to her family, dissecting each phrase, each intonation, making sure that it sounded as if the messages were from her heart. They also showed her tapes of the press conferences given by her family and her fiancé, criticizing them, and further dampening her hopes that they would rescue her.

To keep safe and secret, they decided to move their base of operation. They stuffed Patty into a large, plastic garbage can, rolled it into the trunk of a car, and drove to San Francisco, where they rented an apartment on Golden Gate Avenue, less than a mile from the FBI headquarters. From this site, they delivered their taped communiqués to the media and brazenly ventured out to restaurants, shops, and libraries wearing their disguises of wigs, makeup, and odd clothing.

The army still included Cinque, Nancy Ling Perry (Fahizah), Angela Atwood (Gelina), Patricia Soltysik (Zoya), Willie Wolfe (Cujo), Emily Harris (Yolanda), Bill Harris (Teko), and Camilla Hall (Gabi), who had been the last to join. Maybe Camilla stayed with the SLA in hopes of rekindling her relationship with Patricia (Mizmoon) or perhaps she didn't know where else to go. These eight people and Patty lived in a one-bedroom apartment. In this San Francisco apartment, Patty Hearst would be converted to an urban guerrilla, a revolutionary for the people. Here is where Patty would become "Tania," named for the Russian woman who traveled with the Latin American revolutionary Che Guevara.

The SLA had an open-sex policy, another rebellion against the establishment, particularly against the bourgeoisie. The group lived together as a family. They shared cooking as well as sex. Of course, there were jealousies. Nancy (Fahizah) and Patricia (Zoya) thought that Patty Hearst got too much attention. Cinque and Willie Wolfe both wanted her. Willie fell in love with her. And as far as Patty knew, her captors were the only people who cared about her.

The media speculated that she might be brainwashed, or dead. She answered this theory in another communiqué sent on March 10. In part, she said, "I hope you will believe me and not think that I've been brainwashed or tortured into saying this. I'm speaking honestly from my heart. My father is not even attempting to show a gesture of good faith." She described some of the education she was getting from her captors. "They have given me some newspaper reports to read about the current practices of psycho-surgery and the daily use of drugs and tranquilizers in prisons throughout the country." She discussed the poor prison conditions at San Quentin. "I have been reading a book by George Jackson called *Blood in My Eye*. I'm starting to understand what he means when he talks about fascism in America."

Through these tapes, the nation witnessed the conversion of Patty Hearst. The public didn't know about the closet or the loud music, about being stuffed in garbage cans or the rapes. Her captors used all her senses to break her down. To many people who followed the story, it looked as though she were a spoiled, ungrateful, rich girl who liked the taste of anarchy. Perhaps this was an adventure for her. She was probably bored with her bourgeois existence and this "kidnapping" was a way for her to spit on her family and everything they had worked for. Some people speculated that she had planned her own kidnapping. For some, Patty Hearst was a symbol of all the rebellious youth, the drug culture and the counter-culture, that had permeated the country since the sixties.

Much has been written about the art of "conversion." Eric Hoffer taught that a change usually occurs after a potential convert reaches a level of personal suffering and despair. Sometimes the conversion is permanent.

In one of the SLA's communiqués, Patty said, "I would like to begin this statement by informing the public that I wrote what I am about to say. It's what I feel. I have never been forced to say anything on any tape. Nor have I been brainwashed, drugged, tortured, hypnotized, or in any way confused. As George Jackson wrote, 'It's me, the way I want it, the way I see it.'"

A communiqué delivered on April 4 said, "It should be obvious that people who don't even care about their own children couldn't possibly care about someone else's children. If you and the rest of the corporate state were willing to do this to millions of people to maintain power to serve your needs, you would also kill me if necessary to serve those same needs. How long will it take before white people in this country understand that whatever happens to a black child happens sooner or later to a white child? How long will it be before we all understand that we must fight for our freedom?"

The SLA trusted Patty (Tania) enough to teach her how to wrestle and karate-chop. They taught her how to dismantle and assemble shotguns and rifles. She was in boot camp with the SLA, becoming a full-fledged advocate of their revolution. But the group was running out of money. The Black Panther Party and other radical groups issued statements saying that they did not approve of political kidnapping and would not help the SLA in any way.

So, the SLA was desperate. They planned to commit their most daring and most public crime since the kidnapping. On the morning of April 15, 1974, the Hibernia Bank in San Francisco opened at 9:00 A.M. Four days earlier, the SLA had rented four cars. At about 9:45 A.M., Bill, Emily, Angela, and Willie parked their rented red Hornet across the street from the bank. From here they could see the front door of the bank and cover the street from both directions. Cinque, Nancy, Patricia, Camilla, and Patty pulled up next to the bank in a green station wagon. They wore bulky coats, inappropriate for the warm, sunny morning, as witnesses would later remember. Cinque wore a wide-brimmed, floppy hat.

They strode into the bank in a single line and took their planned positions. Camilla covered the entrance, and Nancy ran around kicking customers and screaming, "SLA. . . . SLA!" Cinque yelled to the guard, "Get on the floor, you mother-fucker, get on the floor!" He stood just behind the rail, which separated the desks of bank officers from the patrons. Patricia (Zoya), who was also kicking patrons and screaming at them, vaulted over the teller's counter and demanded, "Give me the keys!"

Patty wore a thick brown wig with ringlets and a knee-length coat over bell-bottom pants and short boots. Her hand plunged through the hole in her coat where the right pocket had been cut out and swung up her sawed-off carbine with her finger on the trigger. The bank cameras caught the entire scene and the whole country witnessed the first criminal act of Patty Hearst, or Tania, her new persona. They heard her begin her prepared speech,

"This is Tania. . . . Patricia Hearst," but that is all they heard because she forgot the rest of her lines. Cinque was shouting out numbers, indicating that it was time to go, and when he got to number nine, Nancy Ling Perry shot an elderly man with her submachine gun. They jumped over the fallen man and fled from the bank.

By the end of the heist, the SLA had robbed the Hibernia Bank of more than $10,000, shot (not killed) two bystanders, and escaped in two rented cars. They were thrilled with their accomplishment, Cinque exclaiming that now other radical groups would realize that the SLA meant business. Authorities would fear them. They were on their way. Patty feared Cinque's wrath for forgetting her speech for the cameras, but to her relief, he was sympathetic and told her that it was all right.

Patty heard herself described on all the news channels as a member of the SLA and felt sick to her stomach because she knew that she had crossed the line, and that she'd be in as much trouble with the authorities as she was with her captors. She had cut herself off from her family and everyone else on the outside. She was now part of the SLA. Patty decided to take it day by day and prayed that she would survive. At this point, Steve Weed, her fiancé, held a press conference declaring that the photographs he had seen convinced him that Patty had been coerced at gunpoint to participate in the robbery.

Even though Patty Hearst had been kidnapped two months earlier, pictures of the SLA members had still not circulated and the kidnappers had not been fully identified—at least not before the robbery. After the robbery, though, pictures of their faces appeared in post offices and police precincts all over the country. Patty, Cinque, Camilla, Patricia, and Nancy had been photographed inside the bank. Bill, Emily, Angela, and Willie had been in the getaway car, and were not identified.

When it was over, Cinque praised Patty for her performance. Emily later said that Patty had loved the escapade, had "been in her glory." Bill agreed. He said that they had tested her to make sure that she was really one of them. He said she passed all the rigorous tests of physical as well as emotional strength. They were impressed that she was "bright, adaptable, and caught on quickly." And she didn't act spoiled. The bank robbery had been her biggest test of all, a test she passed with flying colors.

Angela became the make-up artist and was in charge of disguising the members of the group before they left their "safehouses." She was good enough to make the white members pass as blacks. She disguised Cinque as a woman before he left the house. She taught him how to walk with a feminine gait, and how to wear lipstick and powder. He had no problems with it. Angela was also in charge of writing the "Tania" scripts.

Since the robbery, they'd become widely recognizable; it would be much harder to hide. Of course, now that Patty Hearst had participated in the bank robbery, the SLA could no longer control the media with their communiqués. On April 24, Patty sent the world another tape. Part of her statement said, "On April 15 my comrades and I expropriated $10,660.02 from the Sunset branch of the Hibernia Bank. Casualties could have been avoided had the persons involved kept out of the way and cooperated with the people's forces until after our departure.

"I was positioned so that I could hold customers and bank personnel who were on the floor. My gun was loaded and at no time did any of my comrades intentionally point their guns at me. Careful examination of the photographs, which were published, clearly shows this was true. Our action on April 15 forced the corporate state to help finance the revolution. As for being brainwashed, the idea is ridiculous to the point of being beyond belief. It's interesting the way early reports characterized me as beautiful, intelligent, liberal, while in more recent reports I'm a homely girl who's been brainwashed. I am a soldier in the people's army. Patria o muerte, Venceremos."

That week, Randolph Hearst offered a $50,000 reward for his daughter.

Cinque monitored police broadcasts and knew of their every

move. The group abandoned their Golden Gate Avenue apartment just before the FBI located it. In early May, Cinque decided that they would pull up stakes and head for Los Angeles. Later, Emily Harris would say that it was the biggest mistake they ever made.

Shootout: Burned Alive

On May 16, 1974, Emily and Bill Harris went into Mel's Sporting Goods Store in the Los Angeles suburb of Inglewood to stock up on clothes and an ammunition belt. As the couple roamed up and down the aisles, checking items off their list, Patty sat in the red-and-white Volkswagen van, reading the afternoon newspaper. Bill, who liked to live on the edge, couldn't resist stuffing a bandolier in the pocket of his hunting jacket. They went up to the cashier to pay for their items and then walked out of the store with their $31.50 of merchandise.

Bill was not aware that a guard had seen him take the bandolier, a wide strap with pockets worn over the shoulder, used to carry ammunition. When the guard followed him out of the store and asked him to please come back in, Bill refused. Bill and the guard got into a fight, both of them falling to the sidewalk. When Emily jumped on the guard's back, he yelled for the other clerks to come to his aid.

Bill pulled out his revolver, but one of the clerks wrestled it away from him, and the guard managed to get a handcuff on one of Bill's wrists. Patty saw the altercation from the window of the van and before anyone knew what was happening, she opened fire with her automatic carbine, shattering store windows. This would be an action that would come back to haunt her.

While the guard and the clerks ducked for their lives, Bill and Emily ran back to the van, hopped in, and the three of them sped away.

Furious, one of the clerks jumped in his car and followed

them. Just a few blocks away, he saw the three fugitives jump out of the van and hijack another car from a terrified, unsuspecting couple. The clerk realized that he was in over his head, backed up and went to a phone to call the police.

When the authorities found the van, they also found evidence of the elusive SLA: a woman's wig and scarf, several .30-caliber cartridges, and clothes. They also found a parking citation for overtime parking from a garage just two blocks from their rented safehouse. Emily had forgotten about the ticket and had stuffed it into the pocket of a gun carrying case, which they had left in the abandoned van.

Because they felt that the cops were in hot pursuit of them, they knew that they could not go back to the SLA safehouse because they would lead authorities to their comrades. They drove around that evening, realizing that they had to get rid of the hijacked car and find more transportation. Emily noticed a "Car For Sale" sign in a yard as they drove by. She left Bill and Patty in the hijacked car, and went up to the house to ask the owner for a test drive.

Eighteen-year-old Thomas Matthews, said sure, and once they got off his block, they stopped to pick up Patty and Bill, who announced to Matthews, "We are from the SLA." Then, Bill showed him his .45 automatic pistol and ordered him to get into the back seat of his car, admonishing him, "If you do what you're told, you won't get hurt."

Matthews lay down on the floor as he was told and they put a blanket over his head. After driving around for about an hour, they stopped at a store and Emily went in to buy a hacksaw to saw the handcuff off of Bill's wrist. When it grew dark, they drove to a drive-in movie, and Matthews successfully removed the handcuff from Bill's wrist and asked if he could keep it for a souvenir. Bill graciously gave it to him. "Sure, kid," he said.

While they were at the movie, Bill and Emily made several trips to the refreshment stand to try to call their comrades. No one answered at the designated number. Frustrated, they left the drive-in and drove around the Hollywood Hills all night long.

Matthews fell asleep in the back seat, and when he awakened it was morning. He overheard the three fugitives discussing how they would steal their next car. It was decided that Patty and Emily would walk up a few blocks and hitchhike.

An unsuspecting man, who they later identified as Frank Sutter, offered them a ride. Emily crawled into the front seat next to him and Patty got in the back. When Sutter pulled away from the curb, Emily pointed her gun at him and told him that they were the SLA and they needed his car. They forced the terrified man to crawl over the driver's seat into the back, and they dashed the car back to where Bill was parked. When they had been alone, Bill had warned Matthews to lie face down on the floor for ten minutes.

When Patty and Emily came by, Bill jumped into the hijacked car, leaving Matthews behind, and they sped away. They drove Mr. Sutter around all day before they purchased a used car. Then, luckily for him, they let him go.

As they patrolled the area, they made frequent stops and left notes underneath sinks in restrooms, phone booths, and other planned spots in case their comrades were looking for them, but the notes went unanswered. The shootout at Mel's Sporting Goods Store had probably been on the news and there was no way they could make contact because that might lead the police to their comrades. Finally, they decided to rest in a motel in Anaheim. On their way to Anaheim, they heard on the car radio that the police had surrounded a suspected SLA safehouse and were planning to assault it.

During the night, Cinque, Patricia Soltysik, Nancy, Willie, Camilla, and Angela had also been driving around, looking for a place to stay. In the middle of the night, they noticed the lights on in a small stucco house on East Fifty-Fourth Street in the Compton neighborhood. Cinque knocked on the door, and a woman answered. He told her in a soft voice that the police were pursuing him and his friends, and they needed a place to stay. She hesitated until he offered her $100. The four occupants of the house were drinking wine, playing dominos, and listening to the radio while two children slept. According to *Voices of Guns,* Cinque and his comrades moved right in, with "sleeping bags, suitcases, cardboard cartons filled with documents, and enough weapons to outfit an infantry platoon." One of the occupants in the house offered to take their van around the block so that it wouldn't be detected.

The next morning, on May 17, the women in the house got nervous as they watched Nancy Ling Perry fill several bottles with gasoline. As they whispered to each other in the kitchen, wondering what to do with these "house guests," the women swallowed some "nerve pills" to calm themselves. Cinque sent someone out for food and beer. The two kids woke up, went off to school, and the women went to bed.

Cinque bragged to the occupants of the house and also a few strangers who dropped by that day that he and his comrades were the SLA. When the visitors left the house, they quickly spread the word that the real SLA was right there in their very own neighborhood. It was almost as if Cinque were begging for a confrontation with the police. Why would he let people come and go as they pleased when he had announced who he was and shown everyone his arsenal? He told one of the occupants that he was aware that police were in the area and that there would probably be a shootout. "We're going to take a lot of motherfucking pigs with us," he said. By now, the cops had gotten word that the SLA was in the Compton neighborhood. They circled the blocks, discovered the van, and were directed to the stucco house where Cinque and his comrades waited.

When the police arrived, they didn't know which SLA members were inside, and they didn't know if Patty Hearst was with them. They staked out the house, and at 5:45 P.M., Captain Mervin King pleaded through his bullhorn, "Come out with your

hands up. Comply immediately and you will not be harmed."
Amazingly, the SLA allowed the two remaining occupants, including a child, to leave. From those people, they got a fair description of Cinque and his comrades. Now they knew that they
had at least five members of the SLA, heavily armed.

Television cameras from every network arrived on the scene.
It was dinnertime, prime-time news. Patty Hearst's kidnappers
were in that house, and if she was with them, there might finally
be an end to the story that the country had been following like a
soap opera for four months. Viewers nationwide gawked at their
television screens, watching as FBI agents unloaded ammunition
from their cars. Perhaps there would finally be closure and answers to Patty Hearst's conversion to Tania.

Television viewers had not seen anything like this since the
riots at the 1968 Democratic National Convention. Then viewers
had seen thousands of people on both sides of the law fighting in
their streets. Now, in the residential Compton neighborhood, only
law enforcement officials were in the eye of the camera, except
for terrified residents running from house to house. There were
537 officers, including 410 Los Angeles police officers and 127 FBI
agents—all of that force against six people in one house.

At 5:53 P.M., the police hurled a tear-gas canister into the
house. Captain King, in charge of the operation, said, "Then
heavy bursts of automatic gunfire came from inside the front and
rear door of the house." He ducked for cover. SWAT teams and
the FBI shot back. When the fire started, police warned the occupants to get out of the house. They couldn't see Cinque, Nancy,
Patricia, Willie, Camilla, or Angela, but as the house began to collapse, automatic gunfire shot out from the air vents in the foundation of the house, which was engulfed in flames.

Then, Nancy Ling Perry, wearing fatigues, climbed out of a
crawl hole at the back of the house. Next, Camilla Hall appeared
at the hole and fired an automatic pistol at one of the SWAT team
officers. He fired back. She dropped to the ground and was
pulled back to the crawl space. Ten feet away from the house,

Nancy turned to her right and fired a pistol. SWAT gunfire riddled her body.

The house was too hot to get close to, but one policeman got close enough to see two people with their clothes on fire in the back of the house. They were wearing bullet-studded bandoliers crisscrossed over their backs and chests. One officer claimed that he had never seen so much ammunition concentrated in a single area in Los Angeles. The police, FBI, and SWAT teams fired 5,371 rounds of ammunition at what would be called the SLA death house, about ten shots per officer.

Even with all the exchanged gunfire, not one of the police officers or federal agents was hit by members of the SLA. At 6:58 P.M., the walls and roof of the Compton house collapsed. Onlookers heard ammunition exploding in the ruins. Finally, fire engines were allowed to put out the flames. All six SLA members in the house were killed.

The horror of that day would stay etched in Captain King's memory. He couldn't believe that the people in the house were shooting at them with automatic weapons, while completely trapped, putting holes in the houses across the street—houses filled with women and children.

Later he would say, "I couldn't understand how people in their right mind would stay in a place and know there's no escaping other than surrendering. I just couldn't visualize why someone didn't say, 'Okay, we're done,' and come out."

Because her lungs showed the least trace of smoke inhalation, Camilla Hall (Gabi) was thought to have perished first. A bullet had gone through the center of her forehead. Her body had not even been found until the next day. Nancy Ling Perry (Fahizah) had fallen next to her, her spinal cord, lungs, and other organs ripped by bullets. She and Camilla had died instantly, before the fire consumed the house. The remaining four, either by using a trap door or frantically hacking a hole in the floorboards, had crowded into the limited crawl space between the ground and the floor.

Patricia Soltysik (Zoya), Willie Wolfe (Cujo) and Angela Atwood (Gelina) succumbed to "noxious gases from the fire." According to the coroner, Dr. Thomas Noguchi, Donald DeFreeze (General Field Marshal, Cinque) put a revolver's two-inch barrel to his own right temple and fired. Noguchi believed that Cinque was the last to die because a greater amount of residue from smoke inhalation was found in his lungs than in any of the other SLA members.

Dr. Noguchi also disclosed that the rubber gas masks worn by the SLA members had melted from their heads and only the metal filters in the masks were found—inches from each of the charred bodies. Noguchi said, "They chose to stay under the floor as the fire burned instead of getting out. In all my years as coroner, I've never seen this kind of behavior in the face of flames."

He also said that clothing fragments found on the charred bodies indicated that all had been wearing military-type fatigue pants with pouches for ammunition. "They were living a fantasy of guerrilla warfare," he said.

In the *Los Angeles Times,* parents of the dead SLA members responded to the violent scenario. Patricia Soltysik's brother, Fred, said that she was one of the victims and he urged the surviving SLA members to surrender: "We would like to make a plea to the rest of the members of the Symbionese Liberation Army to give themselves up so that their parents and families can be spared the sorrow that we have suffered."

Nancy Ling Perry's father said from his home in Santa Rosa, "As for Nancy, yes, it's over for her now. But it's difficult for me to comment. The Nancy we knew and loved is not the same Nancy that has been described in the last few months."

Her ex-husband, Gilbert Perry, acknowledged, "it was a horrible feeling to see your wife murdered on television."

The Reverend George Hall, Camilla's father, a Lutheran minister now living in Chicago, described his daughter as a martyr: "She was not a martyr in the religious sense, but when people die standing up for what they believe, that makes them a martyr."

Willie Wolfe's father from Pennsylvania said that his son had been "an angel, the gentlest person ever born." He added, "The officers did an incredibly stupid thing. They didn't know who was in that house. How the hell would you feel if you were watching television and didn't know if your son was dying in that house?"

Cinque's body was claimed by his mother, Mary, and flown to Cleveland for burial. His brother eulogized him: "My fallen brother died for a nation. That nation might not exist yet, but it will. We have gathered here as a people, and we must have leaders to guide us to that nation. My brother was one."

Patricia Soltysik's mother had her daughter's ashes dropped from a plane over the ocean near Santa Barbara. Her father, who had denounced her in life, did not attend the funeral, but he told her brother, Fred, whom she had remained close to, "I'm sorry, I'm sorry."

There was a memorial service for Nancy at her parents' church in Santa Rosa and a funeral in Oakland put on by her ex-husband, Gilbert Perry. He eulogized her as "a saint." Her brother was there but her parents did not attend. Willie Wolfe and Camilla Hall were cremated, their remains returned to their families.

Angela Atwood's father claimed her body, but final disposition of her remains was withheld pending word from her ex-husband, Gary Atwood, who was still in Indiana. Her sister described her as "a good girl, an A-plus girl. She had a normal life and a regular upbringing."

Russell Little and Joe Remiro were in jail awaiting trial for Marcus Foster's murder when they got word of the deaths of their comrades. The two of them were playing gin rummy. Little laid down his cards and cried. Remiro, who had been described as the most volatile, explosive personality in the SLA, sat like a good soldier, stone-faced, and showed no reaction.

As an all-out search continued for the remaining three SLA members, Patty's two younger sisters made an impassioned plea for her to surrender. In an eight-minute tape given to news reporters outside the Hearst family home, her sisters urged their fugitive sister to turn herself in so she could tell her reasons for joining the SLA.

"If you really feel the SLA is your thing, I don't think you should get yourself killed. Everyone wants to see what you have to say. If you are killed, it would be a waste," said eighteen-year-old Anne. Defending her parents, whom Patty had called "pigs," she added, "Maybe you feel Mom and Dad hadn't done their best, or hadn't tried as hard as they could. But I've been here the whole time and I wouldn't stay here, I'd never put up with it if I thought for a minute they were putting their money ahead of you."

Her seventeen-year-old sister, Vicki, urged Patty not to throw her life away "on a war that doesn't exist. This is the only voice from the family I think you'll trust," she said. "I wouldn't lie to you."

Steve Weed accused the police of conducting a "military tactic," and said if they used the same force again, they had "no right to call themselves professionals."

Patty, Bill, and Emily had watched their comrades die in the inferno on the 6:00 television news from their Anaheim motel room. They were horrified as they sat there helpless, watching their friends burn to death. Cinque, Zoya, Fahizah, Gabi, Cujo, and Gelina were gone and now they were really alone.

In *Every Secret Thing*, Patty Hearst wrote that Emily described the scene as "unreal." She and her husband sobbed in each other's arms. Bill chastised himself, saying if it hadn't been for his shoplifting at Mel's, it wouldn't have happened. Patty huddled alone on the floor by the bed, trembling. They spent several days at the Anaheim motel, then drove fifteen miles west to Costa Mesa and spent another week in a motel. Patty never left the room. Finally, they headed back to Berkeley, but they had no connections, no one to call, and no one to help them—not until June 2, 1974, when Kathy Soliah gave a speech to eulogize her best friend, Angela Atwood, and the other slain members of the Symbionese Liberation Army.

Act Three

"He who holds the ladder is as bad as the thief."

— GERMAN PROVERB

The Second Team

Bill and Emily Harris and Patty Hearst were desperate now. They had just enough money to rent a cheap apartment in Oakland. That would give them a month to try to find help. Now that the authorities knew that Patty had not burned to death in the shoot-out, they intensified their search, knowing that she couldn't be too far away.

On May 31, 1974, the remaining SLA members' spirits were raised when the Weather Underground bombed the California Attorney General's office in Los Angeles and dedicated their attack to "our sisters and brothers of the SLA." It was well known that the Weather Underground had successfully eluded the FBI for years. Perhaps the SLA thought that Bernardine Dohrn would be able to help them. That didn't happen. But their luck changed two days later. The Harrises read in the newspaper that a rally was held at Ho Chi Minh (Francis Willard) Park in Berkeley, a rally to honor the SLA.

The rally took place in a pie-shaped corner of Ho Chi Minh Park on June 2, 1974. The crowd consisted of some former well-known Berkeley radicals and Vietnam War protesters dressed in the Berkeley style of boots and casual clothes. From a nearby building, the FBI filmed the gathering. Someone had lined up bottles of Acadama Plum Wine along the front of the stage, a memorial gesture to Field Marshal Cinque's favorite drink.

Kathy Soliah was twenty-seven years old now, tall and lean, with a firm jaw line and long, straight, light brown hair. She was angry. Cast members at the Emeryville Shakespeare Company, where Kathy had been acting, told the authors of *Voices of Guns* that before Angela Atwood died, Kathy had done beautiful work at the theater, but after the shootout, she changed drastically. They said they knew that she was a supporter of the SLA by the stance she took on the subject. She quit her job.

At the rally she stood at a microphone wearing pink bell-bottoms, a turtleneck sweater, large, round, wire-rimmed sunglasses tinted blue, with both hands clasped over her shoulder-bag strap. She addressed a crowd of about 400 people.

Some of the people in Ho Chi Minh Park that day were well known to the FBI: for instance, Wilbur "Popeye" Jackson, who was the leader of the United Prisoners Coalition. Popeye had played a key role in the Hearst PIN food giveaway. It was rumored that he was trying to bargain with Hearst to locate Patty providing Hearst use his influence to keep Jackson's parole from being revoked for a drug violation. His parole was not revoked and some radicals thought that Popeye's luck was tied to his co-operation with Hearst and also to the FBI. Popeye Jackson was a close "friend" of Sara Jane Moore, who had been assigned by the FBI to spy on Jackson and other radicals working with the program. Jackson told the crowd, "Until we begin to adhere to these things the SLA taught us, we can't say that we are revolutionaries." According to an interview she gave to *Playboy* magazine, in March 1974, Sara Jane Moore had volunteered her accounting services for Randolph Hearst's $2 million food give-away program for Patty's ransom. At the same time, she had been working as a double agent for the FBI. She had infiltrated the radical movement and was "permeated in the SLA."

She knew people who knew its members and would admit later on, "I had a catalog—I was one of the few people around who had a copy of every one of the SLA tapes, every one of its communiqués."

Like Bernardine Dohrn, Sara Jane, born Sara Jane Kahn, had eschewed her Jewish faith. She adopted her mother's name, Moore, became an accountant, married a doctor, and settled into the "blue-blood," country-club life in Charleston, West Virginia. Cinque would have thought her bourgeois.

Like Kathy, Sara Jane Moore had hoped to become an actress and work on the stage, but somewhere along the line, she was enticed by left-wing radicals to leave her husband and children to fight for the downtrodden farmers and for women's causes. Her acting skills were good enough to work both sides of the fence. She could attend a secret Marxist-Leninist study group on one night, and tell FBI agents what she learned the next night. Agents said that she was no Mata Hari. She talked too much. She was perfect for the job because nobody would suspect that she was a spy. Sara Jane Moore would go relatively unnoticed until September 22, 1975, when she tried to assassinate President Gerald Ford.

Kathy had gathered several radical groups together to hear her speech that day, including a group that she and Jim had helped to organize, the Bay Area Research Collective (BARC), a tiny group of SLA sympathizers who had pooled their money to print homemade booklets filled with writings of the SLA and other underground groups. Kathy and Jim thought that the SLA needed help in public relations, and their booklets would draw supporters. BARC had wanted to dig up negative details about Marcus Foster so that they could publicly justify his execution. According to *Rolling Stone* magazine, Kathy had helped them plan a BARC conference entitled, "Eat the Rich, Feed the Poor, SLA Knows the Score."

When Kathy started to speak, the crowd quieted down and listened with rapt attention. She was there to eulogize her SLA friends who had died in the fiery shootout. She explained how she had lost touch with Angela when she had taken her vacation in Mexico. When she came home, Angela, who had changed her name to Gelina, was in the headlines.

Kathy announced, "I am a soldier of the SLA." Some in the crowd cheered, Sara Jane Moore among them. Moore stood right behind Soliah at the podium. Kathy continued, "Angela, Camilla,

Mizmoon,* and Fahizah were among the first white women to fight so righteously for their beliefs and to die for what they believed in." She called Angela a "truly revolutionary woman." "And the amazing thing is that she and her women comrades came from the same background as many of us here. They were white, middle-class people with a lot of advantages who had gotten into the women's struggle and then generalized that struggle to include all people.

"Cinque, Willie, Camilla, Mizmoon, and Fahizah were viciously attacked and murdered by 500 pigs in LA while the whole nation watched," Soliah continued. "I believe that Gelina and her comrades fought until the last minute. And though I would like to have her be here with me right now, I know that she lived and she died happy. And in that sense, I am so very proud of her. SLA soldiers, although I know it's not necessary to say, keep fighting, *I'm* with you. And *we* are with you." With that proclamation, the Harrises knew that help was near at hand. Kathy Soliah then roused the crowd with a charged salute.

Kathy's speech drew the attention of FBI agents who would interview her for four hours two months later. In *Voices of Guns,* it was reported that Marty Soliah had returned from a fishing trip when he learned from friends that his daughter Kathy had been on television giving a pro-SLA speech in Berkeley. He called her immediately to "chew her out." He didn't reach Kathy, but Jo, her sister, who now worked at Oakland's Children's Hospital, answered the phone.

Marty thought of Jo as the dutiful daughter, the one who kept in touch with her family. She told her dad that Steve had advised Kathy not to speak at the rally, but Kathy felt she had to do it for Angela. Later, Kathy called her dad and explained that her speech was personal, not political, and that it was "none of your business." Later, her mother, Elsie, said that Kathy was the only one of

---

*Kathy Soliah referred to Mizmoon, the name that Patricia Soltysik had given up in 1973 when she re-christened herself Zoya.

their children who had the spunk to stand up to Marty when he was angry.

It is possible that Kathy had been one of the SLA's recruits early on, but Patty Hearst said (in *Every Secret Thing*) that Bill Harris thought Kathy was "too flaky to be trusted with the SLA's underground activities." Her speech at the park read like another audition, as if she were competing for a role in a sought-after play. If she were really "a terrorist," why would she risk her freedom to call a rally on behalf of the SLA? It was just too obvious, so the police and the FBI, who filmed her speech and also panned the crowd with their cameras, disregarded her as unimportant.

Emily Harris, however, didn't consider Kathy Soliah unimportant. Patty Hearst wrote that Emily had Kathy's phone number and her address written down in her book. Perhaps Angela Atwood had given it to Emily before she died in the shootout. Emily decided to call on Kathy. She dressed up in a gray wig and a plain outfit, something that an older aunt might wear. The person who answered the door said that Kathy wasn't home, but she gave Emily the name of the Berkeley bookstore about a block from the campus where Kathy worked.

When Emily in her aunt-outfit spotted Kathy at the cash register, she said, "Excuse me dear, but could you tell me what time it is?" Emily's disguise didn't fool Kathy but she looked very surprised to see her, nonetheless. Emily then put a note in Kathy's hand and said, "Oh, would you be good enough to throw this away for me please?" Then Emily walked out of the shop.

Kathy read the note, which said, "Meet me at the church." (There was only one church nearby.) Still friendly with Jim Kilgore, she called him before she left the bookstore, and told him that Emily Harris wanted to see her. She asked him to bring some money, because she was sure that Emily needed help. Jim gathered a small amount of cash and got it over to her before she left for the church. He didn't go with her.

Twenty minutes later, Kathy arrived at the empty church and gave Emily the cash. "I knew you'd need money," she said. She informed Emily that her sister Jo wanted to help too and that she would withdraw money from her savings. Emily was elated. Kathy asked if there was anything else she could do to help, and Emily said she'd get back to her.

That night when Emily told Bill and Patty that they were going to get help, the three of them decided what they would and would not reveal to Kathy Soliah. She was not to know that Bill had stolen anything from Mel's Sporting Goods Store. The next time they met her, they would appear strong, no matter how down they had felt since the shootout. If they wanted Kathy Soliah and her friends to support them, they had better display a united front and not look like sorry victims.

The next night, the trio set up a time to meet Soliah and Kilgore at a drive-in movie in Oakland where *The Sting*, with Robert Redford and Paul Newman, was playing. They arrived at the theater, and as planned on the phone, Emily and Patty met Kathy near the ladies' restroom. Bill did not trust them enough to show them his car, so he met up with the women, and they all went to Jim's car, which was parked in another theater section showing a soft-core porn film called *Teacher's Pet*.

Jim stood outside of his car waiting for them. He resembled the stereotypical, unkempt Berkeley student, about six feet tall, medium-long brown hair, with wire-rimmed glasses, a bristling handlebar moustache, and a wrinkled T-shirt. He got into the driver's seat, and Kathy crawled into the front seat next to him.

The other three crawled into the back seat of Jim's car. Even though it was awkward, Patty, Bill, and Emily reached to the front and hugged Jim and Kathy as if they'd been friends forever. Patty Hearst wrote in *Every Secret Thing* that Kathy lauded over her, exclaiming how much she admired her courage and commitment in joining the SLA. Kathy was so intense that Patty thought she was going to cry.

Kathy emoted about how she had loved Angela (Gelina) and how disappointed she had been that her friend had not invited her to join the SLA. Kathy told Patty that she believed in their cause. She explained again, as she had at Ho Chi Minh Park, that when she'd returned from Mexico, she waited for Gelina to contact her, but she never did. The next thing Kathy knew, her friend was killed in the shootout. Kathy said she felt guilty that she had not been able to help her.

Kathy couldn't seem to stop talking. She explained how she and Jim had been a part of the radical movement in Berkeley for three years and that they knew lots of people who would help. She and Jim had moved to Berkeley in search of people with their same political beliefs, she said, adding, "The people in Berkeley loved the SLA and what it stood for."

Her sister Jo would love to join them too. With that, Kathy handed them the money that Jo had taken from her savings, $1,500. Then she wanted them to know about her brother Steve, as well. Still talking over the back seat, she said that Steve was more a hippie than a radical, and she didn't think he should be told about their activities. They were not to worry, though, because Kathy had other friends in the radical movement who would come to their aid.

Bill finally interrupted, telling her that they were in need of "action, not words." Kathy assured him that she was ready and willing to go underground with the SLA and take part in any actions that were planned. At first, Jim had seemed intellectual and mild mannered, sitting patiently in the driver's seat, waiting for Kathy to be quiet. He got angry then and suggested that they "all lay low until the heat dies down." Then Bill, who did not like people telling him how to run things, added that Jim and Kathy could be more help if they stayed "above ground for the time being."

There was one more thing that they could do to help, Bill added. They were preparing a communiqué in regard to the shootout. They would need a tape recorder. Kathy eagerly assured him that she would get them one and when he asked her if she knew anyone trustworthy enough to deliver the tape to the Pacific radio station in Los Angeles, she said sure.

Now that Bill had their attention, he gave them a rundown of their previous activities, omitting the shoplifting event. He explained that they were "professional revolutionaries." Patty half listened to all of the banter, with one eye on the movie screen. But when Bill mentioned to Kathy that the three of them might have to get out of the Bay Area, Patty was all ears. She wrote in *Every Secret Thing* that Kathy had an answer for that problem too. She knew a man who could help them go wherever they wanted to go. She said that he was a radical sportswriter named Jack Scott who ran an underground railroad for political fugitives. She said that he had helped a number of people "get away from the pigs."

The Human Switzerland

Kathy and Jim's friend Jack Scott, a lanky, balding man, had made many enemies with his brusque, often offensive personal manner over the years, and had been forced out of his job as the athletic director at Oberlin College in Ohio when a new president was named to the school in early 1974. The remainder of his four-year contract had been bought out for $40,000 and, with that, he and his wife, Micki, had moved to New York to start a new life. While he was there, he'd followed the headlines of the Patty Hearst kidnapping by the SLA and had developed a profound interest in the story. He'd decided that he wanted to write a book about the SLA. The timing was perfect.

From her soapbox in the front seat of Jim's car, Kathy Soliah told her audience that Scott was a champion of black athletes and had written a number of books on how blacks were being used and ripped off in organized sports. Bill was impressed and said he wanted to meet Jack. Kathy promised to arrange it. The meeting at the drive-in was over, and Bill basically told Kathy, "Don't call us, we'll call you." He said that he would contact her the next day. When Jim protested that Bill didn't trust them, Kathy admonished him: "They know what they're doing."

Bill Harris gave Kathy and Jim phone instructions, with codes, warning them that phones could be tapped. The three fugitives went back to their own car in *The Sting* section of the parking lot, money in hand, feeling more positive about their future.

The next day, Emily picked up the tape recorder from Kathy. Then she, Bill, and Patty recorded their eulogies, and Bill loved how they sounded. When they were finished, he called Kathy and arranged to meet her at Lake Merritt in Oakland that day to give her the tape. Later that same day, Kathy gave the tape to her brother Steve, who took the tape to the Los Angeles radio station.

Steve felt protective toward his older sister, and he didn't want strange guys giving her unwanted attention. One night when she was walking home from a nearby liquor store, a few weeks after the memorial rally, he heard her screaming and ran out of the house to see what was wrong. A man was assaulting her. When he saw Steve, who was a big, burly guy, coming at him, he tried to flee in his car, but before he got away, Steve grabbed the car door and was dragged about half a block before he let go. Kathy was all right, but Steve was bruised and furious.

As loyal as he was toward his sister, Steve was slow to join her involvement in radical, military politics. He was easygoing and preferred to party with his friends. He had known some of Patty's kidnappers secondhand, Berkeley being the communal town that it was. One of his friends had once roomed with Patricia "Mizmoon" Soltysik, and he also knew that Kathy had waited tables with Angela Atwood. Also, he still painted houses with Jim. Kathy asked Steve if he wanted to meet Bill, Emily, and Patty. He was curious and said yes.

They met at a house in Berkeley where Jim was house-sitting for a friend. Kathy and Jo were there too. When the three fugitives walked in the door, Steve couldn't believe his eyes as the visitors unloaded heavy bags, full of weapons, which they leaned against the walls as naturally as if they were unpacking clothes or groceries. Patty was unappealingly pale and gaunt, and had on baggy clothes, horn-rimmed glasses, and a bouffant wig. He said that she wasn't the kind of woman that men would look twice at. Patty didn't think much more of him on this first meeting. Steve had dirty blond hair and a ragged goatee. "He looked like a spaced-out hippie," she would later tell a friend. Kathy made the introductions and then explained to the fugitives how she and Jo and Steve had all grown up in Palmdale.

Steve half-listened but couldn't take his eyes off the weapons. Perhaps wanting to impress Bill, who by now was ranting about them having to get out of the Bay Area, Steve offered that as a boy he had shot desert rats with a carbine, but as yet, hadn't handled a submachine gun. Now that Steve had met the authors of the tape, which he had personally delivered, he couldn't turn back. He had been drawn into their circle.

The radio station, KPFK, received the tape on June 8, 1974. An anonymous caller had informed them that a cassette was hidden in a rubbish pile behind the station. Stations all over the country patched in, and millions of people heard Bill and Emily Harris and Patty Hearst give a eulogy for their dead SLA comrades.

Patty started the message in a cold voice with, "Greetings to the People." She praised her sisters and brothers and ranted about the fascist pig media. She lauded Willie Wolfe (Cujo) and said how much they'd loved each other. She called Angela Atwood (Gelina), "Beautiful. Fire and joy. She exploded with the desire to kill the pigs." She said that Camilla Hall (Gabi) taught her patience and discipline. Patricia Soltysik (Zoya) taught her, "Keep your ass down and be bad." Then for their leader she said, "Cinque knew that to live was to shoot straight." He taught her to show her love for the People. She ended her eulogy with, "Patria o muerte, Venceremos! Death to the Fascist Insect that Preys upon the Life of the People."

Emily voiced a shorter eulogy on the same note but Bill's was long and arduous. He talked about how they had slipped into LA on May 1, 1974, and then about the Mel's Sporting Goods fiasco. He hadn't stolen anything, he said, perhaps trying to convince himself that he was not at all responsible for his friends' gruesome deaths. He continued, "The SLA is not dead and will not die as long as there is one living, fighting member of any oppressed class, race, sex, or group left on the face of the earth. The pigs have won a battle, but the war of the flea is not over. As our dear comrade Ho Chi Minh once wrote from an imperialist prison, 'Today the locust fights the elephant, but tomorrow the elephant will be disemboweled.'"

Meanwhile, Jack Scott had already come back to San Francisco. Kathy reached him easily, and he was eager to talk. He was short on money and had a scheme to write a book about the SLA, the most famous fugitives in the world. It was sure to be a best-seller, and he'd be rich. They were to meet at the same house in Berkeley where Jim was house-sitting. Kathy, Steve, Jo, Bill, Emily, and Patty waited for Jack Scott's arrival.

When he got there, Kathy introduced him as "a writer and sports director." It didn't take him long to agree to help the three fugitives get out of town. He would not pass up an opportunity like that. As author of a book on the SLA, he would have an exclusive on the Patty Hearst story. Publishers would be calling him!

It was decided that they'd flee to New York. They could stay at the apartment he shared with his wife, Micki, until they found a better place to hide. Scott arranged for Emily's transportation first. Soon after, in late June 1974, Scott, along with his elderly mother and father who lived in Las Vegas, escorted Patty to New York. His father drove the car, and his parents had no idea that the back-seat passenger sitting next to their son was Patty Hearst. She was disguised with a wig and glasses. Their chances of being stopped by police were slim because they would not expect Patty to be in a car with an elderly couple. They stayed in cheap motel rooms and took their meals in the car to reduce the risk of being noticed. After about five days, they arrived in New York. Micki and Emily, and Wendy Yoshimura greeted them at the Scotts' apartment. Scott's parents left the apartment almost immediately.

Jack introduced Wendy to Patty, explaining that he had taken Wendy out East and arranged for her to spend the summer with them in New York after she escaped from the Berkeley bomb factory arrests two years earlier. During her years underground, Wendy had evolved into a committed feminist. Her feminist

views and values would soon begin to influence the impression-
able Patty Hearst.

Scott stayed for a couple of days in New York before flying
back to California to bring Bill to the East. Scott said later that he
felt like a "human Switzerland," apparently referring to his pas-
time of transporting fugitives to safer territories.

Before Scott arrived with the last of his precious cargo, Micki
had searched the want ads and arranged to rent a farmhouse set
on thirty-eight acres in the Pennsylvania Poconos, twenty miles
northeast of Scranton, where Scott had grown up. Micki had explained to the owner that she and her husband were writers and
needed a quiet place to live and work. For $2,000, she got a three-
month lease. The fugitives headed for the Poconos. The two-
story house sat on a bluff overlooking the countryside. Quiet and
secluded, it proved the perfect place to hide. While at the farm,
they relaxed for the first time since the kidnapping. They berry-
picked, sunbathed, and slept.

But they couldn't let down their guard because the "war"
wasn't over. Bill insisted that they keep up their military regimen
with daily calisthenics, jogging, practice sessions with BB guns,
and simulated ambushes. Bill couldn't relax. He always thought
that someone would recognize one of them if they dared to venture out. After a short time he insisted they move to another
place. They found a ramshackle abandoned cheese creamery,
which had gone out of business in the twenties, in the village of
Jeffersonville in rural New York State. To Bill's delight, it was even
more isolated than the first hideout.

Once again, they kept up their daily rituals. A thick wooded lot
surrounded this old abandoned house, and they enjoyed playing
their war games. They trained for battle, crawling on the ground,
learning to move quickly and with stealth.

Now, Bill wanted to write a book too. It would read like a
manifesto such as the one that the Weather Underground had
written. Using a tape recorder, he set up an interview format with
questions and answers. When it was Bill's turn to be interviewed,

however, he lied again about what had happened at Mel's Sporting Goods Store. Emily couldn't squeak out any emotion when she was being interviewed, and Bill told Patty what to say when she was questioned. The interview format wasn't working.

Hearst had become good friends with Yoshimura and during Patty's interview, Wendy became upset because Patty reminded her of a "fuckin vegetable." Patty sounded like a robot, and Wendy wanted her interview to come from her heart. Although Patty had also become a feminist, she was still intimidated by Bill Harris. Bill's chauvinism solidified the women's bond, and this was the beginning of the split between Patty and her former kidnappers.

The tension among these fugitives reached a boiling point. Jack and Micki Scott didn't live with them, but visited often to check up on them and bring supplies. Jack was angry that they had never thanked him for the risks he was taking or the money that he had given them. Most of his $40,000 was gone. When things got so bad that they couldn't stand each other any longer, they all decided it was time to go back to California. Jack Scott agreed to arrange for their transportation west.

From the start of the summer, Wendy had driven Emily into town every third night to call Kathy or Jim to check up on their West Coast activities. They had been faithfully painting houses to finance the revolutionaries' return. When the fugitives got back to California, Kilgore and the Soliahs would help them to reorganize the SLA. They had become the "Second Team."

Sacramento: The Second Team

The Scotts closed down their New York apartment and arranged for Emily, Bill, and Patty to be transported back to California. Scott drove Patty back. An unknown driver took Emily back, and a woman named Margaret Turcich, a friend who had harbored Wendy when she lived in New Jersey, drove her back. According to *Voices of Guns,* Bill was driven back by Kathy Soliah.

The New World Liberation Front (NWLF) was a title first used by Black Panther Eldridge Cleaver in 1969 to describe a political organization of Third World people and radical whites. When he left, Elmer (Geronimo) Pratt became the West Coast leader. New recruits were informed that the NWLF would operate with bombs in the style of the Weather Underground. It was a loose structure, consisting mainly of ex-convicts and young, white dissidents. About half of their members were white women, with a few blacks, Asians, Chicanas and Chicanos. The NWLF had various cells, each consisting of less than half a dozen members, probably not more than twenty in all.

Teko announced that the Second Team of the SLA had aligned themselves with the NWLF and their cell was called the "Malcolm X Combat Unit of the Symbionese Liberation Army." He added that the group wasn't hung up on names, but it had come together with like-minded people in different cells, squads, and military-political units to "eliminate our common enemy by force of arms." They proclaimed, "We proudly take up the banner of the New World Liberation Front."

Even before the SLA fugitives left Pennsylvania, the NWLF had placed bombs all over California. The first bomb attempt of the NWLF had occurred on August 6, 1975, in the Burlingame office of the General Motors Acceptance Corporation. The bomb was faulty and failed to explode. But the NWLF still wanted credit for their efforts. Sometimes they gave phone warnings before the bombs were to explode, and they almost always wrote communiqués, just as their predecessors in the first SLA team had done. The first one said, "Greetings and love to the Symbionese Liberation Army." It read like a "Welcome Home" card. For some reason; however, the police still didn't connect the SLA and the NWLF.

The Second Team had decided to move their operations to Sacramento, California's capital, which was about seventy-five miles from the Bay Area, ninety minutes by car. Jim was to pick up Patty in Las Vegas where Jack Scott had dropped her off, and from there they would take a Greyhound bus to their newest hideout, where they would hole up between October 1974 until May 1975.

In preparation for the fugitives' return from Pennsylvania, Kathy Soliah had rented a safehouse on W Street, a ramshackle place in the heart of Sacramento. It wasn't much more than a wooden shack, divided into two units. A small bedroom faced the street and behind it was a modest-sized living room, kitchen, and bath. Josephine Soliah greeted Patty at the door when she arrived with Jim Kilgore. The Soliahs hadn't seen Patty or the Harrises since June.

This was the second time Steve met Patty, and this time, they both had a more favorable impression of each other. Steve thought Patty looked tan and healthy, and Patty appreciated that Steve's scruffy beard was gone. They hit it off right away. Steve had a serenity about him, and wanted to please—the antithesis of Bill, who was always ranting, raving, and demanding. Patty was tired of Bill's condescending attitude. Steve walked in like a lamb, eager to help in any way he could. And unlike Bill, Steve was a listener. He had genuine sympathy for Patty and quickly became someone she could talk to.

That first night, Patty told him all about their summer in Pennsylvania. In *Every Secret Thing* she wrote, "He was an easy-going man who lived for the day's pleasures and excitement. He did not have his sister Kathy's commitment to the SLA or to the revolution."

According to later court transcripts, Steve stated that Patty confided to him that she didn't want to go home to her parents, that she wanted to stay underground. In her mind, her parents had abandoned her. She described that first night, February 4, 1974, when she had been ripped out of her townhouse and thrown into a garbage can, and how "horrible it was to be kidnapped." She also told him that she didn't get along with the Harrises.

Steve's heart went out to her. But he didn't plan to fall in love with her. He slept on the couch that first night. His sister Kathy shared a bed with Patty. On the second night, Steve and Patty slept together. Though Steve was apprehensive about getting involved with the famous Patty Hearst, it felt right, and they found they were compatible. Nothing seemed to upset Steve. A former roommate said it was impossible to strike up an argument with him, because he just wouldn't go there. He was generous to a fault and could never resist a panhandler's tales of woe, always having to give them money.

These were qualities Patty admired in Steve. Her comrades were always serious, always angry about the state of things, and always bickering. Steve entered the scene with smiles, hugs, and a sense of humor. His friends called him a big teddy bear. He was outdoorsy, liked to bike and jog, and with him Patty could relax and have fun.

All of the Soliahs treated her well, a welcome relief after being ruled by Bill. Patty wasn't used to anyone inquiring about her health or her well-being. The Soliahs talked of their schools, the books they had read, their upbringings, and the state of the world. This "Second Team" expressed their respective opinions that the SLA had been too much into action and too little into fundamentals of the communist and socialist viewpoint of history. To them the SLA propaganda hadn't made sense and that's why they hadn't attracted more followers.

Another benefit of living with the Soliahs was that they ate well. According to Patty Hearst *(Every Secret Thing)* Jim and Kathy were masters at shoplifting: "They came back with steaks and chops and fancy desserts and, according to them, such a diet was all part of the counterculture." (Since the chain markets ripped off the people with their inflated prices, it was appropriate for them to rip off the establishment.)

Kathy and Jim were well known to the FBI because of their radical involvements, and the FBI had questioned both of them several times regarding the whereabouts of the SLA. Kathy told Patty that she had told the pigs, "Get lost ... see my lawyer. ... I've been instructed to say nothing to you at all." She and Jim tried to get the Harrises and Hearst to read more Marxist literature so they could build their ideology on a solid base. Bill balked at that idea, arguing that what they needed was more action. About this time, Bill admitted to the Second Team that he had stolen a bandolier from Mel's Sporting Goods Store. Kathy became furious that he had lied to them. Apparently, she had defended him to her other radical friends in the Bay Area and now she was being told that the "pigs" were right after all. Bill actually wept, and Emily defended him to the group, explaining that they did what they thought was best at the time.

As always, they needed money, and Bill, who had once worked in a post office, remembered that certain stores in Berkeley used the postal system for sending cash receipts to banks and that those cash receipts were picked up by regular mail trucks every day. With their usual meticulous planning, surveillance, maps, and charts, he worked out an action for Jim, Kathy, and Steve.

According to Patty Hearst *(Every Secret Thing)*, Jim followed a mail jeep one day as it picked up a package of money from a Berkeley pharmacy and continued on its regular route. Kathy, looking like an innocent housewife, stood by a roadside mailbox, trying to address and stamp a letter. The mail jeep stopped, and as the driver waited for her letter, she initiated a conversation with him to distract him. "Then Steve rode by silently on a bicycle, dipped his hand into the open jeep, and pedaled away with the money parcel." The mailman had no clue of the theft, and the trio was $1,000 richer.

SLA comrades Little and Remiro, charged with Marcus Foster's murder, had gotten a change of venue and were going to be tried in Sacramento instead of Oakland. Because of all the media coverage in the Bay Area, Bill and his Second Team made plans to help them break out of the Alameda County jail in Oakland before their trial was to start in Sacramento in the spring of 1975. Little and Remiro were held on the tenth floor of the Alameda County Courthouse.

The plan, according to Patty, involved the three Soliahs, Jim Kilgore, and Michael Bortin. The two prisoners had drawn a diagram of the structure and smuggled it out to the Soliahs, who then delivered it to Emily Harris in Sacramento. Assault teams were going to charge into the building with automatic weapons. According to Patty's later interview with the FBI, the team spent two weeks watching the building's tunnel entrances, charting movements of "pig cars." They hadn't forgotten the drills that Cinque had taught them.

After countless meetings in Sacramento, which according to Patty were attended by herself, the Harrises, Kilgore, Bortin, his girlfriend Pat Jean McCarthy, and the Soliahs, they finally decided that the plan was "suicide" and abandoned it altogether. Remiro and Little sent a response to them, "Fuck you—we're going to try anyway."

Things were falling apart on other fronts. By the time the fugitives had returned to California, Wendy Yoshimura could not tolerate Bill Harris anymore and had decided to separate herself from the others and live in San Francisco with Margaret Turcich. She had no more time for Bill's totalitarianism. Bill did accept some aspects of the Women's Liberation movement, such as equal pay for equal work. But other aspects were not convenient for him. Liberation also meant sexual freedom. The Second Team tried to adapt Marxist concepts of the oppression of women, which among other things meant that sex should be "nonexclusive." Nonexclusive also meant that sexual relationships did not have to be heterosexual. According to *Every Secret Thing* and FBI reports, it was during this time that Emily Harris and Kathy Soliah became lovers.

This sexuality concept didn't always work in Bill's favor. He was used to having Emily to himself when he wanted her, and he was used to having Patty if he wanted her. But now that they were all together in Sacramento, Steve Soliah was part of the Second Team, supporting them financially and sleeping with Patty.

By January, the tension was so thick between Patty and the Harrises that they needed a second hideout, a place to get away from each other. The Soliahs raised the needed money from their painting jobs, and using the name "Jessica Henderson," Kathy rented another place on Capitol Avenue.

Using a false name as well, Jim Kilgore got them a third hideout on T Street. This Second Team, a cell of the NWLF, bounced back and forth between the triangle of apartments. All of them, including Mike Bortin, switched between the three houses depending on who was fighting with whom and who was sleeping with whom.

Finding a safehouse was not as easy as just finding a place to live. Certain requirements had to be met. The rent had to be cheap, of course—house painters didn't make much in those days. In Sacramento all three safehouses went for about $85 a month rent. Each had at least two outside entrances, with the rear entrance leading to protected alleyways. Also, windows opened for easy drops to the ground or to adjoining rooftops. The hideouts were usually in neighborhoods that had mostly multi-unit dwellings principally occupied by young people. The fugitives wanted to fit into the neighborhood and be around people their own age, although they rarely went out in the daylight and usually kept the windows covered, either with shades or with old newspapers. The three hideouts in Sacramento all had easy access to Interstate 80 and other major highways and were within short bicycling distance of each other. The Harrises liked to ride their bikes.

Once Jack Scott had delivered his fugitives back to California, he had hoped he would never have to see any of them again, although he still wanted to make a killing on a best-seller book about the SLA and his summer adventure. Unfortunately, he made a huge mistake. Scott had been so proud that he had successfully hidden the most sought-after kidnap victim in the world that he couldn't keep it to himself. The self-described Human Switzerland bragged to his brother, Walter.

On January 31, 1975, forty-one-year-old Walter, an alcoholic and manic-depressive, staggered into the Scranton, Pennsylvania, police station at 2:00 A.M. and slurred that he had information about Patty Hearst. His story was convincing enough that the police called in the local FBI to interrogate him.

He told them enough about the Wayne County farmhouse that agents were able to locate it. During his interrogation, Walter implicated his brother, Jack, his sister-in-law, Micki, and his own parents in the federal crime of harboring fugitives. However, because of his instability, he would not have been a credible witness for the prosecution, thus the government would have no case against any of the Scotts. He did, however, give the FBI their first good lead in seven months. When agents searched the Pennsylvania farmhouse, they found Bill Harris's and Wendy Yoshimura's fingerprints. They had specially trained dogs, called "Patty's dogs," flown in from California to identify Patty's scent and the dogs yelped at the bed she'd slept in.

Because of Jack's brother, Walter Scott, all hell broke loose, and the Scotts, too, went underground. When the San Francisco papers headlined the new discovery about finding Wendy's fingerprints in Pennsylvania, Wendy was afraid of what Bill might do to her. They had all been so careful to wipe their prints from the farmhouse before they'd left, but the night before, there had been a bug in her bed and she had wadded up a newspaper to kill it, then stuffed the newspaper under her mattress and forgotten about it. She had grown close to Patty, however, and decided to rejoin her comrades in Sacramento. She and Patty became roommates.

On February 6, 1975, a pipe bomb exploded at the local KRON-TV station in San Francisco. The NWLF used a familiar phrase in the communiqués that followed: "Death to the Fascist Insect that Preys upon the Life of the People." During that winter, the Bay Area was averaging one bomb every sixteen days. According to Patty's FBI interviews, Bill Harris and the Second Team were behind most of the two dozen NWLF bombings in the Bay Area. Amazingly, no one was hurt or killed in these bombings.

In the meantime, Little and Remiro were planning their breakout. The Second Team still wanted to help but would need a lot of money, more than they could make painting houses. The quickest way to get it was to rob a bank. Still using the techniques that Cinque had taught them, they drew up an outline with fifty-nine points on how to accomplish their goal. Once they narrowed the possibilities down to three banks, they meticulously drew diagrams of the buildings, took pictures, scanned the neighborhoods, and studied possible escape routes. They mapped out the "backup" gun stations and "switch-car" locations before they made their choice. They agreed that the banks would have to be outside the Sacramento city limits, that there could be no surveillance cameras, and that they'd have to have easy escape routes. They called their outline the "Bakery."

Bill supervised practice sessions. The Guild Savings and Loan at the Arden Plaza Shopping Center in suburban north Sacramento met their criteria. A narrow alleyway next to the bank led out of the shopping center into a quiet residential neighborhood—a perfect place to park the getaway car. Since the bank was outside the Sacramento city limits, it was in the Sacramento sheriff's jurisdiction. There were only five deputy sheriffs on duty at any one time, and they were overworked.

Steve had to memorize the route to and from the bank, the name of every street on the route, and the intersection where he would park the rented switch car prior to the robbery. In an ancient Chevy Impala he had bought in San Francisco using a fictitious name, he would drive Mike and Jim to the front of the bank and then drive out of Arden Plaza, around the block, and park at the outside end of the alley alongside the bank, waiting. Bill was relentless in his role-playing and his constant rehearsals, which made Kathy bristle. She was insulted that Bill treated them as if they were stupid. "We do have minds of our own," she insisted.

On February 25 at 9:30 A.M., two men went into the bank and split up. Jim stood by the entrance door and shouted, "This is a robbery!" He ordered customers and employees to lie on the floor, and he counted off the time. Mike demanded cash from the tellers. Once he collected the $3,729 cash, he shouted for everyone to remain on the floor. The two men ran out of the bank and hopped into the old Chevy where Steve Soliah sat with the motor idling. They sped away. Steve Soliah ditched the Chevy a few blocks away and climbed into a waiting switch car. The whole robbery had taken less than three minutes.

According to Patty (Every Secret Thing), Kathy Soliah had her assignment as well. She watched the bank from a nearby store, pretending to look at greeting cards. She was supposed to time the police response. It took five minutes for the sheriff's deputies to arrive with their siren screeching and pull up in front of the bank. Kathy walked over to join the crowd gathered around the bank before strolling into a nearby coffee shop. From there, she phoned a service station and asked that her 1956 Chevy be towed in for repairs. She gave the location and description of the car, saying that the car's registration was in the glove compartment.

Lingering over a cup of coffee, she saw the bank manager enter. "They cleaned us out . . . they took everything," he said. When she heard that, Kathy drove back to the safehouse via the escape route in time to see the tow truck take the Chevy safely away. When they all met up at the safehouse, Bill was furious at her for taking unnecessary risks by going into the coffee shop.

Bank employees had assumed that the robbers had guns, but no one actually saw them. There were no surveillance cameras in the bank, and since the men's faces were partially covered—Mike's with a half-mask that he'd hung around his neck and Jim's with a scarf that he pulled up over his face—no one could give a clear description except that they were white, probably in their mid-twenties, and one of them had red hair. The police wouldn't know who was responsible until one year later when Patty Hearst told the FBI that the two men inside the Guild Savings Bank had been Jim Kilgore and Mike Bortin.

A week later, on March 1, Little and Remiro made an attempt to escape. It was a Saturday and only four guards were on duty. During a scheduled meeting with Little's attorney, Little stabbed one of the deputies, thrusting a pencil four inches into his throat, while Remiro jumped on a sergeant and gouged his eye (they both lived). The other two guards appeared and one of them punched the electric-door lock button, just in time. Remiro had found the right key and had already inserted it into a locker full of loaded guns when he was overpowered. After the escape attempt, Little and Remiro were held under tight security for one month until their transfer to Sacramento for the Marcus Foster murder trial. The night of the escape attempt, another NWLF bomb went off, damaging three Pacific Gas and Electric (PG&E) transmission towers in the hills above Oakland. Fortunately, again, no one was hurt or injured.

By March 1975, Wendy Yoshimura had been underground for almost three years, and the police believed that the Weather Underground was protecting her. The California attorney general's office reported that Wendy had, at times, traveled with Bernardine Dohrn, and now they knew that Yoshimura had been at the Pennsylvania farmhouse with Patty Hearst. It would be several months before the FBI followed up on the Yoshimura

leads, but when they did, they checked the visitors' list at Soledad, where Wendy's boyfriend, Willie Brandt, was housed. The
guest book signatures included Jack Scott, Micki Scott, and Pat
Jean McCarthy (Mike Bortin's girlfriend). Jim Kilgore and Kathy
Soliah—known to the FBI as the two organizers behind the Bay
Area Research Collective (BARC), the group of SLA sympathizers who had organized the 1974 rally at Ho Chi Minh Park—were
also on the list. The FBI was beginning to piece together the first
team of the SLA, which had captured Hearst, with an emerging
picture of the Second Team.

Carmichael:
Myrna Opsahl's Murder

The Scotts learned through their attorneys that the FBI had lost interest in them, and on April 9, 1975, they surfaced and held a press conference in San Francisco. They called the government "morally bankrupt," saying that the government's actions were indefensible. They added that Marcus Foster's murder was no more intolerable than the execution of the six SLA members. When Randolph Hearst read this statement, he contacted them in hopes of getting information about his daughter. Scott agreed to meet with Hearst.

The Second Team was low on finances. The Guild Savings and Loan heist was little more than a dry run. The $3,000 they nabbed was not enough to finance their next bank robbery. They needed getaway cars and, to rent cars, they needed identification and credit cards. Emily checked out the want ads and found that health clubs in the Sacramento area were offering free trial memberships. She and Kathy signed up. According to *Every Secret Thing,* the two women wandered through the locker rooms and stole money, checkbooks, driver's licenses, and credit cards from wallets and purses that had been left unattended.

The Crocker National Bank was located in Carmichael, a suburb seven miles out of Sacramento, and it met the "bakery list" criteria. The bank's rear parking lot abutted the parking area of a large shopping center. The divider was a cyclone fence, which had a "pedestrian hole" to crawl through. Once the police learned that there was a robbery, they would automatically drive to the front of the bank. The getaway car would be in the shopping center parking lot, which was on a completely different street. Now they needed cars. In downtown Sacramento, Jim noticed a blue-gray Mustang on the street, with keys in the ignition, and the motor idling. He hopped in and sped off to hide the car in a garage that Emily had rented.

According to *Voices of Guns,* on April 12, a woman at an open party in Oakland discovered the keys to her car were missing. During the party, she had told Jim Kilgore, who had "dropped in," that she owned a 1967 Pontiac Firebird. When she went outside, her car was gone.

Emily had rented a second garage. This time, she made a serious blunder. The garage owner thought it was odd when she told him that the garage had to have an electrical outlet. He called his friend, a cop, who suspected that this woman might be fronting for an auto-stripping ring and told the owner to call him again when she brought the car in.

Two days after the party, Emily parked the stolen Firebird in the rented garage. The owner saw her drive off with a young man in a newly painted Chevy station wagon, which the Second Team had purchased with cash, and had repainted, after the Guild Savings and Loan robbery. He copied down the license numbers of both cars and called his friend again.

On Sunday, April 20, Jim, Kathy, and Steve drove to the University of California campus in Davis, about a half-hour away from Sacramento, and lifted California license plates from cars parked in the students' parking lot. They replaced them with stolen plates and fixed the new plates to their stolen Firebird and the Mustang, hoping that no one would notice the switch.

Although the Sacramento police periodically drove past the garage in hopes of apprehending the gang when they came back to strip the car, they were not there when the Firebird was moved and parked overnight on a residential street about a mile from the branch office of the Crocker National Bank. The next morning,

Monday, April 21, it was moved again to a shopping center parking lot just behind the bank.

Myrna Opsahl was born in Cheyenne, Wyoming, and had grown up with Midwestern values. While studying to be a nurse at Loma Linda University (then known as the College of Medical Evangelists) in Riverside, California, she had met Trygve Opsahl, a full-blooded Norwegian who had come to the United States in 1949 to study medicine. They married in 1954. Early in their marriage the Opsahls served as medical missionaries in Trinidad; they moved to Carmichael in 1964 to raise their four children.

In 1975, their son Carl was nineteen, their daughter Sonja, seventeen, son Jon, fifteen, and son Roy, thirteen. On the morning of April 21, Jon had stormed out of the house in a typical teenage huff after a tiff with his mom about not having any pens around so that he could do his homework. She said she would pick up some pens that day. He left the house without saying, "I love you."

Myrna was a forty-two-year-old homemaker, active in the Seventh-day Adventist Church. Women in the church divided the duty of counting the church collection and depositing the money in the bank every Monday at the Crocker National Bank in Carmichael. On that Monday, one of the women couldn't go, so Myrna offered to take her place. The other two volunteers were Bernadine Slackman and Beatrice Squier, who was a nurse.

As they entered the bank, the women noticed four figures crawling through the hole in the cyclone fence. They were wearing heavy, bulky clothes and ski hats, odd for such a warm day. One of the four, Mike Bortin, beat the ladies to the door and held it open for them. Mrs. Squier thanked him, and as she did, he pulled a ski mask over his face. Myrna Opsahl was carrying a small plug-in adding machine with both hands. Bortin followed them into the bank, his companions right behind him. It was 9:00 A.M.

Immediately, a woman's stern voice shouted, "Everybody hit the floor. . . . Move!" Beatrice Squier spun around to see four men carrying guns. In *Every Secret Thing*, Patty Hearst would describe what happened in that bank. As always, the plans had been carefully laid out, detailed, and diagrammed. The Second Team each had their assignments. Kathy Soliah was wearing a white Mexican top with embroidery over a green turtleneck sweater, trousers, hiking boots, and in a straw bag she carried her brother's pistol. She was positioned near the tellers' booths, where she screamed obscenities at the bankers and forced the tellers to open the cash drawers with their own special keys. (Josephine Soliah would have known about such procedures from her job at Wells Fargo Bank in San Francisco.)

Mrs. Opsahl turned around, too suddenly perhaps, when she heard the shouting, probably to set down the cumbersome adding machine. Emily, positioned at the door, wearing a heavy coat, light khaki pants, a green-billed cap, sunglasses and a mustache, swung her sawed-off, double-barreled shotgun at her and rocked her with a blast that ripped open her stomach and left torso. Myrna Opsahl slumped to the floor and moaned in pain as her stunned friends stood horrified. Nine pellets were embedded into her left side. Mrs. Squier, who related the story to her own son many times over the years, was close enough to Opsahl to get shotgun wadding in her hair. Because she was a nurse, she knew that her friend would die. "There's a kind of a death gasp when they're expiring."

A man shouted, "Get your noses to the carpet!" No one dared to help Mrs. Opsahl, who lay on the floor bleeding to death. One of the men, who Patty Hearst would later identify as Mike Bortin, hopped over the counter and demanded the cash and traveler's checks. Using a southern drawl, Kathy gave the countdown, "one minute and thirty seconds . . . one minute and forty seconds . . ." as she methodically emptied the cash drawers, including two at the drive-through window. In the process, she kicked a pregnant teller, which sent her into premature labor. (It was reported that she lost the baby because of the injury.) When Kathy's countdown reached three minutes, she shouted, "Time's up . . . let's get out of here!"

Mrs. Opsahl's companions craned to see if she was alive, but they were kicked and told to stay down. The four robbers—Jim, Mike, Emily, and Kathy—fled, one of them hopping over Myrna Opsahl's body, leaving a trail of 9-mm casings. The heist netted them $15,000.

Across the street was a blue Ford Mustang with license plate number 916 LBJ. An astute onlooker had noticed the driver in heavy clothing pacing back and forth outside the car while the robbery was taking place. Since *916* was Sacramento's area code and the letters *LBJ* had become a common presidential reference, the license number was easy to remember. As the robbers fled the building, witnesses saw them take off their masks, pile into the Firebird, and speed off. Bill and Steve, who were waiting as back-ups, took off in the Mustang.

Like the Guild Savings and Loan, Crocker National Bank also lacked security cameras. And since it was hard to tell if the robbers were men or women, identification was almost impossible—until a year later, when Patty Hearst told the FBI what she knew of the robbery.

Patty and Wendy, Hearst said, had not been on the actual scene; they had been assigned to drive the switch cars. Bill and Steve abandoned their Mustang two miles from the bank, and Wendy, who was wearing a blond wig and large sunglasses, picked them up in another rented car. As for Patty, she was parked by a funeral home a few blocks from the bank in a rented VW van. When the getaway Firebird passed her, she followed it. A mile from the bank, the Firebird pulled over, and Emily, Mike, Jim, and Kathy piled into the van that Patty was driving, screaming at her to "Go! Go! Go!" They ripped off their disguises as Patty drove.

Patty heard Kathy mumble something she couldn't understand, and then Emily said, "Maybe she'll live." Jim said it was unlikely. Patty asked what had happened and Emily told her she'd shot a woman, instructing Patty to keep her eye on the road. Patty and Kathy went back to the apartment on Capitol Avenue.

Emily, Mike, and Jim ditched the car and then went back to the T Street safehouse to count the money.

About an hour later, Jim arrived, furious at Emily for her incompetence. He drew a diagram of where everyone had been standing and shouted that he was right in the line of fire and could have been injured or killed. At this point they still did not know if Myrna Opsahl was dead or alive. Jim left and then Emily arrived to explain her side of the story. By now she had heard the news on the radio. Sacramento police had already found the Firebird.

Kathy asked Emily if she thought the woman was all right. Emily said, "Oh, she's dead, but it really doesn't matter. She was a bourgeois pig anyway. Her husband is a doctor." She added, "it will be pretty hot for us around here now that the pigs will be investigating a killing."

Bill arrived and announced that they'd gotten over $15,000. Then he took the brass base of a shotgun shell out of his pocket. "This is the murder round," he boasted. "If it hadn't been for good ol' Myrna, one of our comrades would be dead now. Good ol' Myrna took the buckshot." He said he would bury the remains of the shotgun shell at McKinley Park where no one would ever find it. The other comrade he had referred to was Jim Kilgore. Jim said that Emily had been too nervous, playing with her wristwatch band, not paying attention, and reiterated that he could have been killed. Emily said, "The safety must have slipped; the trigger lock on the shotgun must have accidentally been snapped off." Before the robbery, Jim had warned Emily not to take a shotgun because it had a hair trigger.

Kathy admitted to Patty that she had dropped some 9-mm ammunition from her handgun out of the ammunition pouch during the robbery. Police would later find unexpended 9-mm cartridges on the floor by the tellers' counter.

Dr. Trygve Opsahl was at American River Hospital making his rounds. He got a call that something terrible had happened to his wife and was told to go straight to the bank. He was almost there when the ambulance passed him. At the time, he didn't know how badly she was hurt or whether others had been wounded too. When he went inside the bank, he was told that his wife had just been taken to the hospital. He rushed back to the emergency room to find many doctors there. They told him they had tried everything they could, but she had "completely bled out."

That morning, young Jon Opsahl, his brother, Roy, and their sister, Sonja, were attending a small Seventh-day Adventist school in Carmichael. Carl was away at college. The three were called to the principal's office, and without a word, were driven by the school nurse to American River Hospital. They didn't understand what was happening until they saw the tears in their father's eyes.

"It's Mommy," he told them. "She's been shot."

Jon Opsahl remembers that "everything shut down." His brother and his sister started crying, but he couldn't get the tears out. They all went home and his father insisted that they eat something. They sat down and ate the sack lunches their mother had prepared for them that morning. Dr. Opsahl said, "Bless the hands that prepared it." Jon said that was when he "lost it."

The day after the robbery and murder, Steve Soliah bought a white Ford sedan from a private party in Sacramento. (Later, the car would be identified as the car used by Kathy Soliah, Jim Kilgore, and Bill Harris to drive to Los Angeles on August 8, 1975, to plant pipe bombs underneath police cars.)

According to *Voices of Guns*, police found two fingerprints on the 916 LBJ Mustang when it was identified months later. One of the prints on the rear license plate belonged to Steve Soliah. A print on the front license plate belonged to Jim Kilgore. Since there were no arrest records for these two men, their prints were not on file, and this time, the SLA/NWLF did not send communiqués bragging about their latest conquest. There was no obvious way to connect this robbery to the SLA. The Firebird was identified as the stolen car that the Sacramento police had been looking for. A tan Chevy rented by Kilgore was stored in another rented garage and would not be discovered until the end of Patty Hearst's trial when she gave federal agents a detailed map to the hideaway garage. When FBI agents found the vehicle, their technicians lifted nine fingerprints, all belonging to Steve Soliah.

Myrna Opsahl's murder had the Second Team on edge, and they decided it wasn't a good idea to stay in Sacramento. About one month after the robbery, they relocated to the southern border of San Francisco. Under assumed names, Kathy and Jim rented an apartment for all of them on Geneva Avenue. The others joined them, bringing their weapons, files, clothing, and paraphernalia in two U-Haul trailers. Kathy Soliah began working as a waitress at the Sir Francis Drake Hotel.

Toward the end of June, the Soliahs had a family reunion in Palo Alto, just south of San Francisco. Marty and Elsie came up from Palmdale, and Kathy, Steve, and Jo were there. Jo told her parents that she was a teller at a branch of Wells Fargo Bank. Steve was still painting houses for a living, and Kathy said that she was earning good tips as a waitress. It was wonderful for Marty and Elsie to reconnect with their oldest children and know that they were earning an honest living.

An uncle at the reunion asked Kathy what restaurant she worked at, and she managed to dodge the question. She couldn't say that she was working at the Plate of Brasse restaurant in San Francisco's posh Sir Francis Drake Hotel, or that she was working under the name of Kathleen Anger. There was no point in mentioning that she worked with Margaret Turcich either, Wendy Yoshimura's friend who had given refuge to Wendy in New Jersey.

When the elder Soliahs returned to Palmdale, they felt better about their children than they'd felt in years. Marty said that Kathy had taken him aside and put her arms around him, kissed him on the lips, and said, "I love you Dad." He was moved because they had not been a family to show much affection other than a hug now and then. He said, "It was the first time she'd ever done that." Marty didn't know at the time that the relief over his children's lives would be short-lived.

About a week after the reunion, Jo called home and told him she had quit her job and that she and Kathy were moving into an apartment in San Francisco. She gave him an address and said she'd give her parents the telephone number when they got one. That didn't happen.

While the Second Team remained in turmoil, Jack Scott was busy trying to put a book deal together. Broke, he demanded huge advances from publishing houses, but they weren't interested. He had another idea. Scott had an appointment with Randolph and Catherine Hearst. At the time, he wasn't aware of the Crocker National Bank robbery in Carmichael. If he could unite the Hearsts with their daughter, perhaps he could get a job at one of the Hearst newspapers. Maybe he wouldn't be so subtle; he could tell the Hearsts that he would need a large sum of money for his expenses. Desperate parents might do anything at this point. Their daughter had been missing for almost one and a half years. Randolph was eager to do business with Jack Scott, but Catherine had a bad feeling and was immediately suspicious of his motives. Scott told her that he could probably get to Patty if Catherine were to quit her job on the University of California Board of Regents.

When the meeting was over, Randolph Hearst called the FBI and told them about Scott's offer. According to *Rolling Stone* magazine, a reporter called Catherine on a tip he had heard about the meeting and she told him that, "Yes, Scott was offering a deal, and if she resigned as regent he would appeal for Patty's surrender." She also said that Scott seemed to know how to get in touch with Patty and he was looking for money.

The next day, the *Los Angeles Sunday Times* headlined her explosive comment. Scott was terrified of Bill Harris' reaction when he realized that Scott had met secretly with the Hearsts without his permission. Jack called Randolph, and the next day the paper printed a retraction. Now, the FBI was back on Scott's trail and also on that of everyone he had ever been in contact with. They started with Willie Brandt's visiting list.

Kathy Soliah didn't show up for work at the Sir Francis Drake Hotel after the Crocker National Bank robbery, not even to pick up a waiting paycheck. She didn't call in sick; she just disappeared. Margaret Turcich did show up, though. Soon after she got to work, she was called to the phone, and when she hung up, she took off too. With their visiting list from Willie Brandt's prison, FBI agents appeared at the restaurant showing the employees pictures of Kathy Soliah. They were told that she did work there, but her name wasn't Soliah; it was Kathleen Anger.

The FBI could now connect Kathy to Margaret Turcich, Wendy Yoshimura, and Jack Scott, who were also on Brandt's visitor's list. It was like stringing pearls together. The FBI finally had some clues that might lead them to Patty Hearst and the Second Team of the SLA.

One week later, the Sacramento Police Department requested that the Bureau of Criminal Identification and Intelligence (CI&I) check latent prints from the license plates of the Crocker robbery getaway car against the prints of James William Kilgore, member of the pro-SLA Bay Area Research Collective (BARC). Their fingerprint expert made a positive ID on a right-hand thumbprint found on the license plate. They knew that Jim was Kathy's boyfriend, and now they could connect Kathy Soliah, along with Kilgore, to the murder of Myrna Opsahl.

Explosions

The Second Team took a break in July, apparently because of the tensions between them. Kathy and Emily led a women's discussion group on feminism and continued experimenting with lesbianism. The men split up and found places of their own. All of them were tired of Bill Harris' Hitleresque tactics. He believed that the white nation had to be destroyed, just as the Weathermen had proclaimed in 1969. Bill lived in the past. Perhaps he still needed to prove something to his dead father, to show that he *had* amounted to something and that he *was* a leader. He was Cinque's replacement, the new General Field Marshal. However, remnants of the former SLA, the Second Team, were not impressed. Wendy wrote to Willie Brandt, "These people are totally unable to check out the objective situation and deal with it. They simply do not know how to take a theory and apply it to the reality that exists."

Patty wrote in *Every Secret Thing* that on August 13, 1975, Emily and Steve headed for Emeryville. They had left their apartment in one car, carrying a bomb, destined for a police car, while Kathy and Jim, dressed in their best clothes, left in another car for an observation post in a motel restaurant. Kathy and Jim had heard the explosion from the restaurant where they'd waited, then joined the crowd that gathered to see the wreckage. Perhaps it had become an addiction—and thrill like an arsonist who stands in the bushes watching the building burn. Patty later said that when they returned to the apartment, Kathy "sparkled as she described the destruction caused by the pipe bomb. The police car had been completely demolished; the policemen there were running about in confusion."

The NWLF sent a communiqué, which read in part: "The explosion at the Emeryville Station of Fascist Pig Repression is a warning to the rabid dogs who murder our children in cold blood. Remember pigs: every time you strap on your gun, the next bullet may be speeding towards your head, the next bomb may be under the seat of your car."

According to *Voices of Guns,* shortly after the Emeryville bombing Kathy, Jim, and Josephine went to northern California on a scouting trip, supposedly seeking a mountain stronghold in Mendocino County. "They were gone for over a week, bringing back maps of the Mendocino outback, lists of old abandoned mines—trail notes for future Che's of California;" this information was entered in Wendy's journal. She wrote of her love for Jim Kilgore and was depressed that he was away with his old girlfriend, Kathy. (Twenty-six years later, Wendy's diary would be crucial evidence for "Sara Jane Olson's" defense lawyers, who would claim that Kathy [Sara Jane], was not in Los Angeles on August 21, 1975, when the bombs were planted underneath the police cars. However, the diary now seems to be missing.)

On August 18, an FBI Special Agent Curt Holt dropped in on Marty and Elsie Soliah at their stucco tract home in Palmdale. The chocolate-colored house was in need of paint. Holt lived in nearby Lancaster, and Marty had met him before. Marty was out golfing at the time, so Holt talked to Elsie. He had just told her that they were looking for a young woman, and then proceeded to give her Kathy's description. Just then, much to Elsie's relief, Marty drove up, and he was surprised to see Holt talking to his wife.

Marty had asked Kathy about the SLA at their June reunion in Palo Alto. After having seen her speech at Ho Chi Minh Park on the news, he had naturally asked her if she were involved. Kathy had assured him she had never been a member of the SLA. This had appeased him somewhat. Their relationship had already been strained, partly because Marty disapproved of Kathy living with Jim. Before the reunion, they hadn't spoken for a long time, but Jo, the family peacemaker, had brought them back together.

Agent Holt assured Marty that his kids weren't in trouble, but that they were looking for Margaret Turcich and Wendy Yoshimura. Marty remembered Yoshimura's name from TV news reports. During their conversation, Holt told Marty and Elsie about their daughter's involvement in the Bay Area Research Collective (BARC), and also about Kathy's job at the Plate of Brasse in San Francisco. When he explained that Kathy had been using the name "Kathleen Anger," the elder Soliah's were very disturbed. There had to be a reasonable explanation.

When Agent Holt left, Elsie called the phone operator and tried to get the phone number for the address Jo had given her at the family reunion. Only after she pleaded that she needed to find her children, and a telephone supervisor came to her aid, was she told that the address was not a residence but a business. Marty and Elsie were beside themselves with worry.

If bombs were to explode simultaneously in Los Angeles and San Francisco, the pigs would soon realize that the NWLF was not just a small group of revolutionaries, all located in one city. Like the Weathermen, the NWLF had cells all over the country determined to squash the capitalist ruling class. One of those cells consisted of what was left of the SLA, the "Second Team." Their new scheme was for Emily Harris to lead a Marin County bombing offense and for Bill Harris, Jim Kilgore, and Kathy Soliah to drive down to Los Angeles and find a suitable target there. They would coordinate their actions by telephone.

On August 20, 1975, according to *Every Secret Thing*, the anniversary of George Jackson's death, Steve and Patty left their apartment, and drove across the Golden Gate Bridge into Marin County towards the civic center, a Frank Lloyd Wright building that housed the county courthouse, sheriff's department, county offices, a law library, and a public library. Jim Kilgore had grown up in Marin County—a wealthy, bourgeois neighborhood—a likely target for revolutionaries. Others in the group were familiar with the civic center because they had gone there to get false IDs.

Josephine had done the preliminary work of getting the layout of the building and checking out the security. They planned for two bombs to explode, one under a car in the lower parking lot and another one under a police car in front of the sheriff's office. The one in the parking lot was supposed to go off first. Then, when the sheriff's deputies ran out to see what happened, the second one would explode in their faces. Wendy was appalled at the whole idea, opposed to killing innocent bystanders, and she refused to be a part of this latest offensive. It turned out that the bombs went off in the wrong order, the sheriff's car first and the one in the parking lot next. No one was hurt.

Bill built the bomb for the Los Angeles action. It was more powerful than the ones they had used before, made of hard-to-find, three-inch-diameter pipe. It was twelve inches long, loaded with concrete nails as well as gunpowder, which would produce a more powerful and lethal bang. He described to his group that the concrete nails made it an "anti-personnel bomb." He devised a complex triggering device with a magnet and clothespins so that if the bomb were attached to a police car, it would explode when the car was driven off with one or two "pigs" in it. He was proud of his custom-made bomb.

He and Jim and Kathy had spent most of the time in Los Angeles arguing over their target. Their first idea was to plant it at a convention meeting at the Veterans of Foreign Wars in a midtown hotel. Bill and Jim walked into the meeting carrying the bomb in a briefcase. Apparently, they didn't look like they belonged, and when a security guard followed them, they went back to their car where Kathy was waiting for them. With the bomb in the car, they argued over what to do next. And then they fought.

Patty Hearst stated in *Every Secret Thing* that Kathy had made a disparaging remark about Jim's sexual prowess, and he gave her a black eye. Bill and Jim went at each other, with Kathy sitting in the middle, and when cars started honking their horns at them, they stopped fighting and drove off. That evening, they cruised the streets of a high-crime neighborhood in East Los Angeles until they came upon a parked police car. They put the bomb in a plastic garbage bag and set it to go off when the patrol car was moved. Then they went to another location and planted a second bomb underneath another police car.

On August 21, 1975, Officer James Bryan and his partner, Officer John Hall, stopped at the International House of Pancakes Restaurant (IHOP) on Orange Avenue and Sunset Boulevard in Los Angeles for a bite to eat. It was about 11:15 P.M. They parked their "black-and-white" in an empty space between a yellow car and a blue car. They didn't notice anything unusual as they got out and walked into the restaurant. At midnight, forty-five minutes later, the officers were summoned to a "man-with-a-gun" call. They hurriedly left the restaurant, got into their car, and lurched out of the parking lot.

Soon after, Mervin Morales and a friend parked to the right of the same blue car in the restaurant parking lot and went in to get a cup of coffee. After about fifteen minutes, they returned to their car, but before getting in, they noticed a long, cylindrical object lying on the ground between the yellow and blue cars. Morales thought it looked like a bomb. He remembered seeing another police car earlier, and he ran to find it. He flagged the officers down about two blocks away. In the meantime, his friend ran into the restaurant to tell the manager.

The officers came back to the lot with Morales to examine the object, the end of a pipe wrapped in black plastic. They immediately called their supervisor and were told to secure the area. Within thirty minutes, word was out that a bomb had been discovered in the IHOP parking lot.

Officers Hall and Bryan were summoned back to the area to

help block off traffic on Sunset and the side streets. Field supervisors were called to the scene and all officers were instructed that no radio transmissions be broadcast within a four-block radius.

William Stark was a civilian who worked in community relations at the Hollenbeck Division of the Los Angeles Police Department. On this same date, he drove an unmarked 1969 brown police car with the license plate "Young Tom David—YTD 283," a car that was assigned to the community relations personnel. Stark had parked it back at the Hollenbeck division of the police department after attending a youth baseball game at about 4:00 p.m. that day.

After the bomb was discovered at the IHOP parking lot, Hollywood Captain Mervin King alerted all police divisions to check their cars for explosive devices. The black-and-white police cars were checked first and then officers in every division checked the undercarriages of the unmarked cars.

Another LAPD officer checked the Hollenbeck lot. He found a brownish-green trash liner underneath the brown car with the license plate YTD 283 and when he looked under the plastic, he saw what looked like a bombing device, a pipe with red wires on it. It was under the oil pan. He immediately called his supervisor, and within fifty seconds, a bomb squad was there to deactivate the bomb.

The discovery of these bombs sent shock waves through the Los Angeles Police Department. Captain Mervin King later told *People* magazine, "When a bomber puts a bomb down, he doesn't know if he's going to kill the people he targeted or four kids walking by." King had not yet connected these bombings with the SLA or the police raid on the SLA "safehouse" where the six SLA members died.

Sometime prior to August 21, the day the pipe bombs were discovered, Vita Mele had rented an apartment at 288 Precita Avenue in San Francisco to William and Emily Harris, who used the assumed names Mr. and Mrs. Carswell. Kathy Soliah posed as

Emily's sister. The house on Precita Avenue had been under surveillance by the FBI since Marty's meeting with his kids in San Francisco when Marty had mentioned to the agents that his son Steve worked as a house painter for an independent contractor. The agents had done their homework, checked out all of the independent contractors in the area, and come upon Michael Bortin's company, Able Painting. Of course, Bortin was well known to the FBI.

That week, the elder Soliahs received a chatty, newsy letter from Josephine, telling them she and Kathy had just returned from a fishing trip in Mendocino. Had the Soliahs not known about the false address and that the FBI was looking for their children, they might have felt happy the sisters were off on a carefree vacation together, but they were uneasy. Agents from the FBI reappeared on their doorstep again. Marty showed them Jo's letter, and the agents informed them that the address was actually a "mail-holding outfit," used by people who have no permanent address. When Marty expressed his concern, Special Agent Holt asked him if he would go up to San Francisco and try to contact his children. It was essential that the FBI talk to them. Marty was horrified.

No one wanted to see his children more than he did, but it was as if the FBI wanted him to find them to turn them over to the law, and he didn't believe they'd done anything wrong. They assured him they only wanted to talk about Wendy Yoshimura or Margaret Turcich. Marty remembered that the FBI had questioned Kathy for four hours in July 1974 after the SLA rally eulogy. Finally, he agreed to go to San Francisco to clear this up once and for all.

According to *Voices of Guns,* on August 28, Marty flew up to San Francisco with Agent Holt, who had assured him that if the kids didn't want to talk, he would accept that and leave them alone. That was Marty's condition. The agent's condition was that Marty not tell his children that the FBI was trying to locate them. They all agreed.

Marty and Curt Holt checked into adjoining rooms at the Embassy Hotel near the federal building in the civic center. Two other agents joined them, one of them rather surly. Marty later attributed this to the Crocker bank robbery, which Marty didn't even know about at the time. Marty insisted on paying for his own room, but Agent Holt wouldn't hear of it. That was the least the FBI could do for all of Marty's help. As planned, Marty left a note at the address he'd gotten from Jo, which turned out to be nothing but a small storefront in a seedy part of town. He was even more disheartened. Why would his children ever be in this area, let alone use it for a mailing address? What was going on?

The next day, he went back to the mail-drop and re-dated the note. At 4:00 P.M., his phone rang and it was Jo. She was so excited that he was there, and wondered if her mom had come too. She said that she'd be right over with Kathy; Steve, who was painting houses, would meet them. Marty, Kathy, and Jo all went out for a beer, and when Steve joined them later, they decided to go out for dinner. As they were walking into the first restaurant they saw, Kathy objected, saying that it was too close to the FBI office. Marty was shocked; when he asked her what she was afraid of, she didn't answer him.

His three children were all suspicious, because it was unusual for Marty to go on a trip without Elsie, especially to see the children. Marty realized that he couldn't lie to them. All conditions made with the FBI were off, and he told them everything. He explained that agents from the FBI had been to see him and explained that they were looking for some people that the kids might know and thought that perhaps they could help. "I think you should talk to them," he said, "and tell them if you know anything." Then he assured them that if they didn't want to help, the agents had promised him that they wouldn't bother them.

All three children sat in shock as if he'd dropped a bombshell on them. Josephine cried, Steve sat mutely, and Kathy exploded. "She was furious," Marty later said. "Daddy! How could you?" she demanded. "Don't you know that you can't trust the FBI?"

Marty tried to explain the situation to his children, but while he was talking, he was overcome with guilt, as though he had traded in his own children. Then he accused Kathy of using another name, Anger. "Aren't you proud of your name now?" She answered with, "They're liars. I've never been anybody but Kathy Soliah!" She denied everything, and then she, too, started to sob. She said she didn't know Margaret Turcich or Wendy Yoshimura and insisted that they had nothing to do with the SLA underground or with Patty Hearst. She repeated, "The FBI are liars, liars, liars!"

Marty spent seven hours walking and talking with his three oldest children, but he never reached an understanding of what they were really up to. He asked if they would please speak with Curt Holt, but they refused, saying that they hadn't done anything wrong. He realized that they were not going to give in and he gave up. He begged them all to come home with him, saying he'd put up money for them to start a business. He told them to come home to the desert and breathe some fresh air. "How can you live in a place like this where there's dogshit all over the sidewalks?" Marty remembered it as a very painful evening (*Voices of Guns*). They told him to go home and assured him that it would be over soon. He didn't know what they meant by that and when he asked them, Kathy said, "Don't worry, Dad, there's nothing to worry about."

When they parted that night, Kathy felt that she and Jo were being followed and made Jo give her car to Steve to ditch at the other end of the city. The three Soliahs made their way back to their respective apartments by bus. When Steve met Patty later, he was in a "state of high excitement." He feared that the FBI was on to them and that they were being watched even as they spoke.

The FBI agents were angry at Marty for the way he'd handled the situation. They accused him of "blowing the whole thing." The Soliah siblings never went back to the mail drop. On Saturday morning, August 30, Marty flew home. He was sick with worry. That day, the kids tried to reach him at his hotel, but he'd already checked out. They called Elsie in Palmdale, assuring her that they'd done nothing wrong and that they weren't in any trouble. They promised her they would come home to visit soon.

Wendy Yoshimura's journal, dated August 30, later recovered by the FBI, read: "Well, things look very bad. Where are we to go from here? What or who will feed us, clothe us, and house us? What we had, the little we had is gone. Where is it to go now? Totally confusing period."

As the weeks went on, the sexual relationships changed like the weather. Emily and Kathy were breaking up. Emily was going back to Bill. Jim left Wendy and went back to Kathy, which was very painful for Wendy, who was in love with him. She wrote poignant passages in her journals. Apparently Jim had told her she was too independent. She wrote of being rejected by him and being very depressed.

She wrote a letter to Willie Brandt at Soledad, which he would never receive, telling him, "the group has ceased to be a group." The letter, reprinted in *Voices of Guns,* said that unfortunately Wendy had fallen under Bill Harris' spell, but she now realized how different she was from the Harrises. Politically, she disagreed "very drastically" with them. "They've no understanding of what it really means by 'third world leadership' [sic] their blind insistence of third world leadership (black) is clearly coming from white guilt. They believe that armed struggle is the only valid answer and anything else is irrelevant." The Harrises had weak egos, she wrote, and lacked a "sense of themselves." They obviously felt guilt for the death of their comrades, particularly since Bill "fucked up at the sporting goods store," and guilt for being white. Yoshimura added that she hoped Brandt would be able to meet Patty Hearst some day. "She is incredible! She amazes me! I swear only the toughest would have come out of it as she did. What an ordeal she went through!!" This unfinished letter never reached Brandt. It was found on the kitchen table the day that Wendy and Patty Hearst were arrested.

Act Four

"Injustice is relatively easy to bear. What stings, is justice."

↗ H. L. MENCKEN,
 PREJUDICES: THIRD SERIES (1922), 3.

Capture: September 1975

The Harrises settled into their Precita Avenue apartment, and the Soliah sisters moved in with them temporarily. Since none of them got along they needed another house. The Harrises rented another flat at 625 Morse Street in San Francisco's Mission District, a poor, working-class neighborhood about two and a half miles from the Harris's safehouse on Precita. Bill used the name "Charles Adams," and said that he'd be staying there with his Oriental wife [Wendy], and "Emily," his sister.

Two days later, on September 9, Steve, Wendy, and Patty moved in. Neighbors commented that they were a strange group, often peeking out the windows, and the women rarely came outside during the day. The Harrises, though, made friends with their neighbors on Precita Avenue and were thought of as open and friendly. Though they jogged daily and appeared like any other couple outside the house, inside they were stocking their apartment with cases of files, manuscripts, lists of phone numbers, and names.

According to *Voices of Guns,* the apartment also became a well-equipped bomb factory stocked with boxes of alarm clocks, reels of wire, batteries, and stacks of iron pipe with caps drilled for fuse wires. The authors wrote, "There were jugs of gasoline, three pounds of high-explosive gunpowder; four .38-caliber pistols; three military-model M-1 rifles, one with a cut-down barrel, and all converted to fully automatic weapons; two 12-gauge shotguns; and one Marksman twenty-shot BB repeater air pistol."

The tension between the Harrises and Wendy and Patty

became significant enough that Wendy decided to seek the council of Kathy Soliah. Kathy had been avoiding the two safehouses, waiting for the FBI to lose interest in her, but the dispute was so bad that it required immediate attention. And, Kathy began to feel that the FBI had no more interest in her since her meeting with Marty in San Francisco. Feeling cocky and safe, Kathy began commuting between the two houses, acting as mediator in the dispute.

On September 14, the Harrises and Kathy Soliah attended a rally in San Francisco's Golden Gate Park for the "San Quentin Six," the prison inmates who were standing trial in Marin County for conspiracy-murder. They had been charged with George Jackson's escape attempt in 1971 from the San Quentin Adjustment Center, when three guards and two white inmates had been murdered, and Jackson himself was killed. "Doc" Holliday was at the rally too. He was the thirty-three-year-old former leader of the Black Guerrilla Family at San Quentin and had been a key prison contact for the early SLA. Angela Atwood and Emily Harris had visited him in 1974 on the day that Remiro and Little were arrested. Now he was on parole after serving fourteen years of a life sentence for robbery and murder.

Sources said that Kathy approached Doc Holliday at the rally and explained that the Harrises wanted to meet with him. They subsequently met with him and told him that the SLA wanted to reorganize and needed a famed prison revolutionary to galvanize the leadership. Apparently Doc was not impressed because he refused. There would not be a reorganization of the SLA. Unbeknownst to what was left of the SLA, on September 15, the FBI had located the Soliahs.

Two months earlier, in July, Michael Bortin had taken a painting job at a large apartment complex in Pacifica, a coastal bedroom community on the peninsula just south of San Francisco. Mike, Steve, and Jim were all painting the units. The FBI, alerted to the Soliahs' contract work, had the job site under surveillance. The authors of *Voices of Guns* describe the stakeout:

At about 9:00 A.M. on September 15, FBI agents interviewed the manager of the Pacifica apartments, Bill Ozgood. They showed him photographs of Mike Bortin, and Ozgood recognized him, although Bortin was using a different name. Ozgood informed them that a couple of girls were also on the painting crew. The agents asked Ozgood not to mention their visit.

At 10:30 A.M., as they sat in position in their unmarked government car, the agents saw Kathy and Josephine arrive at one of the painting jobs. The agents radioed their findings to headquarters and were told to lay low.

At 5:30 P.M., a man thought to be Kilgore quit painting for the day; he and the two girls left Pacifica and headed north on the freeway back into San Francisco and directly to their safehouse on Morse Street, where Patty was living. A little after six, the threesome piled into the house as FBI agents circled the block. The agents broke for the night. At about 10:30 the next morning, while agents waited in their cars, Steve came out of the house, got into his car, and drove off. Agents followed him to Precita Avenue. Steve pulled up to the house and waited. A few minutes later, Kathy and Jo appeared in their painting overalls, and they all drove back to Pacifica. The girls must have gone to the Precita address during the night after the agents had left.

At quitting time, the painters piled into the car again. Steve drove to the Precita address and dropped off Kathy and Jo. He then drove back to the safehouse on Morse Street. Now the FBI had the two addresses where the remaining remnants of the SLA were living. The agents assumed that Kathy and Josephine lived on Precita and that Steve lived at Morse. They decided to stake out Precita because they believed Kathy was a key figure and any connections would have been made through her. The FBI watched the house around the clock.

On the morning of September 17, at 7:00 A.M., an agent spotted Steve's car parked a block away. At 10:00 A.M., agents who were parked on Precita in a camper truck bearing Utah license plates observed Kathy and Jo walk out of the house and around the corner to Steve's car. They drove off, apparently headed for work. The agents didn't follow them, but remained in position at the Precita address. Then they got their break.

For the first time since Patty Hearst's kidnapping, the agents saw Bill Harris, one of the FBI's Three Most Wanted. At 10:50 A.M., Harris, wearing cut-off jeans, T-shirt, and tennis shoes, came down the steps, stretched, and went back inside. At first, they weren't positive that it was him, although he fit the description—right age, height and weight—but his hair was jet black, not brown. He also had a bushy black beard. They didn't expect a beard, or the black hair, but they knew that the SLA members were big on disguises.

At 11:15 A.M., Bill Harris left the apartment again with a short-haired woman who fit the description of Emily Harris. They were going out for their daily jog, down the block, through the park, and back again. Twenty minutes. Another agent appeared on the scene and watched as Bill strolled to the grocery store a block away and bought the morning *Chronicle.* He was reading it as he sauntered back to the apartment. The camper had a camera with a telephoto lens, with which they snapped pictures of Bill Harris, General Field Marshal Teko.

He emerged from the apartment once again at 4:35 P.M. carrying a white cloth laundry bag, walked two blocks to a self-service Laundromat, and went in. He was sorting his shirts and underwear when an FBI agent walked past him over to a pay phone. The agent had to be sure he had the right man. He noticed a surgical scar just below Bill's cut-off jeans. Harris' Marine Corps records noted that he had had an operation on that knee. The agent returned to his car to wait an hour for Bill to finish his laundry and finally walk back to the Precita address.

At 6:15 that evening, the woman who had been jogging earlier with Bill emerged from the apartment and proceeded to the grocery store. The agent followed her in as if he were a customer, smiled as he passed her, and came to the conclusion that this person was not Emily Harris.

At 7:10 P.M., Steve dropped Jo and Kathy off at the Precita apartment. The agents could still not positively identify the Harrises. The FBI had earlier earned a reputation for raiding the wrong houses on SLA "sightings" and couldn't risk another mistake. They didn't need any more bad publicity or lawsuits against the agency.

The next morning, on September 18, at 8:00 A.M., Charles Bates, the FBI's San Francisco Bureau Chief, met with agents at the federal building. They decided that if these people were, in fact, the Harrises, then Patty must be with them. They believed that the SLA members always lived together, moved in unit strength, and they had no reason to believe it was any different now. Bates ordered his men to "Take them while they're jogging, because they would be unarmed."

At 10:02 that morning, Kathy and Jo left the Precita apartment. They were not followed. They spent the day with Jim and Steve painting in Pacifica. At 12:50 P.M., Bill and Emily came out of the house, Bill in purple track shorts and a green polo shirt, and Emily all in white, tennis shorts and a T-shirt. The agents watched as they broke into their run. The men were ordered into position. Bates himself was parked on a hill a few blocks away, listening as other agents gave spot reports on the couple's progress.

At 1:12 P.M., the agents got a flash that the suspects were jogging home. Four agents in a sedan pulled up and double-parked on Precita a few doors down from 288. Bill and Emily rounded the corner, walking and chatting, apparently carefree, and as they passed the government car, the four doors sprang open. "We're the FBI," the agents announced. Bill stopped in his tracks, but Emily pulled back and tried to sprint toward the corner. She almost bumped into two more agents, one of them with a shotgun; a third agent was on her heels. She ran a few paces before they grabbed her. She struggled and shouted, "You motherfuckin' sons of bitches!" They hustled her into a car and drove away before her ranting could alert anyone else in the house.

Bill remained silent. One of the senior agents grabbed his

hands and peered at the loops and whorls on his fingertips. "It's him," he said. Harris was pushed inside the car, and another agent quickly inked Bill's fingers, rolling them onto a five-by-eight print card. Identification was positive. The FBI finally had Bill Harris.

The other agents rushed up to the house, which was padlocked, and yelled, "FBI . . . OPEN UP!" One of the agents smashed the window with the butt of his shotgun, reached through, unlocked the window and yanked it open. "FBI!" he yelled again. They all hurriedly climbed through the window and fanned out into the apartment. After a couple of minutes, it was obvious to them that Patty Hearst was not there. The house was empty except for cases of papers, books, guns and bombs.

The Harrises were taken downtown. Now teams of agents were sent out to collect the rest of the SLA. Everyone was disappointed that Hearst was not in the house. Charles Bates had conducted the "Hearnap" investigation from the beginning, and this was another huge letdown. Patty had slipped by them again.

Jim Kilgore, Josephine, and Kathy were supposed to paint two apartments that morning. At about 11:00 A.M., Ozgood, the apartment manager, checked in the first apartment as he often did and saw they were doing their job.

After the Harrises' arrest, FBI agents showed up at the apartment complex and informed Ozgood that they were looking for Josephine and Kathy. Ozgood confirmed that the crew was working that day and asked the agents to wait while he went to find them. When he opened the apartment they were supposed to be painting, only about forty percent of it was painted. There was no sign of the Soliahs or Kilgore. Opened buckets of paint sat in the kitchen. Painting clothes had been dropped on the floor. The Soliahs and Kilgore had vanished.

The FBI still had not found Patty. She'd probably slipped out of the Precita apartment when the Harrises were nabbed. No one really believed that she would be at the Morse Street address, but it was the best shot the agents had. Two officers from the San

Francisco Police Department accompanied the FBI agents to the Morse address. One of them had been on the Hibernia Bank robbery case, and he wanted Patty Hearst as much as the FBI did. He'd been acting on SLA sightings for the past seventeen months. The two agents and officers drove past the place a few times and learned there were only two ways in and out. They wouldn't need help. The building's owner was working in one of the underground garages and told the officers that no one lived on the second floor, but the third floor was occupied by new tenants, a young man and a couple of girls. He thought the girls were upstairs now. When the agents showed him photographs, he didn't recognize Wendy or Patty, but he did Emily. When asked, he described the layout of the apartment; he told them that if they went up the back stairs, the back door was half glass. One FBI agent and one SFPD officer headed to the back stairway. The other two covered the front of the house.

Guns in hand, the agents proceeded up the stairs. When they got to the top landing, they froze. The FBI agent found himself face to face with Wendy Yoshimura on the other side of the Dutch door. She was standing up.

"FBI . . . Freeze!" he shouted.

Patty, who had been sitting at the kitchen table, stood up and backed toward the bedroom. The FBI agent yelled at her to "Freeze or I'll blow her head off!" pointing his gun at Yoshimura's head. An officer from the SFPD burst in through the door and, as Patty was making her way out of the room, called out, "Patty!" She turned around and he told her not to move. She looked pale and scared. He went over and handcuffed her, later reporting that, "she didn't give any trouble."

The agent removed a loaded revolver from Patty's purse and a loaded pistol from Wendy's. In the bedrooms, they found another pistol, a shotgun, and two sawed-off rifles, one of which was later identified as the carbine Patty Hearst had carried into the Hibernia Bank. In the refrigerator, wrapped in aluminum foil, nestled next to the eggs, they discovered a packet of eighty-four $1 bills.

One of the bills bore Serial Number L07097168D—a "bait bill" stolen from the Crocker Bank in Carmichael.

Before they left, Wendy asked if she could get her contact lenses, which were on the kitchen table where she had been writing another letter to Willie Brandt. As they were leaving, Patty asked the police officer, very politely, if she could change her clothes. She had wet her pants. It was September 18, 1975. The seventeen-month odyssey for Patty Hearst was finally over.

Steve Soliah heard of the Harrises' capture on the radio. He raced to the house on Morse Street hoping to rescue Patty before the police got there. He was too late; two waiting FBI agents arrested him on the front steps of the house.

He would see Patty the next day in San Francisco's federal courthouse. Patty, handcuffed, saw him in a cell and kissed him through the bars. They would pass love notes through her original lawyers. But when F. Lee Bailey took over her defense, their relationship ended. Steve was saddened that Patty faced a jail term. "She was a victim," he said.

Catherine Hearst learned of her daughter's arrest about twenty-five minutes later. "God has answered our prayers," she cried. "Today everything is wiped out—all the despair, I'm terribly happy," she told the *Los Angeles Times*.

Randolph Hearst was in New York on business. He was in a barber's chair when he heard on the radio that SLA fugitives William and Emily Harris had been apprehended. He went back to his apartment in the Essex House and phoned Charles Bates, who said, "Patty's okay." That was the first he knew of his daughter's apprehension.

Interviewed by a *Los Angeles Times* reporter on the TWA flight back to San Francisco, Hearst spoke of his daughter: "She is going to have to go through a difficult period now. I assume she will have to stand trial, but I believe she will be exonerated. I don't think she has too much to fear."

On the subject of brainwashing, he said his daughter underwent "the spell" that Charles Manson cast over the members of his "family." "Who knows what kind of a spell some people can cast over others?" he asked.

Above all, he said, he was heartened that his daughter was "alive and well. I would have been happier had she given herself up, but I'm gratified that during the capture she wasn't harmed physically. She can have all the help she wants from her parents. All she has to do is ask for it."

Four days later, on September 22, Wendy Yoshimura was arraigned on the 1973 indictment for the Berkeley Bomb Factory, charging her with possession of explosives, possession of a machine gun, possession of materials to make destructive devices, and possession of explosive devices, with intent to do injury and destroy public property. On the same day, in another Los Angeles courtroom, Russell Little and Joseph Remiro won the right to act as their own attorneys for Marcus Foster's murder.

On the night of the arrests, warrants had been put out for Kathy and Josephine Soliah. The all-points bulletin listed them as "armed and dangerous." They were wanted in connection with the explosives discovered in the house at 288 Precita.

Charles Bates, the FBI's San Francisco Bureau Chief, spoke to the press at length. He explained that after a lot of digging the FBI had found out where the Soliahs were living and that is what had led them to Patty Hearst. He gave the details of the surveillance of the Harrises at the Precita address and how that subsequently led them to the Morse address where they found Wendy and Patty sitting in the kitchen.

FBI officials met with the Sacramento authorities to review evidence that had been discovered at the Precita address, evidence that would further implicate the Soliahs in the Crocker bank robbery and the murder of Myrna Opsahl. Among the items was an unsent communiqué by the NWLF claiming responsibility for the robbery. Now authorities could make a definite connection between the SLA and the NWLF. Fingerprints of Jim Kilgore and Steve Soliah were found on stolen license plates.

A police sketch of a woman involved in the holdup and shooting bore a strong resemblance to photographs of Kathy Soliah, and a green scarf similar to the one worn by a suspect in the robbery was also found.

Evidence uncovered at the Morse address where Patty and Wendy were arrested included a 9-mm automatic pistol and live ammunition (9-mm bullets had been found on the floor of the bank after the robbery) and a red notebook with notations about San Francisco banks, along with six pages ripped out of a San Francisco telephone directory listing San Francisco banks. They also recovered detailed plans for the bank robberies.

Steve Soliah was indicted in late September by a federal grand jury on counts of harboring a fugitive, of being an accessory after the fact to bank robbery, and violating federal firearms laws. The judge set his bail at $75,000.

Marty Soliah seemed bewildered by the sudden national prominence of his son and two daughters. At first he refused to talk to reporters, but as he watched the television news, he realized he'd have to talk to someone eventually, and, against Elsie's wishes, he finally relented when a *Los Angeles Times* reporter showed up at his house. Marty stated he was "positive" that neither daughter was involved in the Hearst case, but declined to say how long it had been since he had been in touch with them. Now Marty's main concern was trying to get his son's $75,000 bail reduced. "I have no idea how I can raise $75,000," he told the reporter.

Showing the reporter two framed photographs from the wall, graduation pictures of Kathy and Steve (the latter sporting a crewcut), Marty couldn't hide the pride he felt for his children, children who had turned into people he didn't know anymore. "Beautiful aren't they?" he asked.

Marty explained that although he was still teaching, he had quit coaching when Steve became a senior in order to avoid accusations of favoritism. He took another swallow of his beer and proceeded to blame the San Francisco Bay Area for the radical influences that his children had bought into. "At home they were good, right-wing Republicans, who got up every morning and pledged allegiance to the flag. How do you figure it?" He said that his fourth child, Lance, was attending college in Iowa. "We tried three kids in California schools," he continued, "and they went to shit. So we sent this one to Iowa."

Regarding Josephine, Marty said, "She's just tagging along with Kathleen. She's totally innocent, has nothing to do with all this. She's up there now, scared...."

He added, "I've got to go up to San Francisco to talk to the judge about getting bail reduced so I can get my boy home." He thought the judge would listen when he told him what kind of a person he was, "If I tell them about my philosophy, tell them I'm a good Republican and that I'll vote for Nixon again if he comes back."

Elsie, who looked thin and nervous during the interview, finally spoke up. "We can't talk about anything. Why don't you leave!"

Steve Soliah pleaded innocent to the charges of bank robbery.

Patty's Trial: February 1976

The Harrises' capture had already been on the news, and now the media learned that Patty Hearst had also been arrested. As Patty, Wendy, and FBI agents approached the downtown federal building, which housed the San Francisco FBI headquarters where they were to be arraigned, a huge crowd of reporters and photographers greeted them. In true revolutionary style, the only style she knew now, Patty Hearst smiled and raised a clenched fist in salute. Wendy sat next to her looking as if she might throw up. In *Every Secret Thing*, Patty said that some of the photographers jumped on the hood of the car in hopes of a better picture. They banged on the windows and shouted questions.

The car drove into the garage and agents escorted the two women up to the FBI floor where the corridors were filled with employees waiting to see the "famous fugitive." At five feet four inches, Patty weighed only ninety pounds and wore corduroy pants, a striped lavender T-shirt, and rubber-soled thongs on her feet. She was led into a small room, fingerprinted, photographed, and strip-searched. On the way to a large conference room where six or seven agents would interrogate her, she caught a glimpse of Emily Harris. One of the agents proudly announced that this room had been devoted to Patty, the room where they had done all the work on her kidnapping case. The walls were lined with "Wanted" posters of her. An agent read Patty the Miranda rights, informing her that she had the right to remain silent, etc. He then asked her to sign something called a "Waiver of Rights." She refused. She remembered Cinque's advice: "Never sign anything,

Kathy Soliah, Third grade: The center candy cane in school play. *Courtesy of family*

Kathy Soliah: Third grade
Courtesy of family

Two of his most ardent fans share their dad's elation with Coach Marty Soliah as they read headlines telling of the Trojan victory over Moorhead, which sent Barnesville's team into the finals of the District 23 tournament in Moorhead. Steven and Kathleen Soliah, ages 6 and 8, are mighty proud of their pop, even if the Detroit Lakes team did defeat the Trojans in the final game.
—*Moorhead Daily News Photo*

Marty Soliah, March 1955, with Kathy 8, Steven 6
Courtesy of Barnesville Record Review

William and Emily Harris and Angela Atwood kidnapped Patty Hearst from this Berkeley townhouse on February 4, 1974. *Courtesy of Bruce Hendry*

Peking House on Chabot Road in Berkeley, where the SLA came together in 1973. *Courtesy of Bruce Hendry*

Patricia Hearst and her fiancé Bernard Shaw leaving federal prison, February 1, 1979. She is carrying what she called her "clemency blanket," which she crocheted during her internment with the Symbionese Liberation Army (SLA). *Courtesy of the Sacramento Bee newspaper*

A federal warrant was issued on February 27, 1976, in Los Angeles, California, charging Kathleen Soliah with unlawful interstate flight to avoid prosecution for the crime of a destructive device with intent to commit murder (Title 18, U.S. Code, Section 1073). *FBI Photo*

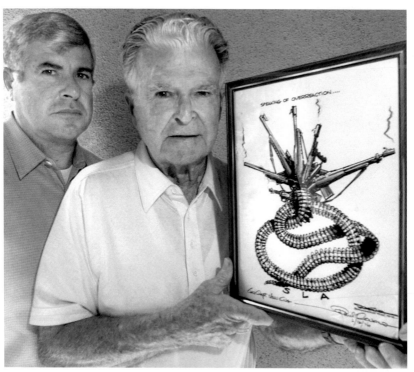

Tom and Mervin King (LAPD) holding a picture of the SLA slogan, seven-headed cobra. *Courtesy of San Gabriel Valley newspaper.*

Wanted Poster for James William Kilgore, 1976. *FBI Photo*

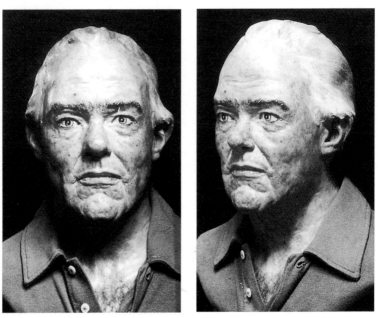

Bust of James William (Jim) Kilgore (Age enhanced). If you have seen this man
(he may wear glasses), CALL 415-553-7400 or 1-800-CRIMETV. *Courtesy of FBI*

April 27, 1976: A happy Steven Soliah hugged his girlfriend Emily Toback following a news conference in Sacramento after he was found not guilty of bank robbery charges. *Courtesy of A/P Wide World Photos*

August 9, 1975: William and Emily Harris were found guilty in a Los Angeles, California court of kidnapping and robbery. The Harrises were also acquitted of six assault charges credited to Patricia Hearst. *Courtesy of A/P Wide World Photos*

Myrna Opsahl

The Opsahl
family, 1965

The Opsahl
family, 2001

1976: Dr. Trygve Opsahl of Carmichael, California, holds a picture of his wife Myrna. *Courtesy of A/P Wide World Photos*

2002: Dr. Jon Opsahl smiles during a press conference in Sacramento after the arrests of Bill Harris, Emily (Harris) Montague, Michael Bortin, and Sara Jane Olson. *Courtesy of A/P Wide World Photos*

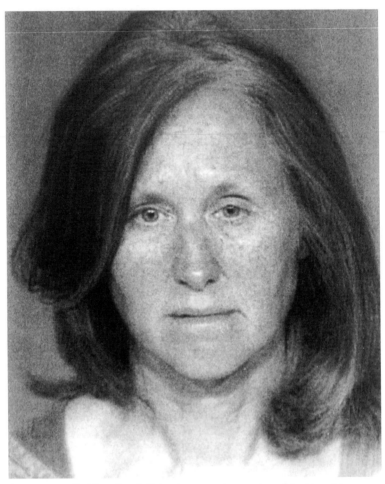

June 16, 1999: Kathleen Ann Soliah, a long-sought member of the terrorist group, Symbionese Liberation Army, in a police booking photo following her arrest in St. Paul, Minnesota. Soliah, who was known in St. Paul as Sara Jane Olson, was indicted February 26, 1976, by a grand jury in Los Angeles on felony chages including conspiracy to commit murder of police officers and possession of explosives. *Courtesy of A/P Wide World Photos*

November 19, 1999: Dr. Gerald Frederick Peterson, right, husband of former Symbionese Liberation Army fugitive Sara Jane Olson, and Olson's sister, Josephine Soliah Bortin listen during a hearing where motions to dismiss Olson's indictment were denied in Los Angeles Criminal Court. Olson's trial was pushed back one month to give the defense time to analyze explosive evidence. *Courtesy of A/P Wide World Photos*

July 20, 1999: Kathleen Soliah (Sara Jane Olson) and her husband Fred Peterson smile outside the Los Angeles county jail. Friends of Soliah posted her $1 million bail, allowing her to return to Minnesota to await trial on charges she planted bombs under police cars during the 1970s. *Courtesy of A/P Wide World Photos*

February 2000: Sara Jane Olson and her husband Fred Peterson at Olson's defense rally at Lake Harriet Community Church in Minneapolis.
Courtesy of Bruce Hendry

February 2000: Bernardine Dohrn and Stuart Hanlon at Olson's defense rally at Lake Harriet Community Church in Minneapolis. *Courtesy of Bruce Hendry*

Wendy Yoshimura with her watercolors. Berkeley, 2001. *Courtesy of Bruce Hendry*

Judge Larry Paul Fidler

May 17, 2001: Defense attorneys Tony Serra and Shawn Chapman argue their motion to recuse themselves as attorneys for Sara Jane Olson, citing conflict of interest, during a hearing to defend themselves on criminal charges. They had both been arraigned on misdemeanor charges related to the release of witness information. *Courtesy of A/P Wide World Photos*

January 16, 2002: William Harris after his arrest in Oakland, California. *Courtesy of Sacramento Bee newspaper*

January 16, 2002: Emily (Harris) Montague after her arrest in Altadena, California. *Courtesy of Sacramento Bee newspaper*

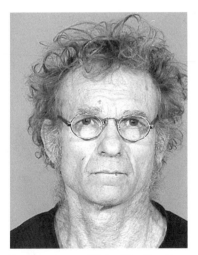

January 16, 2002: Michael Bortin after his arrest in Portland, Oregon. *Courtesy of Sacramento Bee newspaper*

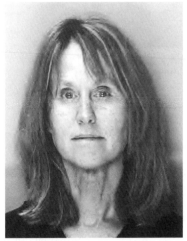

January 16, 2002: Sara Jane Olson after her arrest in Beverly Hills, California. *Courtesy of Sacramento Bee newspaper*

Former Symbionese Liberation Army members—from left: Michael Bortin, William Harris, Sara Jane Olson and Emily Harris. *Courtesy of the Sacramento Bee newspaper*

never say anything, when the pigs've got you." Next, a doctor appeared, which scared her more than anything else. She thought they were going to send her to a mental institution. She refused to talk to him too. When the FBI realized that she would not speak to them, they gave up on her, and let her out of the room. She saw Wendy, who whispered to her that Bill and Emily had been arrested.

Patty and Wendy were led to an elevator that brought them to the nineteenth floor of the U.S. Marshal's office. Patty was put into a wire-mesh cell designed so that she could see out, but others could not see in. It was known as a conference cage. She sat there alone for about six hours. Wendy was in a standard, barred holding cell to Patty's right, and Emily was in the next corner cell on Patty's left. Bill was in a cell next to hers. They were able to converse, and the Harrises told Patty about their arrest. They explained to her how the FBI had traced them through the Soliahs and their painting jobs. Bill said, "If only we could have got to our guns, we could have blasted our way out of there."

Wendy was taken out of the holding cell, shackled in heavy chains wrapped around her waist and attached to cuffs on her wrists and ankles. She was going to Oakland for arraignment in the Alameda County courthouse. In *Every Secret Thing* Patty observed, "In all those chains, Wendy looked so tiny and helpless, like a Roman slave girl being led to auction. She was crying."

Finally, Patty was introduced to an attorney, Terence Hallinan, a known defender of liberal and left-wing causes. As they rushed to a courtroom filled with people, he assured her he would take care of everything. She was then led to a table before a judge and the charges were read: armed bank robbery and the use of a firearm to commit a felony, in connection with the robbery of the Hibernia Bank on April 15, 1974. In her book, Patty recalled that she was chewing gum, and she took it out of her mouth and stuck it under the table. Her lawyer pleaded "Not guilty."

She was taken to San Mateo County Jail, not far from her parents' house in Hillsborough, where she had grown up. Like Wendy,

Patty was secured with chains around her waist, her wrists hand-cuffed to the chains. When they arrived, she was again finger-printed, photographed, and booked into jail. When they asked her what her occupation was, she answered, "Urban Guerrilla." The next day, that response was the headline in newspapers throughout the country.

After a routine delousing shower and another strip-search, Patty Hearst was dressed in a coarse cotton, pink hospital gown that just covered her bare buttocks—that would be her outfit for the entire next week. Her cell was six by nine feet with a double bunk bed and a plastic commode, which combined a toilet and a sink. The walls were cement, and the cell door was made of steel bars with an opening for passing food inside. Emily was brought in and put in the cell next to her. That night, Patty was told she had visitors. She was led to a room where her mother, father, and two sisters, Vicki and Anne, waited. She hadn't seen them for al-most two years.

Her mother handed her a bouquet of long-stemmed yellow roses. It was awkward at first. Her sister Vicki was twenty and had blossomed into a young woman from the seventeen-year-old Patty remembered. She knew that she looked different too with her gaunt features and tinted red hair. Her mother went on about how happy she was to see her and assured her that she would be coming home soon.

Patty barely remembered the visit, but later she was told that she had "curled up in a ball, like a fetus, and barely managed to mumble in a weak, disembodied tone of voice." All she knew was that she was a prisoner again, and Cinque had promised her that if she were ever caught, she would be "beaten and tortured, put on trial, and sent to jail." She had no reason to doubt him.

She and Emily spent hours whispering from their cells. Emily warned her not to talk to the authorities: "You can't trust them." She lectured Patty on their defense.

When more lawyers hired by her father arrived the next day, however, Patty decided she'd better tell them everything. They took notes and seemed surprised to hear what she'd been through. She was surprised herself when tears fell out of her eyes as she related her story to them. As the days went on, her situation got worse. At night, she would listen to the warnings of Emily, and during the day, she would be bombarded with questions from lawyers who demanded that she sign affidavits she was afraid to sign. Prisoners strolled by her cell to get a look at her, and prison guards asked for her autograph. She was sure her lawyers were going to make her plead insanity. Her parents were getting nervous as well. When she told her lawyer that Emily wouldn't leave her alone, Randolph Hearst ordered a guard placed outside their cells so they could not communicate. Emily was furious and managed to hiss one night, "I knew we should have killed you way back when. . . ."

Patty spent her time in the San Mateo County Jail reading and crocheting. She began to feel that jail was better than being a POW in the SLA. She learned how to get along in the jailhouse, mingling with the other inmates and listening to their stories. Although she was told she was safer in jail than on the streets, she hoped she could get an appeal, or be offered bail so she could go home to her family, at least for a while.

There were hundreds of letters a day, one from Charles Manson saying, "You write me." He promised to help her if she would do everything he told her to do. Most of the letters she received condemned her for deserting her country and her heritage, for having sex with black men and hippies, and for being a rich, spoiled bitch. She now knew how much she was hated.

Randolph Hearst hired F. Lee Bailey, famed for saving the Boston Strangler from the death penalty and for winning an acquittal for Dr. Sam Sheppard for the murder of his wife. Bailey's associate Albert Johnson would take over her case. Bailey urged Hearst to cooperate with the court-appointed psychiatrists who were to determine whether she was competent to stand trial. Her previous attorney, Hallinan, had given her opposite advice, and she was at the point where she didn't care what she did anymore.

The government had pictures of her robbing the Hibernia Bank, and they had the tape of her bragging about it. In her mind, she was going to jail for a long time, no matter how many psychiatrists tried to prove that she had been coerced or brainwashed.

Bailey did not want to put her on the stand, believing that it was important for impartial psychiatrists to explain all that had happened to her to the jury. That was fine with Patty, because she believed that if she testified against anyone in the SLA, they would kill her. Bailey admonished her to remember that she was only being tried for the Hibernia Bank robbery, not that of the Crocker National Bank in Carmichael where Myrna Opsahl had been murdered. She was not to talk about anything that happened in Sacramento or in San Francisco. All she could think about when Bailey left the jail was Cinque telling her, "There is no such thing as a fair trial in this fascist state. We're revolutionaries, and they've got to put us down, if they can."

Negative publicity against Patty continued. The majority of people thought she had voluntarily joined the SLA and that she should go to prison. Half of the people polled believed that she planned her own kidnapping. This was devastating to Patty because at this time, the Harrises, through successful plea bargaining, were only being charged for their part in the shoplifting/shooting incident at Mel's Sporting Goods and for kidnapping the young driver of the hijacked car, Tom Matthews. Patty would be charged with those crimes too, after this trial was over. The prosecutor in her case would be the Chief U.S. Attorney for northern California, James R. Browning Jr.

Eleven days after her arrest, the first psychiatrist came to see her. During their long consultation, she was forced to "go back to the closet" and to relive her time with the SLA. She said that she wept more in that session than she wept when she had been locked away in the closet. It was the first time since her kidnapping that she allowed herself to truly *feel*. During hours and hours of painful extraction, the doctor had her relive the threats, the metallic clicking of the rifles outside of the closet, the rapes, the bank robberies, the Criticism-Self-Criticism meetings, the combat drills, the weapons and, worst of all, the fear that she had experienced for all of those months.

There were more psychiatrists and more tests. Patty's IQ had been 130 when she was in high school, but now it registered 90. A 20 to 40–point variance in anyone indicates that a serious change has taken place. Other tests revealed that she was "sad, hopeless, withdrawn, emotionally distressed, and expressing a silent cry for help." During her psychotherapy, Patty learned about the various methods of brainwashing. The "modern" preferred technique was to "weaken your prisoner gradually by depriving her of proper food, sleep, exercise, and then browbeating her through continual, unrelenting questioning until she agreed to what the captors wanted her to say or do and had, in fact, come to believe it herself." She learned of the Maoist formula of thought reform, which her psychiatrist called the three Ds—Debility, Dependency, and Dread.

She had been weakened by her confinement in the closet, deprived of sight, decent food, regular sleep, and exercise, with the radio blaring at her. She had been dependent on her captors for the necessities of life and any information from the outside world. The SLA were the only people with whom she had communicated, and they threatened to kill her while warning her that the FBI would kill her as well if agents ever found her.

After one month in jail, Patty was let out of solitary confinement and allowed to eat meals with the other prisoners. She spent her life waiting—waiting for lawyers and waiting for visits from her family, which were difficult because everything was taped and they were separated by a glass partition.

Hearst's trial began on February 4, 1976, two years to the day after she'd been dragged out of her Berkeley townhouse. After days of testimony about the bank robbery, Patty learned that she would have to get on the stand after all, despite Bailey's promise that she wouldn't have to testify.

In a hearing, without jurors present, she explained to her

defense lawyers and prosecution lawyers that Angela Atwood had written the tape about the bank robbery and that she had only read it. She testified that she had told Tom Matthews about the robbery because Bill Harris had instructed her to recite her regular spiel for outsiders. She further testified that the Harrises had supervised the SLA manuscript for the book Jack Scott and the Harrises had hoped to write, which contained the "Patty Interview," and was supposed to show how great the SLA was. She explained to Browning her fear for her life from both the SLA and the FBI and hoped he would accept that as good reason for her not running away when she had the opportunities.

The forty-three-year-old prosecutor, Browning, who was a Nixon appointee and had not tried a case in seven years, was not impressed. He made sure that the jury heard Patty's voice on the tapes saying, "Greetings to the People. This is Tania. On April 15 my comrades and I expropriated $10,660.02 from the Sunset branch of the Hibernia Bank. . . . My gun was loaded and at no time did any of my comrades intentionally point their guns at me." They relived the shoplifting incident at Mel's Sporting Goods Store where Patty leaned out from the Volkswagen van's window and fired a volley of shots. They heard testimony from Tom Matthews telling of being kidnapped by the Harrises and Patty.

On February 9, the court had to take an unscheduled recess after a phone call was received stating that a bomb had been placed near the courtroom in the federal building. No device was found, but a couple of hours later, another man called the *San Francisco Examiner,* claiming to represent the NWLF and saying that a bomb had been set to "demolish" the courtroom where the Hearst trial was being held. Again, no bomb was found.

On February 12, the day before Patty took the stand in her defense, a bomb exploded in one of the three guesthouses at her parents' San Simeon estate. The bomb had apparently been left there while a group of nearly 60 people were taking a guided tour, and was timed to go off after they left. Apparently some of Patty's former "comrades" had managed to join the group of tourists. No one was hurt, but a side wall was blown out, along with furniture. Damage was estimated at approximately $1 million.

The NWLF sent a communiqué claiming responsibility for the bomb, and demanding that Randolph Hearst pay $250,000 for the legal defenses of the Harrises. It threatened further bombings and violence if their demands were not met within forty-eight hours. (During this same time, the Harrises were giving interviews from their jail cells stating that Patty was a turncoat and that she had voluntarily joined the SLA.)

Days later another bomb went off at the New York City offices of the Hearst magazines. Patty heard about it on the ten o'clock news and the jury was informed of it the next day during her testimony.

During her testimony, Browning asked her, "About the bombing last night, do you have any idea who did it?"

"I wish I did," she answered gravely.

"Who are these people who are not in custody?"

"James Kilgore, Josephine Soliah, and Kathy Soliah."

"Didn't you testify just the other day that you were not in fear of Kathy?"

"I have reason to believe now that I should be very much in fear of her," Patty stated.

Shana Alexander wrote in her book *Anyone's Daughter, The Times and Trials of Patty Hearst* that Kathy's name had been linked to the San Simeon bombing. All SLA sympathizers were suspects. Patty refused to answer any questions regarding the "Second Team," or questions concerning what was now referred to as the "missing year"—1975—when she had been hidden and transported to Pennsylvania and back to California with the help of the Harrises, the Soliahs, Jim Kilgore, and Michael Bortin.

Since the judge had decided to allow testimony of events that occurred after the Hibernia Bank robbery, a whole new Pandora's box could be opened. Hearst asked Bailey if she could tell the story of the Crocker National Bank robbery in Carmichael because if she didn't, she feared the jury would think she had more things to hide, but Bailey was in charge, and he instructed her to give yes or no answers and nothing else. She was to follow his signals. Her pat answer was to be, "I refuse to answer."

Browning asked her, "Was James Kilgore a member of the NWLF? What was your relationship with Steven Soliah? With Kathleen Soliah? Were you and those persons, as allies, not in fact engaged in a program of armed struggle?"

"I refuse to answer."

Bailey instructed her to give that response forty-two times. The seven women and five men on the jury probably imagined she was covering up even more criminal activities with the SLA, including the Crocker Bank robbery. In hindsight it was apparent that Bailey should not have put Patty on the witness stand in the first place, but since he did he should have let her answer the prosecutor's questions.

Ironically, as she refused to answer the questions in her own trial, she was privately telling all to another U.S. attorney in regard to the Crocker Bank robbery. The chief federal prosecutor of Sacramento and his assistants were preparing their case against Steve Soliah. She told all she knew in exchange for "use immunity," meaning that the government could not use anything she told them against her in any further proceedings.

Patty's trial was still in progress when Steve's trial began on March 10, 1976. The government could not prosecute her in San Francisco and at the same time use her as their witness in Sacramento; this would undermine the credibility of her testimony against Steve. Instead, they chose to try to prove that Steve Soliah was inside the bank in spite of the fact that Patty had repeatedly told them that he was outside the bank as a backup during the robbery.

During the course of the trial, Patty came to the conclusion that the whole thing was a farce. The government portrayed her as a symbol of the rebellious radical youth movement of the sixties. But in truth, Patty was not a child *of* the sixties; she was a child *in* the sixties. In 1960 she'd been six years old. If that wasn't enough, the old and frail judge sometimes referred to the participants as Patricia Harris, and Bill and Emily Hearst. His confusion did not boost her confidence of the possible outcome.

Patty's trial was a media event and worse, a circus. Bill and Emily Harris appeared from jail on the *Today* show talking about how Patty joined them of her own free will. At the same time, Hearst properties were being bombed by the NWLF, and Patty's parents had bodyguards escorting them to and from court every day.

Patty also suffered verbal abuse from the other prisoners and repeated threats to her life. On her twenty-second birthday, the marshals took one threat seriously enough to transport her in an unmarked car, taking a completely different route to the courthouse. She was still being housed in the San Mateo County Jail. (At the time, Sara Jane Moore, who had tried to assassinate President Ford, was there as well. Moore spent her time trying to get close to Patty while Patty, who was very depressed, spent her time trying to avoid Moore. She would actually slam her cell door in Sara Jane Moore's face.)

In closing arguments, Browning outlined for the jury all of the evidence that had been presented. His summation flowed, and he put the pieces together like a fine tapestry. After the luncheon recess, it was the famous F. Lee Bailey's turn. Patty expected him to unravel Browning's tapestry, to tell the jury the real story, to prove to them that Patty was innocent. She would be sorely disappointed.

Bailey rose from the defense table to offer his summation grabbing an unruly stack of notes. Patty noticed that his hands were shaking. His hair was messy, and his face was blood red. She wondered if he'd been drinking at lunch. He detached the microphone from its stand and began to address the jury, seemingly forgetting that he had the notes in his hand. He rambled on and on about things that had nothing to do with the case. He talked at length about himself and about the difficult tasks of lawyers.

As he swept his arm up in a gesture, he knocked a glass of water off the podium, which dribbled down the front of his pants. Patty was appalled as some members of the jury giggled.

F. Lee Bailey kept rambling as if the front of his pants were not wet and as if he hadn't seen the judge smile. It was a disjointed closure that went on for forty-five minutes, even though Bailey had preached that a closing argument should be no longer than twenty minutes. In Patty's mind, it went on for a lifetime. When it was over, she asked Bailey's assistant, Al Johnson, what had happened. He hung his head and said that he didn't know.

The next day, the judge instructed the jury on the law applicable to the case. Catherine Hearst sat in the front row where she had spent every day of the trial crying. Patty wondered how much more her mother could take. At approximately 11:00 A.M., the jury filed out of the courtroom to begin their deliberations. Patty waited in the holding cell in the courthouse until 5:00 P.M., when she was taken back to San Mateo County Jail. She was told by all the people surrounding her to expect an acquittal. Her prison guard, Janey Jimenez, said they'd go out for a drink the following weekend. Patty didn't believe any of them. In her heart she thought that if her case hadn't been lost by the testimony, it had certainly been lost after Bailey's last performance.

The next day, Thursday, March 11, 1976, another bomb exploded at the Wyntoon estate in northern California, another Hearst family retreat. The bomb was defective and did little damage but it was clear that the Hearsts were under siege.

According to *Rolling Stone* magazine, in an article titled, "The Lost Year of the SLA": "That month, towards the end of Patty's trial, a Berkeley radio station KPFA had received a communiqué signed by Jim Kilgore, Josephine Soliah, and Kathy Soliah, who had vanished into the underground. They still wanted a voice, though, and they wanted to separate themselves from the old SLA style.

'We are not gun-toting militarists,' they wrote. 'We are serious political people with much important work confronting us as we try to help build the revolutionary movement in this country.'

The communiqué continued: 'We are proud to be among those fighting the U.S. Empire. We are proud to have uncompromisingly supportive people who have taken up arms against the enemy.' Apparently, they were angry about Patty Hearst's testimony at her trial, even though she pleaded the Fifth Amendment forty-two times rather than incriminate them. Their communiqué contained a quote from F. Scott Fitzgerald's book *The Great Gatsby*: "Let me tell you about the very rich. Even when they enter deep into our world or sink below us, they still think they are better than we are."

On March 20, 1976, as Patty waited in the courthouse with her family, she was told that the jury had reached a verdict. It seemed too soon, only twelve hours. It took two hours to get everyone together to go back to the courtroom. When they were finally all seated, the jury stared straight ahead, refusing to meet Patty's eyes. Bailey whispered to her, "It's bad." Once the judge received the piece of paper with the verdict written on it, he read it to himself, then handed it back to the clerk who read it to the open court:

"We the jury, find the defendant guilty on the first count and guilty on the second count."

Janey Jimenez, Patty's prison guard who had grown very close to her, burst into tears.

Patty said to the dazed Bailey, "I never had a chance." He didn't bother to answer her.

One week after her conviction in San Francisco, Patty was flown to Los Angeles to be arraigned on the same charges that the Harrises faced: eleven counts of robbery and kidnapping resulting from the events surrounding the shoplifting/shootout at Mel's Sporting Goods Store. She received the maximum sentence—twenty-five years for the robbery, plus ten on the firearms charge. Patty would have to go through a ninety-day psychiatric study by the Bureau of Prisons. The judge would pass the final sentence after he reviewed their report. Her attorneys would appeal.

In April 1976, the FBI and federal prosecutors questioned her again and this time she told them about the "missing year." She decided to help authorities in the prosecution of SLA members and their associates in return for a lighter sentence. She also hoped to get immunity in connection with the SLA robbery of the Crocker National Bank in Carmichael. Patty identified everyone connected with that robbery, including Emily Harris, who, she said, pulled the trigger on Myrna Opsahl. On this same day, Steve Soliah was identified by witnesses at his trial as having been inside the bank. Patty had always maintained that Steve had waited outside the bank.

Patty was jockeyed back and forth from the Federal Correctional Institution in Pleasanton, California, where she was supposed to receive her ninety-day psychological evaluation, and a prison in San Diego. Patty read in the newspapers that they blamed the whole fiasco at Mel's Sporting Goods Store on her. Bill Harris denied shoplifting. The Harrises' defense lawyer said that Patty Hearst had endangered their lives. Their trial was in its third week when Patty was taken to the Los Angeles Superior Court for a hearing on the eleven-count indictment over the Mel's shootout.

Kathleen Soliah: Indictment

Kathy Soliah and Jim Kilgore had vanished, but when the authorities had cleaned out the Precita Avenue apartment where the Harrises had been arrested, they'd found enough evidence to connect both of them with the bombings of the Los Angeles police cars. Charges would never be brought against Josephine, but Kathy and Jim would both be indicted for the crimes. Kathy Soliah was charged with attempted "Explosion of a Destructive Device with Intent to Murder."

For the prosecution of such crimes, an indictment before a grand jury was required. An indictment is a formal accusation presented by a grand jury consisting of twelve or more people assigned to inquire into alleged violations of the law in order to ascertain whether the evidence is sufficient to warrant a trial by a jury. Prosecutors had to determine whether they had enough evidence to try Kathy and Jim on conspiracy charges.

Conspiracy laws are based on the premise that organized criminals are more dangerous than those who act as individuals. Some recent examples of conspiracy cases were the prosecutions in the World Trade Center bombing in 1993, where six people were killed and 1,000 injured. Another conspiracy case was that of the Oklahoma City bombing of the federal building in 1995 where 168 people were killed.

To win the conspiracy conviction, prosecutors would have had to prove that Kathy Soliah entered into an agreement with others to commit a crime. Because conspiracies are almost always hatched in secrecy, prosecutors have broad leeway in using circumstantial evidence to prove the existence of these hidden agreements. Conspiracy laws also allow testimony that would be inadmissible as hearsay in a non-conspiracy case. A pattern of criminal activity by co-conspirators would also be allowed as evidence, even if Kathy Soliah had played no immediate role in her conspirator's crimes. For instance, if the judge decided to allow the criminal history of the Symbionese Liberation Army (SLA) as evidence, Kathleen Soliah could be held responsible as well.

On February 18, 19, and 26 of 1976, the grand jury met to hear the case against Kathleen Soliah in the California Criminal Courts Building in Los Angeles. There were twenty-seven witnesses.

First they heard from James Marshall, who worked for the Larsen Supply Company, a wholesale plumbing business. He had helped a woman and a man when they came into his store on August 20, 1975, one day before the bombs were discovered underneath the police cars.

He described the woman as about five feet two inches and slightly plump with long, light brown hair, curled under. The most prominent thing on her face was her nose. "I recognized that the bridge of her nose was kind of wide and rounded, and she was very quiet. She didn't speak, didn't smile or anything." He guessed she was about twenty-five-years old.

She and the unidentified man had purchased two [3″ x 12″] long, galvanized pipes and one [3″] galvanized cap. The man said that he had actually wanted four caps, one for each end of the galvanized pipe, but Marshall told him that they only had one. The man said he'd take it and that they'd buy the others someplace else. From a police line-up photo, Marshall identified Kathy Soliah as the woman who had purchased the pipe.

Later, an unidentified man called the Imperial Pipe & Supply Company and spoke with Irving Lebow. Lebow thought that the voice on the phone was high-pitched and that the caller must be a young person. The man told Lebow that he was looking for three-inch caps and specified screw caps, not slip-fitting caps, the type that fit over the end of the pipe and have no internal threads. (During the testimony, caps of the same variety were marked Exhibits 9-A, B, and C.) Later that day, August 20, an unidentified man came into the Imperial Pipe & Supply Company and purchased these types of caps.

Lebow described the man as Caucasian with dirty, blond-colored long hair, about five feet, eleven inches tall, weighing about 175 pounds. The description fit Jim Kilgore's physical appearance. Lebow was surprised when he heard the man speak, because his high voice (the same Lebow had heard on the phone) didn't seem to fit his build and age. One of the pipefittings that Lebow sold this man turned out to be defective, and the man returned the next day to exchange it for another one.

Fred Smith, chief of the explosives unit for the FBI, identified photos of the bombs found one day later, on the morning of August 22, 1975. He explained some of the terminology so the grand jury could understand.

An "IED" stands for *Improvised Explosive Device,* a common term used by technicians in the explosives business to characterize homemade bombs or destructive devices. None of the materials in an IED were by themselves originally constructed for the purpose of being part of an explosive device. This was in contrast to military bombs where each piece was specifically manufactured for the bomb mechanism. Smith and others testified to the fact that the bomb-making materials found in the Precita Avenue apartment in San Francisco, where Kathy's fingerprints had been found, were consistent with the bombs found under the Los Angeles police vehicles.

In court documents, one LAPD officer described how the bomb found at the Hollenbeck Division was *supposed* to operate:

"The device was attached to the bottom of the police vehicle with a magnet. As the car was driven away, the monofilament line or fish line would become taut and pull a wood shim out from between a clothespin—two clothespin jaws. These provided electrical contacts; when the wood shim was removed from the clothespin jaws, the clothespin jaws would shut, making electrical contact with the two screw heads providing your electrical current to your blasting cap.

"In the position it was placed, if the device had detonated, it would have completely totaled the engine compartment of the vehicle and severely injured, probably killed, the two occupants in the vehicle."

The officer then explained how the bomb was constructed, describing how the pipe was filled with concrete nails and almost two pounds of smokeless powder. A six-volt lantern battery acted as the power source and was embedded in the pipe with the powder and nails.

Officer Lawrence Baggett from the LAPD in the Scientific Investigation Division, Firearms Identification and Explosives Unit explained how the bombs worked: "The battery is the power source, which is necessary to fire an electric blasting cap . . . the clothespin switch and wedge is the firing switch. The manner in which it works is this, with the small wooden wedge stuck between the jaws of the clothespin, the two metal screws, which go one through each side of the jaws of the clothespin, cannot come in contact; therefore, the circuit is open.

"If the screws had come together while I was disarming the bomb," Officer Baggett continued, "the device would have detonated and I would probably be dead now." He based his opinion on the overall size of the device, the amount of powder in it, the metal in the pipe, and the approximately 120 concrete nails contained within it.

The officer explained, "the only malfunction that I can see is the fact that when I approached the device the two screw heads, instead of being together, were just slightly apart from each other. It appears as though the jaws of the clothespin had torqued slightly when the wedge was removed and the screws barely failed to come back together.

"If the bomb had detonated, the odds are that the persons sitting in the seats above the bomb would be gravely injured if not killed." Just that morning of the grand jury proceedings, Officer Baggett and other LA police officers had detonated a device similar to the bombs found in Los Angeles at one of the explosive ranges at the El Toro Marine Air Corp facility.

The bomb had been placed underneath a police car of the same type and year as the car in the IHOP parking lot with two mannequins in the front seats. The bomb ripped a number of big holes in the floor of the car and sent fragmentation through the floor of the vehicle, through the seats, and through the roof of the car. Nails blasted through the hood; the driver mannequin was also moved around and distorted. The passenger mannequin was shoved up into the ceiling.

Arleigh McCree was the officer who found the pipe bomb at the apartment on Precita Avenue. During his testimony, he identified in photographs the two bombs found underneath the LA police cars as being of the same type as the one he found in the apartment at Precita Avenue. McCree's credentials were impressive. He had spent eight years in the United States military and was considered a specialist in explosives, booby traps, demolition techniques, machine guns, and automatic weapons. He'd then been to bomb technicians' school, was a graduate of the International Association of Chiefs of Police Advanced Bomb Technology School, and the bomb-scene officers' school.

He had joined the police department in 1965, which he described as the "formative period of the bombing campaign that we are seeing in this country today." The police needed him to assist in investigations involving explosives and military items. McCree had been a squad leader in the Criminal Conspiracy Section of the Los Angeles Police Department since 1969.

At the time of his testimony, he was a professor at Cal State Long Beach, where he taught a peace officers' standards and training class on bomb-scene investigation. He also taught a similar class at Mt. San Antonio Junior College. As the intelligence officer for the International Association of Bomb Technicians and Investigators, he lectured around the country and internationally in this field. He'd been on approximately 350 bomb investigations.

When asked if he had any opinion as to whether the persons who occupied the apartment at 288 Precita Avenue were responsible or were involved in the making of the devices he'd identified in the photographs, he said, "No sir, not the people."

But when the question was rephrased, "Do you have any opinion as to whether the persons who had access to that apartment could have been responsible in the manufacture of the two Los Angeles devices shown in the photographs, he said, "Yes, sir, I do."

Then he was asked to explain what the difference was.

"Access and occupancy," he said, ". . . it is different because I can't say that those people who lived there actually built the bombs. But I can say, due to the unique nature of the materials found in that closet, that some individual who had access to those materials did build these three bombs."

He explained his reasoning. "First of all, when we talk about the assembly of a bomb, to equate it to something that the average person is familiar with, it is like a fly fisherman tying flies. If I tie a fly, you can tell the fly that I tie from someone else's, at least I can tell the one I tie.

"If one of the ladies is a seamstress, you can have five or six dresses that appear to be identical to the untrained individual, . . . but a seamstress can tell she sewed that dress; a carpenter, the same thing.

"It is what I call fabrication technique. . . . When people start to take and assemble items together, they use techniques that are successful for them, just as if you were sewing a dress or building a cabinet, you use those techniques that are successful for you, that work well.

"And the devices exhibit a number of fabrication techniques that remain consistent for all three of the bombs, particularly the two devices under the cars in Los Angeles. Even to the untrained eye, there are many, many fabrication features that you can see very clearly that literally jump at you.

"The device that was in the closet in San Francisco exhibits many of these similarities. The use of the pipe, just in and of itself, large pipe, the way the holes are drilled in the ends of the pipes."

"Do you mean the endcap portion?"

"Yes, sir, the endcaps of the pipes. What you are dealing with is a person drilling an eighth of an inch hole. Well, that is a consistent feature with all three of these bombs." The jury listened carefully, finding this witness extremely credible.

He explained that the way the individual leads his wires through this small opening; the way that he affixes the batteries to the pipes; the excessive use of tape; the very methodical and intricate method that he uses to overlap the tape; and the positioning of the battery on the pipe itself, were unique.

"While, on one hand, with the Precita Avenue address [bomb] we are dealing with two and a half inch pipe; we are dealing with three-inch pipe here in the two situations in Los Angeles. However, the bomb found at the Precita location had the same kind of tape as a safety to hold the knife switch down as the bomb found at the Hollenbeck location." He also noticed the types of wire used and the selections of the filler material for the actual bombs.

"For example, we had two different types of explosives used in the bombs in Los Angeles. We had Red Dot used in one and Green Dot used in the other. Now, these are what we refer to as double-based smokeless powders. In other words, they contain nitroglycerin.

"Now, the device in Precita Avenue had Green Dot adhering to the threads of the endcap. The way the individual assembled the device; he positioned the knife switch slightly different in the Precita Avenue device. However, he was going to use a clock to fire that device, as opposed to motion to fire the device here in Los Angeles, and it just happened to work, in my opinion, to his advantage to fire the one here on motion and to fire the one there on time.

"Obviously, the purpose of the two devices was different. He intended to use this device as a planted device inside a structure and this device was meant to kill because it does work on anti-motion. There is a booby-trap, if you will."

The fact that the bombs were set to go off differently did not affect McCree's opinion at all. "It is just a tactical consideration of the bomber. It doesn't have anything to do with fabrication technique used on the bomb itself."

When asked if someone else familiar with the manufacture of a destructive device could just by happenstance come onto this same fabrication technique, McCree said no. There could not be copying or "modeling" to this extent. These fabrications are too unique.

"The way he lays the tape over when he is affixing the battery to the pipe—he goes around the central axis of the pipe, and in others then he goes the length of the pipe when he comes back and puts a piece of one-inch tape over half, three-quarter inch tape along a wire that runs the length of the pipe.

"And the way he separates and cuts a lot of the tape with a knife to come between the leaves of the knife switch to affix the knife switch to the pipe itself; the loop he throws in his line.

"The insulated wiring on the two devices here is approximately the same size in both instances and he did a similar type of thing in the Precita bomb as well. Additionally in all three instances, there is no tape on one end of the bomb. That of course, would facilitate filling the explosive into the pipe itself, but it is a unique feature of the individual.

"The magnets were affixed with fishing line. The individual would go through the hole several times in his wraps, and it was always the same amount of wraps as he went through it, and the way he tied the knot to hold the fishing line to the magnet was the same.

"It is a very methodical person that does these kinds of things.

These three bombs are highly individualized items, and I believe they were made by the same person."

On February 26, 1976, the federal grand jury proceedings concluded. Kathleen Soliah was indicted on "Charges of Conspiracy to Commit Murder." James Kilgore was also indicted on the same charges. He was thought to have been the actual bomb-maker with Kathy as his accomplice. By this time, the couple had disappeared into the underground, and authorities would not see Kathy Soliah until her arrest twenty-three years later.

With the more sensational trials going on in 1976—those of Patty Hearst, Bill and Emily Harris, and Wendy Yoshimura—the indictments of Soliah and Kilgore were barely noticed by the press. They were not newsworthy. No one would have guessed, at that time, that twenty-five years later, the former Kathy Soliah would replace Patty Hearst on the front pages, or that Patty Hearst, if subpoenaed to testify, would have to relive her kidnapping and her time spent in prison once again. The country would experience a rerun of the seventies. Only this time, the star would be Kathleen Soliah, *aka* Sara Jane Olson.

Steve Soliah Trial

A month after Kathy went underground, her brother Steve was put on trial, five months after he had been indicted by another federal grand jury on a charge of participating in the robbery of the Crocker National Bank in Carmichael where Myrna Opsahl was killed. (So far no one had been charged for her murder.) The charge of "harboring a fugitive" [Patty] had been dismissed when the government decided to prosecute him for bank robbery.

One day after Steve Soliah's arrest, Steffan Imhoff was appointed to defend him. Imhoff was thirty-four years old and had been practicing law in California for nine years. He had been involved in the defense of Native Americans in the Wounded Knee case in South Dakota and had worked with other activist lawyers.

Because Steve was charged with a capital offense, the court allowed a second attorney to be appointed. Sheldon Otis took over the primary duties. Otis had had a stormy career, which included running for judge, suspension of his license in Michigan, and a prosecution against him in California on grand theft charges. He had worked on the Angela Davis trial in 1971. While working on that defense team, he was charged with embezzling $10,000 from the San Mateo Legal Aid Society of which he was executive director.

Steven Soliah was twenty-seven years old when his trial began on March 10, 1976.

During the jury selection, Steve, who sat next to Otis, was dressed in a suit and tie, his blond hair neatly trimmed. Although his father, Marty, had tried his best, the judge had refused to reduce Steve's bail, stating that he was "not impressed" that Soliah would "keep his bargain." "Bail reduction denied!" he declared. Steve's mother, Elsie, who had pledged their home in Palmdale for his $75,000 bail, was seated behind him in the courtroom.

An FBI expert testified in court that a fingerprint found on the stolen license plate from a stolen car, a blue Mustang, which was used as a backup car in the Crocker Bank holdup, belonged to Steven Soliah. Another FBI expert noted that pistol cartridges found at the scene of the fatal bank robbery matched shells discovered in the San Francisco Morse Street apartment, where Steven lived with Patty. Two eyewitness bank employees identified Steve in the courtroom as one of the gun-wielding robbers who had shouted obscenities at them.

After the court heard several witnesses for the defense and for the prosecution, Steve was called to testify on Thursday, April 22, 1976. Wearing a powder-blue suit with a vest, he became flushed in the hot federal courtroom. He grasped the microphone in his left hand, looked directly at the questioner, and traced his life with special emphasis on events after the shootout on May 17, 1974.

He told the jury that he had spent the previous summer sleeping with Patricia Hearst: "I lived with her. I slept with her." Patty Hearst and Bill and Emily Harris had changed his life. He talked about his empathy for Patty during time he spent with her. "We had a close relationship," he said, adding that she'd even painted houses with him and the crew.

"When I first met them," he stated, "I still had the memory of the untimely death of Angela Atwood. I was of the state of mind that the same thing might happen to them." He testified that he didn't particularly like the Harrises, but he agreed to help because of Patty.

When his attorney Sheldon Otis asked him about his feelings about the SLA and Angela Atwood, Steve said, "I felt that what they had done was wrong. She [Atwood] didn't seem like the type of person who would get involved in that sort of thing. The whole thing didn't make any sense to me."

After the rally at Ho Chi Minh Park, he gave the Harrises $100 at Kathy's request. "I really don't know why I gave them any money," Steve said. "Maybe I shouldn't have, but I did. I told them I thought what they were doing was crazy. About a week later in Berkeley, Kathy came over to my house. She asked me if I wanted to meet the Harrises. I said I did."

When Otis asked him why, Steve said, "I was curious. I wanted to see what they were like."

Steve recalled that at his first meeting, Patty looked like a "dowdy housewife." He remembered how nervous they had been when they'd walked in the door with their bags of weapons, pacing the floor and peering out the corners of the windows. They were friendly to him, but admitted they were anxious to get out of the area. That was the last time they would see each other until their return in August from out East.

Kathy had asked Steve to help her find an apartment for them, near, but not in, the Bay Area. He agreed to help her, and they rented a house at 1721 W Street. At the beginning of September, Steve met Patty and Jim Kilgore again when they arrived from Las Vegas. Patty told him about her summer and emphasized that she wanted to stay underground. She didn't want to go home to her parents. He explained that the first night, he slept on the couch while Kathy and Patty slept on the bed. The Harrises arrived later.

Otis asked what they discussed. Steve said that he remembered the twenty-one-year-old Patty talking about her parents and about how "horrible it was to be kidnapped and how horrible the whole thing was."

"I felt sorry for her," Steve testified. "I wanted to help her. She said that she had a hard time with Bill and Emily Harris . . . and she told me at some point that she hated her parents. She felt that they had abandoned her, and she didn't want to go back with them. It just seemed to me that she was in a situation at that time that was—it was really difficult for her to deal with. It really made me feel sorry for her."

He explained how he visited the house on W Street frequently because he wanted to see Patty. They took long walks in the neighborhood, and she cried on his shoulder. She told him that if she had a choice, she'd move. She wanted to get away from the Harrises. Steve promised to talk to Jim and Kathy about ways to make her life easier.

He said that in February 1975, he and Patty went up to Oregon but couldn't find a place to stay, so they came back to Sacramento. On March 5, 1975, he had been in a car accident fracturing five ribs and cutting the bridge of his nose. He said that he felt miserable and moved to San Francisco with his old girlfriend, Emily Toback.

He continued with his testimony to say that on April 17 or 18, Jim went to his place and told him that Patty had asked about him. On that day, Jim asked Steve to go to Sacramento with him. He told Steve that he was bringing some license plates and camping equipment to the fugitives who were becoming edgy about the revelations surrounding Jack Scott and the uncovering of the Pennsylvania farm hideout.

He told the jury that it was on that trip that he touched the license plates (which he admitted had been in a paper bag), to offer an explanation about why his fingerprint had shown up on the stolen license plate on one of the stolen cars used in the bank holdup. Kilgore took him to another safehouse in downtown Sacramento where he met Bill Harris, who was cool to him and asked him to leave. This made Steve angry, because he'd hoped to see Patty and was told she didn't want to see him. He left Kilgore there and took his car back to San Francisco.

He returned to the apartment about a week later on April 28. He had purchased a car for them, using a phony name, with money that Emily had given him. He spent that night with Patty and went back to the Bay Area the next day. The Harrises asked him and Kilgore to rent them two more apartments in San Francisco. At this time, Jim was "Wanted," as were Kathy and Josephine. Although the warrants were still outstanding, charges would never be pressed against Jo or Margaret Turcich, perhaps for lack of evidence against them.

Steve complied and helped the Harrises and Patty move in a U-haul trailer. Once they settled in their two places, the Harrises lived together and Steve and Patty lived together. "We did things together. We took walks," he said. He and Kilgore and his sisters painted houses to earn a living.

During the trial, Steve insisted that he was a "victim of a tangled web of circumstances" in the robbery investigation. He insisted that he had been in San Francisco living with his old girlfriend, Emily Toback, and that he was with her while the robbery was taking place.

One of the final witnesses for the defense was Emily Toback, the twenty-six-year-old San Francisco masseuse who worked at the Body and Mind Clinic. She indicated that Steve might have been in her home during the robbery, but she had "no specific recollection." She said that on the night of April 20, she and Steve went to dinner, drank beer, and returned to her home "and we went to sleep." She said that she left the house around 11:00 A.M. the next morning to go to a noon class. She said that she wasn't sure if he was there when she left the house, but he was there that night when she got home. Steve had sworn on the stand that he was there on April 21, 1975, the morning of the holdup.

The prosecutor got her to admit that she had testified as a defense witness in another San Francisco murder trial and that she was a frequent visitor to Folsom Prison. At this point of the trial, no one knew why that would prove to be so important.

At the end of the seven-week trial, the prosecutor told the jury that Steven Soliah had traded a life of athletics for a life of "phony names, coded phone numbers and lies." In his final argument, he accused Steve of taking part in the Crocker National Bank robbery where $15,000 was stolen and where Myrna Opsahl was murdered. He called Emily Toback "really a prize. She was called to give an alibi, which she couldn't give." He reminded the jury of Steve's fingerprint on the stolen license plate of the stolen Mustang that was involved in the holdup. He asked the jury to recall the statements of the two eyewitnesses who had been reluctant to testify, but swore that Steve Soliah was the man they saw brandishing the shotgun in front of the bank.

Patty Hearst, who was still in prison, was never called to testify. Apparently, prosecutors did not think that her testimony would be credible. On April 27, 1976, just six and one half-hours after the jury had gone into deliberation, Steven Soliah was acquitted.

Just moments before the verdict was read, it was discovered by the State Department of Corrections that Emily Toback's name had been recorded on the visitor's registration card at Folsom prison on April 21, 1975. She was there to visit a convicted robber and had signed in at 9:30 A.M. and signed out at 2:30 P.M. Folsom prison, located approximately twelve miles from the Crocker National Bank, is about a hundred miles from San Francisco, where she claimed to be at the time of the robbery. This new, incriminating information could not be admitted because the jury was already sequestered and couldn't be disturbed.

When questioned about this latest finding, Otis said he found that bit of information "puzzling."

Toback never faced perjury charges.

On April 27, Steve Soliah was found innocent of taking part in the bank robbery. Emily Toback, who had spent the trial sitting in the first row of the gallery, gave him a big hug.

Elsie, Steve's mom, cried, "I just feel so wonderful," she said.

Steve talked to reporters at his hotel room. "I am really happy," he told them. "It was the right thing. I didn't know what to expect, but I am glad it happened." When asked if he was going to see Patty, he said he couldn't talk about that.

When a reporter from the *Sacramento Union* asked what he was going to do next, he said he didn't know. Elsie said, "I'm sure he'll relax for awhile. I would like to see him go back to college. I can't tell him what to do. He's a big boy now." And then she added, "I never gave up hope. I knew he was innocent." She called Marty at Palmdale High School where he was teaching to tell him the news. His response was, "Now I can eat again." Elsie said that her husband had been so nervous that he had difficulty keeping food down.

Steve was now free of all charges that the federal government had brought against him. State charges had not been brought against him. No other members of the SLA were ever charged with the Crocker Bank holdup.

Otis commented, "This is one of those rare instances in our history where the jury system worked, it doesn't happen a lot. It doesn't happen for a lot of people. A lot of people in our prisons today, who similarly had been mistakenly convicted, do not have the benefit of the court-appointed and paid-for counsel that Steven had."

Dr. Trygve Opsahl and his children were in a state of shock when they got the news. All he could say was, "All those responsible for my wife's death should be brought to justice."

Trials

Six months after Steve's trial, it was Wendy Yoshimura's turn. Four years had passed since Jack Scott had helped her flee to the East Coast after arms and explosives were discovered in the Berkeley garage she had rented for Willie Brandt, using the name Annie Wong. She got support from a group that called itself the Wendy Yoshimura Fair Trial Committee, composed of people from the Japanese-American community. They raised $25,000 for her bail, so she had been free since her indictment on December 19, 1975. Wendy's trial began on October 18, 1976.

By now Patty Hearst had been in jail for one year waiting for her second trial to begin. On November 19, 1976, Patty was granted bail ($1,250,000—fifty times more than Wendy's) and was released to the custody of her parents, who were told to provide around-the-clock bodyguards for her.

In the beginning, Wendy's case seemed encouraging for her. The judge ruled that the police search of her apartment in Oakland in 1972, after Willie Brandt, Mike Bortin, and Paul Rubenstein were arrested, was illegal. He said that the mere suspicion of evidence in her apartment did not justify their entering and searching the premises. This was a gift for the defense.

Wendy, thirty-three years old now, and a consummate chronicler, took copious notes as she sat at the defense table wearing a denim skirt, a tan blazer, and flat-heeled shoes. Her parents, Frank and Fumiye Yoshimura, who lived in Fresno and worked as gardeners, attended the trial in support of their daughter as much as possible.

After five weeks of jury selection, the trial finally began on November 28, 1976. The DA told the jury of a damaging piece of evidence found in the Berkeley garage. It was a dossier on Robert McNamara, the former defense secretary, which included the habits and athletic abilities of some of his family members, as well as twenty-four photographs of the McNamara's vacation home in Aspen, Colorado. There were also maps of the surrounding terrain and maps of the interior of the house. In addition, the police had discovered that other targets of these "Berkeley Bombers" were the Naval Architecture Building and the Space Sciences Laboratory at UC Berkeley. The Volkswagen at the Berkeley garage had been registered in Wendy's father, Frank Yoshimura's, name.

This was the first day Wendy's parents had been in court, and they sat placidly in the front row of the spectator's section. The DA explained evidence that had been found in the apartment, which included a "working library on how to conduct a campaign of underground guerrilla warfare and terrorism" and brochures on where to get more information on the subject. Wendy's fingerprints were on artist supplies and a copy of *Quotations from Chairman Mao*. There were piles of clothing in Wendy's size, many of them of Oriental design. The jury listened as the DA discussed their daughter's months with Patty Hearst in Pennsylvania, her letters, and her diaries.

Wendy's lawyer tried to convince the jury that even though she had rented the Berkeley garage, she didn't know anything about a criminal conspiracy. She was doing it for her boyfriend, Brandt, who had told her he was the subject of an FBI inquiry because of his antiwar activities.

Her lawyer described Wendy's life from her birth at Manzanar to her family's relocation in Japan, then their return to California where her father worked as a farm laborer and her mother worked as a cook until they could save enough money to start their own garden business. He got into the "context of the times" explaining how Wendy had been an apolitical art student at California College of Arts and Crafts but got caught up in the protests that surrounded her. The murders at Kent State had affected her deeply. Brandt's arrest scared her. She was afraid she would have to testify against this man she loved. So she fled. She only came back to California because she missed her parents, he said. But when her fingerprints were discovered at the Pennsylvania farmhouse, she was afraid and decided to reconnect with Patty and the Harrises.

When it was Wendy's turn to testify, she refused to talk about her years underground. Unlike Patty, she did not plead the Fifth Amendment because her lawyer cautioned her that it would look like she had something to hide. After Patty's trial, it was obvious that he was right. But Wendy did not want to incriminate anyone who had helped her. That was Japanese tradition. However, that worked against her because the judge ruled that she could not pick and choose what questions she wanted to respond to. It was all or nothing. So in the end, all of Wendy's testimony was thrown out.

The case went to the jury on January 13. Eight women and four men deliberated for forty-four hours over a six-day period. On January 20, 1977, Wendy Yoshimura was found guilty of three counts of illegal possession of explosives, bomb parts, and an automatic weapon. When the verdict was read, Wendy patted her attorney's shoulder as if to say, "You did the best you could."

On March 18, 1977, she was sentenced to a prison term of one to fifteen years. Her attorney said, "People change. Miss Yoshimura is a different person sitting here in this court today than she was in April of 1972, or in September 1975." Kathy Soliah's *aka* Sara Jane Olson's attorneys prepared to drive this same argument home twenty-three years later, should she be brought to trial.

Wendy would spend less than one year in prison.

Leonard Weinglass, who had defended the Chicago Seven with William Kunstler, was chosen by the Harrises to defend them. Susan Jordan, who twenty-three years later would be hired to represent Kathy Soliah, *aka* Sara Jane Olson, would work with him to defend Emily.

Prior to the trial, Weinglass successfully argued to the judge that 1,000 items that were recovered from the Precita Avenue apartment on the day the Harrises were arrested had to be thrown out as evidence because FBI agents had had the apartment under surveillance for thirty hours *before* the arrest. However, they had failed to obtain a search warrant until twenty-four hours *after* the Harrises had been taken into custody. Since some of the items taken connected Kathy Soliah to the crimes, there was concern among the authorities that the judge's ruling could have an adverse effect on her indictment.

In April 1976, the Harrises still had not gone to trial. They had been charged with nineteen counts each of kidnapping, robbery, and assault with a deadly weapon, and false imprisonment. These charges came just twenty-four hours after Patty Hearst agreed to cooperate with authorities in return for possible immunity and a more lenient sentence for her bank-robbery conviction. She was angry that the Harrises were publicly blaming her for their troubles. Emily exclaimed to the press that Patty's defense was designed as much to discredit revolutionaries as it was for her acquittal. "Now she has no one," Emily stated. After the Harrises learned that Patty was going to cooperate, they decided not to present a defense, which meant that the prosecution could not call Patty to testify against them.

Bill and Emily Harris had been behind bars since their arrest on September 18, 1975. On August 31, 1978, after a two-year delay of successful legal maneuvers, they pled guilty in Oakland to four of the thirteen counts against them. This surprised everyone. It paid off. With a plea bargain, the other nine counts were dropped, including the kidnapping with bodily harm, which could have sent them to jail for life without possibility of parole.

The Harrises were sentenced on October 3, 1978, to one to twenty-five years in prison. However, both the defense and prosecuting attorneys decided that the Community Release Board, a group of political appointees newly formed in California, would determine the final sentence. It was thought that they would serve at least ten years. The "time already served" was in question. Emily's attorney, Susan Jordan, praised both of the sentences and the Harrises, calling them "quiet, sensitive and serious, considerate, and well-motivated, intelligent people." The Harrises, she said, are "committed to social change in this country—they chose a very spectacular means to demonstrate that. But now," she said, "I think the era is over."

After the sentence, Bill Harris, thirty-three years old, wearing a windbreaker jacket, jeans, and desert boots exclaimed, "La lucha continua, Venceremos," which translates from the Spanish into, "The struggle continues. We shall overcome." A *San Francisco Chronicle* reporter described him as "fresh-faced and younger looking than his thirty-one-year-old wife."

Emily wore a floral-patterned dress and entered the courtroom as if entering a stage, smiling broadly and blowing kisses to her friends in the courtroom. She had been housed at the Santa Rita Rehabilitation Center but would now be sent to the California Institute for Women at Frontera. Bill would continue his sentence at San Quentin's high-security adjustment center where his former SLA comrade Russell Little was serving his life sentence for murdering Marcus Foster.

Bill Harris was given permission in court to address a group of about forty supporters: "The plea doesn't mean we have feelings of remorse. Instead we feel pride in what these actions were able to accomplish." He then bragged that he and Emily would be "back on the streets" by 1983. Emily's comment to the press was, "We exposed the ruling class. We returned to the people what's theirs," apparently referring to the People in Need (PIN) program that the SLA had initiated after Patty Hearst's kidnapping.

Patty was still serving her sentence in Pleasanton when the plea agreement was reached. Through one of Patty Hearst's bodyguards, Bernard Shaw, she met and hired a new attorney,

George Martinez. He stated that she was relieved and gratified to have at least one aspect of the matter behind her.

On the day that she had been sent to Pleasanton Correctional Institute to resume her prison sentence, Hearst's family and friends started the "Campaign to Free Patty." The authorities allowed Patty to give two interviews a month to the press. In these interviews, she talked about human-interest stories of her experiences in prison and expressed her hopes for the future. The American public learned that Patty Hearst was a warm human being, not a murderous revolutionary. Public opinion did a 180 degree turn in her favor.

In just six months, the Committee for the Release of Patty Hearst had taken on a life of its own. Every state had a group of people trying to help her. Friends and family went on TV and radio talk shows. "FREE PATTY" bumper stickers, pins, and T-shirts were distributed nationwide. Patty's T-shirt said on the front, "Pardon Me", and on the back, "Being Kidnapped Means Always Having to Say You're Sorry." Tens of thousands of letters were sent to the pardon attorney's office, which became one of the largest campaigns for clemency in the history of the United States.

Politicians from all over the country, including Ronald Reagan, called for Patty's release. Six of the jurors from her trial agreed that she had suffered enough, and editorials from all over the country urged President Jimmy Carter to set her free. In the first week of August, Martinez filed two motions in federal court: one, to modify her sentence to time already served, and two, to overturn her conviction, alleging that her former attorneys did not defend her adequately.

During the last week of January 1979, President Carter's sister, Ruth Carter Stapleton, visited Patty in prison. On the very next day, her attorney informed her that President Carter had commuted her sentence.

The White House's press announcement on commuting her sentence read: "It is the consensus of all of those most familiar with this case that but for the extraordinary criminal and degrading experiences that the petitioner suffered as a victim of the SLA she would not have become a participant in the criminal acts for which she stands convicted and sentenced, and would not have suffered the punishment and other consequences she has endured." So on February 1, 1979, Patty Hearst was set free, almost five years from the day of her kidnapping, having spent almost two years in prison. That year, Patty Hearst married her bodyguard, Bernard Shaw, and they settled in Connecticut. They had two daughters.

The SLA had a short life, only twenty-two months. In that time, they murdered Marcus Foster, kidnapped Patty Hearst, robbed several banks, and killed innocent people. Even the most liberal minded people never understood why. What had they really hoped to achieve? They liked to think of themselves as having a cause like the Students for a Democratic Society, but in reality, their revolutionist agenda had no effect on the social or political system.

Many of them had acted in college and they still needed the applause, approval, and to create their own stage, their own environment. They wanted the power to be who *they* wanted to be in ultimate freedom—to create their roles, their rules, their lives, their own drama, their own press reports. They thrived on this power. So, what happened to each of them after the curtain closed?

In 1979, the year Patty's sentence was commuted, Joseph Remiro was serving time in San Quentin for Marcus Foster's murder. Russell Little had been released, having been acquitted of the murder charges in 1976. The prosecution had not been able to prove their case against him. Yoshimura had been released from prison and was leading a quiet life as an artist in Berkeley— where it had all started. Bill and Emily Harris were in their separate prison facilities for kidnapping Patty Hearst. They would be released in 1983 and would divorce in 1984 to go their separate ways.

About five years later, after failed marriages to other people, Josephine Soliah and Michael Bortin would marry. No charges were ever brought against them for the bank robbery or the bombs.

Thero Wheeler had escaped from Vacaville four months after Cinque escaped from Soledad prison and had moved in with Patricia (Zoya), Nancy (Fahizah), and Cinque in an Oakland apartment. According to him, he "split" when he heard Cinque's plans to execute Marcus Foster. Although it was thought that he had participated in Patty Hearst's kidnapping, Wheeler was never charged with the crime. In 1975 he was arrested in Houston on other, "unknown" charges.

Jack Scott would stay in the background until later.

Steven Soliah reportedly lived a "hippie" lifestyle with his girlfriend in Berkeley. Of course, Cinque, Nancy Ling Perry, Patricia Soltysik, Willie Wolfe, Camilla Hall, and Angela Atwood had burned to death. As yet, no one had been charged in the Crocker National Bank robbery or for Myrna Opsahl's murder. Jim Kilgore and Kathy Soliah had vanished.

Act Five

> "We are so accustomed to disguise ourselves to others, that in the end we become disguised to ourselves.
>
> ↗ LA ROCHEFOUCAULD, MAXIMS (1665). TR. KENNETH PRATT

Underground

The SLA trials received sensational, national attention from all forms of media. Still no one reported that they had seen or heard from Kathy or Jim. It is not known whether or not Kathy tried to contact her family during Steve's trial. It must have been difficult for her to stay away, knowing that he could spend much of his life in prison if he were to be convicted. Nevertheless, she did not come to his aid.

In February 1976, the NWLF issued a "declaration of war" backed up with bombs and demands against a hit list of "scumlords," according to the *San Francisco Chronicle*. A number of bombs were discovered in San Francisco—near Francis Drake Boulevard, Marin County; at Pacific Gas & Electric; at Pebble Beach; and at the home of the chairman of the board of the Bank of California. Only one bomb exploded, in San Francisco, damaging a car of one of the property owners whose name was on the hit list.

The NWLF message ordered that all rental dwellings in San Francisco that did not meet fire and safety standards be immediately brought up to codes. Failure to comply would lead to plantings of more bombs, said the communiqué. Before the NWLF statement, a powerful bomb, composed of dynamite sticks, had been disarmed outside the home of an apartment owner, also named on the hit list.

During the fall of 1976, Kathy had spent about one year in Seattle, where she supported herself as a waitress and appeared in two feminist plays using the name Nancy Bennett. She disappeared after four performances. She met someone who told her that Minnesota had a thriving theater community and in January 1977, she returned to her home state. (Although there were reportedly "Jim Kilgore sightings" in Seattle, the couple apparently went their separate ways according to *People* magazine).

Kathy hadn't been back to Minnesota since she was eight years old, but she arrived in Minneapolis with a social security card that identified her as Sara Jane Olson and a birth date that shaved over two years off of her age.

Kathy Soliah may have been "underground," but a low profile was not in her makeup, nor was it a lifestyle to which the new Sara Jane Olson would subscribe. Kathy did not change her appearance but kept her long, strawberry blond hair, looking much like the same young woman who graced the stage lined with Acadama plum wine bottles in Ho Chi Minh Park in 1974. If she worried about being discovered, she hid it well.

Sara Jane Olson was hired as a live-in cook at a University of Minnesota fraternity house. Melding into the campus scene came naturally to her. She also taught a theater course in public schools for nine months. She volunteered at the Arise Bookstore and Resource Center, which had a large mural depicting a female factory worker with her fist raised in defiance. Here, she hooked up with a group of counterculture activists. She also acted in a small theater's local production, Shakespeare's *Two Gentleman of Verona*. It was at about this time that Sara Jane moved next door to a young doctor, Gerald Frederick (Fred) Peterson.

Born in Mason City, Iowa, in 1949, Fred was two years younger than Sara Jane. He'd graduated from Mason City High School, and then from Harvard University. In 1974, about the time that Kathy gave her speech at Ho Chi Minh Park, Fred earned his medical degree from Albert Einstein College of Medicine in New York. Between 1975, when the bombs had been planted under the police cars in Los Angeles, and 1976, when Kathy Soliah had been indicted, Fred had been working as an intern at Hennepin County Medical Center in Minneapolis.

Sara Jane and Fred shared a passion for jogging, good food, music, and dancing. Soon they were living together. Her new cause was for the people struggling for independence in Rhodesia (its name during white rule), today's Zimbabwe.

In 1978, a group of Zimbabwe students studying at the University of Minnesota were organizing to assist more than half a million refugees who had escaped from Rhodesia [because of the war raging in neighboring Mozambique]. Sara Jane and Fred attended some of those meetings. The discussions centered on ways to assist those displaced people. Life for a black person in Rhodesia was unbearable, said one of the speakers, Farayi Albert Munyuki. The white regime of Ian Smith had been brutal. The black citizens were not allowed to vote, and schools and hospitals were segregated. Farayi was shocked that white people would be interested in his work, but Sara Jane and Fred were there to help. The refugees needed clothing, medicine, food, shelter, books, and other necessities to sustain life in a most difficult situation.

Tony Mtero, a refugee then studying at the University of Minnesota, said that the couple was always at meetings and raising money for Zimbabwe's refugees. "She was eager to know and learn," said Mtero.

The couple married in Minneapolis on March 12, 1980, four years after her indictment. Sara Jane did not take Fred's surname, Peterson, but kept the name Olson. It is not known whether or not Fred knew Sara Jane's true identity. It seems likely that she married him without full disclosure of her previous life.

In *The Secret Life of Families*, Evan Imber-Black, Ph.D., writes: "The decision to create and keep a secret has deep and complicated roots. Intimidation by others may drive and underpin our silences. The fear of losing a spouse, a dear friend, a job, or one's own sense of self may lead us to nail the closet door shut. Relationships that would ordinarily change and grow become frozen in time, as the presence of a secret locks people in place."

In February 1981, five months after their first child, a daughter, was born, the family moved to the newly independent

African nation of Zimbabwe. According to the *Star Tribune* in Minneapolis, Sara Jane had borrowed a friend's passport.

Zimbabwe is a landlocked country in south-central Africa and is slightly smaller than California. The official language is English, and Shona and Ndebele are the prominent native languages. Ninety-eight percent of the population is indigenous, the Shona group being predominant. The Republic of Zimbabwe had won independence in April 1980, when Robert Mugabe's Patriotic Front Party won the elections by a landslide. Mugabe became prime minister and eventually established a one-party socialist state.

Sara Jane and Fred worked through the international charity Oxfam GB in England, and were placed in Mount Darwin, a tiny northeastern outpost near the Mozambique border. They were reunited with some of the former University of Minnesota students, who were thrilled to see them.

Mount Darwin, located in the most remote part of the country, about 100 kilometers north of Harare, Zimbabwe's capital, had been most affected by the civil war; hospitals and schools had been destroyed. Fred was posted as the resident doctor, and according to their friend Farayi Albert Munyuki, Sara Jane was hired as a schoolteacher, "becoming the first white lady to teach Chimimba School in Mount Darwin." This was a poverty-stricken school where the kids went without shoes, were poorly clothed, and considered themselves lucky when they got a meal. Sara Jane would later write that she also worked in rural well-baby clinics in Zimbabwe that helped underfed children. Food had been used as a weapon during the country's civil war and now there was a food shortage. She wrote that the Zimbabweans admired her little girl because she was fat and healthy. The natives considered Sara Jane a "good" mother because her daughter was chubby, while the whites worried that she would grow up to be a fat adult.

Mount Darwin had no library; some children had never seen a television or radio, and many homes had no running water or electricity. There were not enough textbooks. Children had to share a pencil, and parents struggled to get school fees for their children. Teachers at Chimimba School had to create their own teaching materials.

Sara Jane was at home among the very poor people of Zimbabwe. She set up women's clubs where she taught them how to keep their homes clean, mend or make clothes for their children and husbands. Ninety percent of the people were illiterate, and Sara Jane dedicated herself to teaching them "functional literacy." She encouraged them to grow crop food so their children could eat.

Munyuki was extremely impressed with Sara Jane. He said that it must have been unbearable for her, coming from America where luxury was commonplace, to a home in Mount Darwin that he said had no electricity, no bathtub, and no carpets. Sara Jane had no washing machine or television because the country's television signal was weak and could not reach Mount Darwin.

According to a friend from Zimbabwe, Sara Jane had a tremendous impact on the community. Some of her students still have cherished memories of her.

Elisa Marama was assigned by the local Catholic diocese to work with Dr. Fred Peterson. Elisa praised Fred's dedication. His assignment was to re-establish health care in the villages and missions of the war-ravaged countryside. He attended to pregnant women, as well as lepers, people with snakebites, tuberculosis, and malaria. He worked at an open-air hospital where there were no beds, inadequately trained staff, and a short supply of medicine.

Marama said that Sara Jane, who was called Mrs. Peterson by the local Zimbabwe people, conducted her classes under a tree. She often accompanied Fred and Elisa on their trips into the bush, rumbling down dirt roads in a mine-proof Land Rover—sometimes with their daughter in tow. Both Fred and Sara Jane worked in a mosquito-ridden area, where Fred battled against lethal tropical ailments such as water-borne diseases, malnutrition, and yellow fever. He traveled to areas where poisonous snakes were the order of the day and no doctors were available. He also organized a campaign to arrest the spread of whooping cough, polio, and diphtheria. He and his assistant inoculated thousands of kids in the area and were later praised by the Zimbabwe government. Thousands of villagers traveled ten to fifteen kilometers by foot to attend his clinics. Fred was described as a modern-day Dr. David Livingston.

Elisa Marama particularly remembered Sara Jane's work with the poor. "She handed out things and helped to weigh the children," he said. "She also volunteered to teach English and drama at a middle school." Marama gave Sara Jane a rave review. Sara Jane worked after hours, helped with the problem children in school, and held discussion groups with the young people as well as the old.

Sara Jane Olson had found a new life. It was unlikely that authorities would be looking for her in Zimbabwe. She had a devoted husband, a beautiful daughter, and in April 1982, while they lived in Zimbabwe, a second daughter was born at a hospital in Bindura, near Mount Darwin. Her parents gave her a Shona middle name—Shorai.

In September of that year, the Olson-Peterson family left Africa and eventually relocated in Baltimore. Sara Jane seemed to have reinvented herself, and quite possibly thought that she had nothing to fear by moving back to the United States. While living in Baltimore, Fred studied in the environmental health department at Johns Hopkins Medical School.

Sara Jane had been interested in food and cooking from her childhood. Now she decided to enroll in the Baltimore International Culinary Arts Institute, where she became immersed in the world of soup stocks and meat identification. Here she wore a white jacket, scarf, and a white chef's hat. She was twice the age of most of her fellow students. One of those students, Randy McGuffin, who was eighteen at the time, remembered her as "an older, red-haired woman with an artistic flair who cheerfully did everything that was assigned to her, from washing dishes at L'Ecole, the sixty-seat student restaurant, to sweeping the parking lot." McGuffin, who now runs two trendy Arkansas restaurants, said that while most of the students were going to school seeking professions in the cooking industry, Sara Jane did not have that desire. He said that she just wanted to learn to be a better cook for her husband.

McGuffin also said that she got on very well with her fellow classmates and that she would often tag along to a local bar for an after-class beer. He added that he soon realized what topics to avoid: "You just didn't go in the direction of politics, anything like that, because she was very strong headed," he said. "It would just ruin everything."

In 1985, soon after Sara Jane had earned her restaurant-skills certificate and Fred had earned a master's degree, the family returned to the Twin Cities. They settled in a bungalow on a quiet Minneapolis block near the Mississippi River. Sara Jane went about her new life, taking more classes, volunteering, and acting in local theater productions. Life was good, except that she missed the rest of her family. Occasionally, she sent messages to them.

Sometime in the late 1980s, Sara Jane, Fred, and their two daughters went to California to see her parents. They met in a park in Santa Clarita, a town between Palmdale and Los Angeles. Sara Jane's mother, Elsie, told *Time South Pacific* magazine in June 1999, that they only visited for "an hour or two." She said, "She was so frightened because she was in California. It was hard to say good-bye because we didn't know when we would see her again." After that reunion, a lawyer advised Sara Jane that she was being too casual and, according to Elsie, she cut off most contact with her parents after that. At about this time, she was trying to work out a plea bargain agreement through intermediaries. When she was told that prosecutors would not rule out prison time, the bargain fell through. Sara Jane carried on with her new life.

When Fred and Sara Jane's third daughter was born in 1987, the family of five crossed the river and moved into an ivy-covered Tudor home in St. Paul's Highland Park, one of the city's more upscale neighborhoods. The house interior was Craftsman-style with a center hall, five rooms on the ground floor, three bedrooms, and a bath on the upper floor. The living room had a half bath, a fireplace, and built-in bookcases. The remodeled kitchen was top-of-the-line with all of the newest appliances, fit for a gourmet chef. It was a welcoming home. Stoneware jars filled with Hershey's Kisses were always available. One guest described the house as a "mix of decors" that included middle-class touches, such as Sears-type family portraits on the walls, and landscape photographs. Knitted lap blankets were placed tastefully on sofas. The house was comfortable for the family as well as for all of the guests they entertained.

By now, Fred was a well-regarded emergency-room physician at St. Paul's United Hospital. He and Sara Jane still enjoyed jogging and were often seen on their neighborhood route. They were a typical Midwestern, middle-class family, throwing fundraisers for their youngest daughter's soccer team, hosting lavish parties for Fred's medical associates and Sara Jane's acting associates, and entertaining their mixed group of politically liberal friends.

Sara Jane was a devoted mother to her three daughters and acted in local productions. Her resumé for Theater in the Round in Minneapolis had stated that she had come to Minnesota from California in 1983 and was active in the anti-apartheid movement. (In 1987, the *Star Tribune* had published a letter to the editor from Sara Jane Olson that protested South Africa's occupation of its neighbor Namibia.)

She played many roles at Theater in the Round, including a liberal American who has a nervous breakdown over apartheid in *A Fair Country*. Pam Nice, who directed the play, said, "Sara Jane was right for the role because her character was extremely intense and Sara Jane was like that—you notice her intensity right away. She understood her character being on edge emotionally and she captured that very well."

In 1997, she played a "Medusa-like Queen Eleanor," in *The Lion in Winter,* Miss Havisham in *Great Expectations,* and a conniving daughter in *King Lear.* Local papers gave her mixed reviews for all of her roles.

A Guthrie Theater veteran actor, Stephen Pelinski, told the *Jewish World Review* that the entire local theater community supported Sara Jane. He said that she was "one of our most advanced actors." Lynn Musgrave, an actress and director, called Sara Jane "a pacifist and liberal Democrat who supports gun control."

Finally Sara Jane got to repeat her role as queen of the protagonists in Shakespeare's *Macbeth,* which she had played in high school.

The saying that art imitates life applies to some of her roles. *Macbeth*—a story of murder, deception, guilt, and eventual atonement—must have resonated somewhere in Sara Jane Olson's mind, especially in the lead character's line: "False face must hide what the false heart doth know." A line in the third scene of *Macbeth* is just as eerie, considering the SLA's penchant for calling police "pigs," and the fact that, later on, Sara Jane Olson would contend that she was the subject of a "witch hunt:" "Where has thou been, sister?" asks the first witch, as the thunder rolls. "Killing swine," comes the second's reply (*Minnesota Monthly*).

None of Sara Jane's fellow actors could name Sara Jane's close friends. Lynn Musgrave said, "I don't know who brought her [opening night] bouquets."

Sara Jane auditioned for a role in "Paradise Inn," a pilot sitcom about gay characters that debuted during the Twin Cities Pride Festival of 1997. She had read for a major part, but didn't get it. Greg Allen, the executive producer/creator of the sitcom, said that the force of her reading struck him: "It was our first full day of auditions, so it was quite memorable. She was good, but her intensity was a little too much for us. She was interesting enough that we hung on to her tape in case we might need her for something else."

Experts pointed out that although it may have been foolhardy for Sara Jane to take to the stage, to have her face appear on theater posters, and in local newspapers, fugitives who attempt to change their lifestyles too dramatically seldom avoid authorities for long. Those who make it year after year under the weight of an arrest warrant create an identity with its roots in the truth. Jim McCandless, who had studied theater with her in college, told *People* magazine, "She had great accents. She was a master of disguise."

America's Most Wanted

Many magazine and newspaper articles would later refer to Sara Jane's modus operandi as "hiding in plain sight." Since college, Sara Jane had seemed to enjoy living on the edge. Were her public appearances a cry to "catch me," because this was too hard? Or were they meant to dare authorities to arrest her when she could prove that she had become a stellar member of society? Perhaps she thought that the political friends whom she had financially supported would come to her aid if she were ever caught.

Other people who had spent years underground had turned themselves in, perhaps because the stress of leading a life with a false identity was too difficult. Bernardine Dohrn, former leader of the Weathermen, turned herself in in 1980. She had been allowed to plead guilty to lesser counts relating to antiwar demonstrations, had been fined $1,500, and placed on probation. When Dohrn surrendered she said, "I was shocked at the anger toward me. I think part of it [is] reserved for women. You stepped out of the role of the good girl."

In 1993 another fugitive, Katherine Ann Power, gave herself up to authorities. Power had driven a car during a Boston bank robbery in which a police officer, Walter Schroeder, father of nine, was killed. Power had assumed a new identity in Oregon. After twenty-three years in hiding, the same amount of time as Sara Jane Olson, Power surrendered to the Massachusetts police, pleaded guilty to manslaughter, and was sentenced to eight to twelve years in prison.

In an interview with the *New York Times* about Power, Dohrn waxed nostalgic about the earlier days of protest, violence, and social division: "Everyone tries to make it finally over. But it is far from over."

Former *New York Times* columnist and author Anna Quindlen wrote about Katherine Power, calling her "the embodiment of the chasm between the sixties and nineties, like someone with a multiple personality disorder. It is almost as though a different Kathy [Power] drove three ex-cons . . . to the scene of the crime. The other personalities, the cook, the mother, the middle-aged woman, perhaps feel as if they scarcely know her, as we scarcely know our younger selves." Quindlen also talked about how the press emphasized the pain of Katherine Ann Power, surrendering after a lifetime on the run. "But a man died; his wife was left alone; his children grew up without him," she wrote. "If the last twenty-three years have given us a sense of proportion, then surely we all understand that they are the point of the story."

The similarities between Katherine Ann Power and Kathleen Ann Soliah were almost eerie. They were both fugitives for twenty-three years and allegedly responsible for someone's death. Myrna Opsahl's family in California could probably identify with the Schroeder family. Power turned herself in because she had been receiving therapy and was exhausted by the effort required to sustain a false existence. Kathleen Soliah, however, handled things differently.

"When crime is down, we don't go to the golf course, we dust off old cases," former Hollywood police Captain Mervin King told a reporter for the *Star Tribune.*

In the late 1990s, crime was down in Los Angeles. Mervin King had investigated the Soliah bombing case in 1975. Now, with a still-solid build, wavy, white hair, and wire-rimmed glasses, he was in his eighties, but age hadn't changed his belief that the LAPD had a moral and judicial imperative to pursue the Kathleen Soliah case. He had spent years hashing it over with his son, Tom, also a detective for the LAPD. Tom, who had inherited his father's commitment and determination, had learned about the booby-trapped police cars from other cops too. "These were very large bombs," Tom said. "They were intended to kill police officers, and they would have killed bystanders too." The case needed closure.

In 1999, Officer Tom King had almost despaired of ever solving the case, but enlisted the help of David Reyes, who had grown up in lower middle-class East Los Angeles and was an up-and-coming elite-unit LAPD detective. Reyes, in his early forties with expressive brown eyes, dark hair parted down the middle, and a full mustache, vowed to Tom King, "I'm gonna find her [Kathy]. And when I do, I'm gonna have your old man sign the booking approval." Reyes and his partner, Mike Fanning, had been thirteen years old when the bombing attempts had taken place.

So much time had elapsed that it would be a tough case to prove, but Reyes and Fanning sorted through two large boxes of investigatory material put together by a generation of cops—old notebooks, press clippings, books on the SLA, the old indictment—and they became hooked. The two detectives thought the research was like "reading a novel."

They both realized that they were going to need help, so Reyes contacted Rick Denny, an FBI agent who had collaborated with him on a recent hate-crime case. They also brought in Denny's former partner, Mary Hogan, and the four of them decided to "rattle the trees and see what falls out."

According to John Walsh's book *Public Enemies,* Special Agent Mary Hogan, a details-oriented person who read all the documentation relating to her cases, looked at the SLA as a history lesson, and wanted to pursue the case. She had the FBI issue a UFAP ("Unlawful Flight to Avoid Prosecution") for Kathleen Soliah and James Kilgore. Hogan realized that she would need national coverage to reignite interest in the case, and she contacted *America's Most Wanted.*

In March 1999, Sharon Greene, the West Coast bureau chief of *AMW,* was given some background information on the SLA along with the wanted posters for Kathleen Soliah and Jim Kilgore before meeting with the FBI. She was skeptical about airing this case. She was already working on twelve other segments, and this was such an old story. But after she read the file, she changed her mind.

Greene was too young to remember the story firsthand, but she interviewed people who had lived through the SLA's terror and Patty Hearst's kidnapping. They told her about the wave of bombings in Los Angeles and how they lived in fear of just "walking down the street." Greene assigned freelance producer Margaret Roberts to do further research. Roberts was skeptical at first until she read Patty Hearst's memoir, *Every Secret Thing*. It was a revelation to her. She agreed to meet with Detective Reyes and his partner, Mike Fanning. Reyes and Fanning brought a replica of the bomb that was planted underneath the police cars. Seeing the bomb and imagining what would have happened to those policemen if it had gone off stunned her. It made her think of the crime from the victim's perspective.

Some of *AMW*'s decision makers had doubts about airing the segment, reminding the producers of "the context of the times." They had lived in the sixties and seventies and had also protested against the Vietnam War. They too had been repulsed by Johnson's and then Nixon's escalation of the war. There were many meetings and arguments over the subject. Greene wanted to know if the cause of peace was advanced by the Symbionese Liberation Army execution of Marcus Foster, who had been trying to make classrooms a safe place for kids. Or the many bombs that could have killed numerous innocent people? And what about the thousands of rounds of ammunition shot in the residential Compton neighborhood, where somebody could have been killed, just because the SLA would not surrender?

One of the producers said, "But no one was hurt."

Sharon Greene corrected him. Officer James Bryan was so emotionally devastated after finding the bomb under his car that he had to quit his job as a policeman, which had been his lifelong ambition. Officer Hall still had trouble getting into a car without checking to see if someone was going to blow him up. Greene wondered where you draw the line. In the end, she won out, and *America's Most Wanted* decided to help the FBI in finding Kathleen Soliah and Jim Kilgore. After a few weeks of gathering pictures and information, the show was ready to be put on the air.

Two sets of cops called on Kathy's parents, Marty and Elsie Soliah, now an elderly couple who still resided in Palmdale. By this time, *America's Most Wanted* had decided to run a segment to coincide with the twenty-fifth anniversary of the SLA shootout in May 1974, and in that segment, they were going to profile the missing fugitives, Soliah and Kilgore.

The Soliahs weren't at their house, but the investigative team found them at the home of their youngest daughter, Martha Soliah Conaway. Martha lived in a Spanish-theme development not far from the elder Soliahs' home. She answered the door, invited them in, and they all sat down to talk. Marty, his hair thin and gray, was dressed in Bermuda shorts and a striped golf shirt. His voice quivering, he asked the police officers who were wearing suits, "So, are you guys Mormons?" Age hadn't diminished his wit.

During their conversation, the police learned that Kathy had been close to her younger brother Lance, who lived in Iowa. Marty, now eighty-one, had sent his fourth child to Luther College in Decorah, Iowa, and he had settled there.

Reyes felt guilty that he was disturbing these nice elderly people, but there was no turning back. "Kathy's had twenty-five years to come forward; don't you want all this to be over?" he asked them. No answer.

Then he showed the Soliahs the 1974 "wanted" poster of their daughter, which now also had a digitally altered photograph to approximate her present appearance. Elsie, a trim woman with brilliant white hair, wearing slacks and a long, white shirt, took a second look at the composite, and said, "Oh no, she doesn't look like that," and reached into her wallet to pull out a family photograph taken two years before. "This is what she looks like."

As reported in the *Los Angeles Magazine,* after seeing her picture, the four cops tried to hide their excitement, and casually asked, "Where was this taken? When?" They told the Soliahs that if they could talk with Kathy and get a dialogue started, *America's Most Wanted* would not air the segment. Martha Conaway called her older sister Josephine and her husband, Michael Bortin, in Portland, to see what they thought, but Bortin's message to her was, "Tell the cops not to bother to come up here."

Now that they were on the track, Reyes and Fanning disregarded Bortin's angry rebuff and flew to Portland to interview him. The authorities already had him on surveillance. That morning, as they were leaving the airport hotel, Reyes got a call from veteran *San Francisco Examiner* reporter Larry Hatfield, who was writing an article about the twenty-fifth anniversary of the SLA shootout in Los Angeles. Hatfield wanted them to know that he could relay messages between the police and Kathy Soliah. He never spoke with her directly. Hatfield's contact, possibly Michael Bortin, was interested in arranging a deal for Kathy, much like the one that Bernardine Dohrn had received. Hatfield called again and the negotiations began. Phone calls were traded between Hatfield and his source, and Reyes and the DA's office through the LAPD. However, the Los Angeles Police Department was not willing to offer a deal with no jail time. Reyes tried to get Hatfield to put him in direct contact with Kathy, but Hatfield apparently didn't trust him, and the negotiations collapsed on Monday, May 17.

Hatfield had interviewed Michael Bortin ten years earlier for an article he had been writing for the *San Francisco Examiner* concerning the bank robbery in Carmichael. Bortin had given him information that had led him to believe that Kathy Soliah was living in the Midwest, married to a professional, the mother of two daughters.

On May 15, 1999, *America's Most Wanted* aired their segment as planned. The host, John Walsh, announced, "Tonight's story has new details that could put, of all people, Patty Hearst back under investigation for her days as an urban terrorist. It was May 17, 1974, twenty-five years ago this week that LA police got a tip that the most wanted fugitives in America might be hiding in this Compton neighborhood." As Walsh narrated, viewers watched the standoff between the Los Angeles cops, FBI agents, SWAT teams, and six members of the SLA holed up in the little stucco house.

Walsh continued, "The LAPD closed in. Inside this house were six terrorist members of the Symbionese Liberation Army who were wanted for murdering a school superintendent and kidnapping heiress Patty Hearst, who later joined them and was caught on tape robbing a bank. Now they were cornered. It was one of the fiercest police shootouts ever."

David Reyes, who was interviewed for the segment said, "It was a residential area, and they [SLA] didn't care who got in the way. 'This is where we're going to make our stand.'"

Next there were scenes from the shootout: women running from their houses, screaming, ducking, flailing their arms, and holding their terrified children. The LA police crouched under windows, cops ran in a frenzy from car to car. Flames shot out the windows and black smoked spewed out of the roof of the SLA house.

"The SLA and the LA police fired more than 9,000 rounds of ammunition," exclaimed Walsh. "The house caught fire, but the SLA refused to surrender. When the shootout was over, six people inside were dead." Remarkably, no one outside of the house was killed.

Walsh continued, "Now, the SLA was down to only three members, William and Emily Harris and Patricia Hearst. They desperately needed new recruits. They found them in San Francisco. Radical activist Kathleen Soliah and her boyfriend, James Kilgore, eagerly joined the SLA. According to LA police, they played a major role in the SLA's next wave of terrorism."

David Reyes added in the interview that the SLA planned a bloody payback against the LAPD. "James [Kilgore] would actually experiment, with Kathy at his side, with different types of bombs and different types of mechanisms to set them off," he said.

Officer John Hall faced the camera and said, "The night that the pipe bombs were planted, the movies were just letting out, and there were a lot of families in the International House of Pancakes restaurant. The tables were full." Viewers then saw a re-enactment of someone placing a bomb underneath Officer Hall's car. It was chilling to realize that the man telling the story could have been blown up in that car.

Officer Marty Feinmark had been twenty-four years old at the time. At the Hollenbeck Station, he and his partner had gotten onto their hands and knees to check the undercarriages of the cars. They'd found nothing until they decided to check the unmarked cars parked on the street. Under one of the police cars, Feinmark saw a piece of plastic, and lifted it up. Underneath was a pipe bomb with the wires exposed. He said his heart was beating 1,000 miles a minute. He and his partner backed off and ran into the station to report the bomb.

Walsh explained to the viewers that the bomb would have caused death or injury to anyone within hundreds of feet. Next, *America's Most Wanted* continued with a videotape re-enactment of a police car exploding, a car that had the same type of pipe bomb placed in its undercarriage as the one that Kathy Soliah had been accused of placing back in 1975.

"Wanted" posters of Kathy Soliah and Jim Kilgore filled the screen along with digitalized, age-enhanced photographs of how they might now look. *America's Most Wanted* displayed their website, AMW.com, and the hotline number to call if anyone had seen "this woman": 1-800-CRIME-TV.

The hotline received nineteen tips the night of the broadcast and one other tip after that. Mary Hogan read the tip sheets that the phone operators filled out as they received the calls. She knew that *America's Most Wanted* was about to chalk up capture number 570.

Although Kathy Soliah's hair was short and curly in the Wanted Poster, viewers told the hotline that the eyes and mouth of the woman in the broadcast bore a striking resemblance to fifty-two-year-old Sara Jane Olson, who now had long, straight, strawberry blond hair, and lived in the Highland Park neighborhood of St. Paul, Minnesota.

Olson was a doctor's wife, the mother of three daughters—ages eighteen, seventeen, and twelve—a church goer and an avid community activist. She was a jogger and had completed a marathon. She was a soccer mom, a gourmet cook (her neighbors dubbed her Martha Stewart), and a local actress. She hosted teas for a Democratic congressman. She followed foreign affairs and read everything from Charles Dickens to *The Economist*. She supported gun-control efforts. How could Kathy Soliah and Sara Jane Olson be one and the same? It seemed impossible. The tips were anonymous, but perhaps one of the callers was a neighbor of Sara Jane's, a member of her church, someone with whom she had performed in a local play, or a fellow volunteer. In any case, these tips led Detective Reyes and his team to Minnesota.

According to the *Los Angeles Times* magazine, Tom King arranged for Reyes and Fanning to take the red-eye flight into Minneapolis and join two other officers, who, along with local FBI agents and St. Paul police, had already placed the Olson-Peterson's ivy-covered stone house on Hillcrest Avenue under surveillance. The word was that on June 16, anyone answering to Soliah's description who exited the Olson-Peterson house was to be pulled over a few streets away by the St. Paul Police on the pretext of a traffic violation. If the suspect's driver's license read "Sara Jane Olson," she would be compared to a photograph of Kathleen Soliah. If that checked out, she'd be arrested.

That Wednesday morning in June, a lawyer who lived in her neighborhood was driving his eight-year-old son to daycare when he pulled up to a stop sign and looked to the left. He saw the minivan being pulled over at the intersection of Edgcumbe and Niles. One St. Paul police car pulled in front of it and another pulled in behind it. At 8:21 A.M., FBI Agent Mary Hogan approached Sara Jane's car and she rolled down the window.

Sara Jane looked calm. "What's wrong, Officer?" she asked. Then she looked in the rearview mirror and saw the other cars pull up. "People were jumping out of their cars," she said later, and then, "I thought, oh, oh. I seemed to disappear. I was in shock."

FBI Agent Mary Hogan said that it all happened very fast. After she presented her credentials, Kathy realized that her past had caught up with her.

Hogan said, "FBI, Kathleen, it's over."

Reyes and Fanning from the LAPD had parked their rental car on a maple-lined street near the Olson-Peterson house. All of a sudden, they saw FBI agents who had been parked nearby racing off in their vehicles. Frantically switching police-band frequencies to find out what was going on, the LA cops discovered that a suspect believed to be Soliah was in St. Paul police custody a few blocks away. Reyes said, "When we arrived on the scene, we're like, 'Hey, Kathy, how's it going?' Then we asked her, 'You want to go by Kathy or Sara Jane?'"

Her answer came in a "dramatically trained voice, full of range and expressiveness, 'I want to speak to my lawyer.'" Sara Jane Olson was taken to the Adult Detention Center at the Ramsey County Jail and fingerprinted.

That night, Kathy Soliah, *aka* Sara Jane Olson, was the lead story on all of the Twin Cities' nightly news shows. Sara Jane's family, friends, and everyone who knew her or thought they did, were stunned.

Dr. Fred Peterson told Minneapolis Police Captain Michael Jordan that he was totally shocked. "He sounded sincere," Jordan said. "He said that he didn't know about her background. He couldn't believe it." Neither could anyone else.

Her children had only known their mother as Sara Jane Olson. She was devoted to them, an integral part of their lives. Her neighbors knew her as the gourmet cook and fantastic entertainer. Her theater colleagues knew her as a good actress. Although Sara Jane had been acclaimed for her supporting roles in local plays, it would soon become apparent that Kathleen Soliah had played a starring role for twenty-three years. "Sara Jane Olson" was the performance of a lifetime.

Four hours after her arrest, the FBI proved that, yes, Kathy Soliah and Sara Jane Olson were one and the same. The fingerprints matched.

The next day, after spending the night in jail, Sara Jane faced a judge in the Ramsey County courthouse wearing a prison orange jumpsuit for her bail hearing. After deliberating with the attorneys, the Ramsey County district judge explained, "Anyone with a twenty-three year history of fleeing police is a flight risk." She ordered Sara Jane Olson held without bail. The court had to investigate whether "Conspiracy to Commit Murder" was an offense punishable by life imprisonment in California. The defense and prosecuting attorneys had until noon to give her an answer.

They discovered that the maximum penalty for the conspiracy charge in California is life imprisonment with the possibility of parole, the same as it was in 1976 when Kathleen Soliah had been indicted. There would be no bail, and Sara Jane Olson would remain in jail until it was decided whether she would be returned to California to face charges. Her attorney, Howard Bass, stated that if it was proven that Sara Jane Olson was actually Kathleen Soliah, his client might waive extradition.

Evan Imber-Black wrote in *The Secret Life of Families*: "Sometimes we keep secrets to protect the people we love, mired in a confusing morass of protection and deception that erodes the very relationships we were hoping to preserve. And sometimes we keep secrets to protect ourselves or to secure power, and in so doing betray spouses, parents, siblings, children, or friends." If Sara Jane had kept her secret in order to protect those people she loved, it appeared that she had made a poor decision; she had betrayed them in doing so.

At the hearing, Sara Jane's three daughters sat in the front row of the courtroom. With her head on her father's shoulder, her twelve-year old, wearing glittery butterfly barrettes in her strawberry blond hair, and braces on her teeth, cried through the whole ordeal. Her two oldest daughters were sobbing. When it was over, as if on stage, Sara Jane turned around and smiled at the courtroom audience, her family, and friends, as if to say, "Thank you for coming." Photographers from the *Star Tribune* and the *St. Paul Pioneer Press* caught the emotions of the day. The front pages depicted a stunned Sara Jane, tears in her eyes, hands covering her face. The most heart-wrenching photograph was of Fred with his arms around his sobbing twelve-year-old, who had her arms stretched out to her mother as she was being led to her prison cell.

Sara Jane remained in jail for five weeks without bail, waiting for the extradition papers to be sent from California. During her time there, she remained taciturn and appeared rueful, if the newspaper pictures were any indication. Photos depicted the shell-shocked expressions of Fred and her three daughters. Tearful photos of Sara Jane revealed a middle-aged woman who, if relieved that it was over, had now come to realize that it was not over at all. It was just beginning.

Outside of the jail, friends of her family rallied. Supporters from her church, various volunteer groups, and fellow actors defended her on television, radio, in the print media. Sara Jane had detractors as well.

Two websites, www.soliah.com by Greg Lang from Minneapolis and www.lektrik.com/sinc/ by Jack Golan from Sacramento were registered almost immediately after her arrest and would post daily news articles, link discussion groups with local newspapers, and keep literally thousands of people informed of the latest news on Sara Jane's case.

University of Minnesota psychologist Marti Hope Gonzales thought that some of Sara Jane's critics were as turned off by her deception as they were by her alleged misdeeds. In an interview for *Minnesota Monthly,* Gonzales commented, "There's something in humans as social animals that we just don't like people who are not genuine." She continued, "So it may well be that [criticism of Olson] has less to do with the act she's accused of having perpetrated, and has more to do with the fact that this woman who is a fake, is someone other than what she claims to be. Human beings," she added, "find that very unsettling. I think it also has to do with the fact that by virtue of engaging in this deceit, she has not paid the price of retribution for her actions."

Michael Bortin, now in his fifties, was living in southeast Portland with his wife, Kathy's sister Josephine, whom he had married in 1988. He hadn't strayed much from his "radical days" profession. He still worked as a contractor laying hardwood floors and Josephine was a nurse. They were raising their four children in a large Victorian-style house that they were refurbishing. He was furious about his sister-in-law's arrest.

He told reporters for the *Guardian Unlimited*: "For fifteen years, we've been making fun of her for being such a goody two-shoes. All of a sudden, she gets arrested, and she's a terrorist! It's so hard. They've lost all their money. Their kids are freaked out. They're not going to college; they want to stay close to home."

He added, "Olson is not the woman prosecutors are portraying. Everybody gets vilified and turned into these monsters. You don't go from your twenties and thirties following Charles Manson to reading to the blind in your fifties. Everybody knows something is wrong. Someone is lying. People change, but not like that. It defies common sense."

He accused the Los Angeles prosecutor of "grandstanding," apparently referring to their "celebrating" the silver anniversary of the SLA's fiery demise. Bortin said, "We figured they knew where she [Sara Jane] was. She's been a pretty up-front member of the community. She's been in plays, and there were write-ups in the papers about her. I don't understand what all the hoopla is about unless it's some kind of political thing in Los Angeles. They're getting big media points: 'Hey, look what we did!'"

He added that although the FBI had always known where she

was, they didn't want to look for her. He said they'd been sorely embarrassed by their failures in the Patty Hearst kidnapping investigation, and he believed that the FBI passed on information about "Kathy's" whereabouts to the LAPD in the guise of a tip generated by *America's Most Wanted.*

Josephine Soliah Bortin said that the arrest was very hard on her family: "My parents are old, and they aren't well. *America's Most Wanted* tried to break into their house Wednesday night. They had to physically push them out. My parents are in their eighties for God's sake." She added, "We love and support her [Kathy], but we are wondering, why after twenty-five years this was something the FBI and LAPD had to pursue?"

Bortin added in disgust, "Three weeks ago [before the arrest], Reyes and another cop from the LA Red Squad [a term used by critics for King's division] and an FBI agent barged into Marty and Elsie Soliah's house in Palmdale. This was after, years ago, the Feds telling them that Kathy was not wanted." He said that the authorities had been trying to negotiate a deal the day before the TV show aired and this was just part of a "police game" to trick her into capture. He told a reporter that Kathy had nothing to do with the pipe bombs placed underneath the police cars. "The thing she's charged with is a total joke," he stated. "They're just creating a big circus here. They don't have a case, so they're trying her now.

"Kathleen Soliah and others who confronted authorities over the war in Vietnam and related issues in the early 1970s were very moral people," he explained, "and most—like my sister-in-law—have lived admirable lives since. These people gave up careers, and sometimes more, over one war in Southeast Asia. And when it ended, it all ended. What is this stampede with her now? We're all proud of her. What do they do when they pick someone up and find out she's a saint?" he asked. "This is so typical of the LA police that it's unreal. Look at a person's record. Look at how Kathy leads her life now. That's what's real." He said that he was tired of it and that the case had haunted his family and his in-laws, "like a deranged relative knocking at your door every few years."

Bortin, who had previously served prison time on explosives charges, also said that he was confident that if either Soliah or Kilgore faced trial on the charges currently pending against them, they would not be convicted. "Who cares about a bunch of people running around with bombs twenty-five years ago?" he asked. "If they do find Kilgore, and they do charge him, they'll never convict him, because I'll testify and a few others will that it was our bomb."

After his sister's arrest, Steve Soliah called his parents from his home in Berkeley and assured them, "We were not part of that group. We were helping those people, and I'm sorry we got involved. We made a mistake."

Elsie was positive that her children were never members of the SLA. Kathy's mother, who had been shy of the press in the past now wrote a statement for her daughter's defense website. In part, she stated, "When my husband, Marty, was a schoolteacher and coach in Barnesville, there was another young man teaching and coaching in Moorhead, Minnesota. Although he and Marty had never formally met, he eventually became an FBI agent and moved to Lancaster, California, eight miles from Palmdale where Marty taught and coached until his retirement.

"After my son Steve's trial for the Carmichael Bank robbery ended in acquittal (due to a false indictment rather than a lying girlfriend as the media has been saying), this agent came to Marty and me with what he called 'good news.' He said that the FBI didn't want our daughter Kathy anymore and that she wasn't being looked for as a fugitive. According to him, the Bureau said that they were done with our family. He said that the agents went to LA and informed the DA and LAPD that she was no longer wanted, that the LA charges were considered minor, and that since no one was hurt, why not drop the charges. "LA [sic] said, 'Never! We will always want her.'

"This whole case could have been done with in the late 1970s if the LAPD had listened to the FBI. But after they've spent so much money and time, I suppose they feel they have to get her for something."

Marty Soliah said that maybe it was a relief for his daughter to finally be able to stop hiding. He said that he and Elsie were just trying to stay busy and "keep ourselves occupied." They hired an attorney, but Marty wouldn't elaborate. "We take one-hour hikes in the desert daily," said Marty. "I do my calisthenics and she works in the garden." He added that his daughter was never a member of the SLA. "They would drop the charges if they had any sense. They told me they had nothing to hold her on."

Sara Jane Olson and Kathy Soliah became the subject of many philosophical debates. If she were guilty, how responsible was she? Were her actions simply a "normal" response to violent times? One successful businesswoman who was about Sara Jane's age and had protested the Vietnam War in her youth, explained to the author how a peaceful protester could turn to violence: "We were in our twenties," she said. "So much of what we did depended on who we hung out with, who we were sleeping with, and what drugs we were using." She continued, "I could walk in one door and paint signs for an upcoming protest, or I could walk in the next door and learn how to make bombs. To be violent or nonviolent was only the difference between a door jamb."

Another woman of the same age agreed. "I was newly married, teaching high school and going to grad school in the sixties. I was passionately opposed to the war and participated in demonstrations and on committees planning demonstrations. I never did anything illegal, but I was prepared to be sympathetic to people who did. I thought I could have been one of the Kent State victims, and I was furious at the police behavior at the Chicago Convention. So the slogan, 'Off the Pigs' was not offensive to me. I felt powerless and enraged at authority for what I considered unconscionable behavior in Vietnam and in our own country with respect to protesters."

A woman psychologist with a liberal bent, also about Sara Jane's age, explained her views when asked, "What would make a nonviolent person turn to violence?" She thought for a few seconds before answering, as if it was not the first time that this question had been posed to her. Her answer was well thought out: "It's an unresolved authority issue," she stated. "It's rebellion. People rebel against government because they believe that the government is trying to control their lives. It's ironic because in their rebellion, these protesters are also trying to control other people's lives."

A University of Minnesota professor told the author that he believed that the "door jamb" theory was a cheap shot. He said, "It's easy to forget the context of the times." His parents had lived during the depression in the 1920s and '30s. He said it was "logical" for people then to join the Communist Party. "If we could recapture part of that time, we might better understand why people become radicalized," he stated.

With the news of Kathy Soliah's reappearance, it looked for a while as though Sara Jane might become a symbol for the turbulent sixties and seventies, a martyr of the times. But it would soon become evident that opinions on Sara Jane Olson's arrest would be as polarized as the 2000 Presidential election between Al Gore and George W. Bush—and just as ambiguous.

Extradition

Sara Jane Olson was ordered to remain in jail until her extradition hearing, which would be held on July 15. She hired Susan Jordan, the San Francisco attorney who had represented Bill and Emily Harris back in the seventies, to defend her. According to *The Recorder/Cal Law,* Jordan claimed to have a "long-standing interest and passion for defending the political underdog." She said that her client, Sara Jane, was a victim of the political climate of the times. "The origin of this prosecution is in the politics of law enforcement in the seventies: Go after anybody associated with any political group left of center."

Jordan teamed up with Stuart Hanlon, who shared an office with other criminal defense lawyers in San Francisco in a modest, unincorporated house located on the edge of the Castro. At fifty-two, Hanlon had a middle-aged gut and admitted to a reporter for the *San Francisco Weekly* that he didn't always like his clients, but he made a good living "representing drug dealers and murderers."

Hanlon already had experience working with former associates of the SLA. In the late seventies, Russell Little had been retried and acquitted for the murder of Marcus Foster thanks to Hanlon. Since Bill Harris' parole in 1983, he had worked for Hanlon as a secretary. Yet, Sara Jane Olson and Bill and Emily Harris signed documents saying that they didn't believe there was a conflict of interest for Hanlon to represent Sara Jane, even though she had lived with the Harrises when the bombs were planted in 1975, as long as the prosecution did not call the Harrises to testify.

Hanlon said that sympathy for Soliah could go a long way if the case goes to trial. "Most people look back and say this was a time of total political turmoil," he said. "They shouldn't be prosecuted for it. If she did what she's being accused of, young people then did really stupid things. They didn't do this because they were criminals. They did it because they were motivated politically. It just seems they're prosecuting the wrong person at the wrong time."

Not everyone agreed with him. Later, on November 11, 2001, two months after the collapse of the World Trade Center's Twin Towers, Todd Gitlin who wrote *The Sixties: Years of Hope, Days of Rage,* told the *New York Times* that the country had become impatient with the claims that violence can contribute to the political good. "It's a hard sell today," he said. "Acts that seemed to make sense back then seem senseless to us now." He referred to the Symbionese Liberation Army as "a farcical footnote to a footnote, a cartoon," and he worried that Sara Jane Olson's case might sabotage everything that the well-meaning protestors fought for in the sixties. He added, "This will turn out to have been very bad political theater if it just provides some clownish grist for people who have harbored this grudge against the sixties. Nobody needs to rescue those days, but nobody needs to sabotage them either."

Local Minnesota democratic politicians, however, flocked to Sara Jane's side. State Representative Andy Dawkins had known Fred and Sara Jane for twenty years. (He met Olson through friends in the Cooperative Commonwealth Co-Rec Softball League.) Peterson played a trumpet in a reggae band called the Pressure Cooker, and Dawkins had met him through mutual friends who also played in the band. The couple was living together by then in a house in South Minneapolis where Dawkins said friends would get together, roll up the carpet, push back the furniture, and dance all night. Prior to moving to Africa in the early eighties, Fred and Sara Jane asked Dawkins, an attorney, to represent them in regard to their "civil affairs." When Dawkins first ran for office in 1987, Sara Jane, Fred, and their daughters passed out literature and helped him with his campaign. Dawkins claimed that he had no idea about Sara Jane's true identity and had never seen her passport. If the allegations against her proved to be true, he hoped that the authorities would consider how she had reformed herself. "The Sara Jane we've known for twenty years in Minnesota," he said, "is the real person, the real Sara Olson."

Senator Sandy Pappas made this comment in the Minneapolis *Star Tribune*: "Don't they have any real crimes to fight? Those were such turbulent times all those years ago, and some people were pulled over the line. We were all going to protests and demonstrations, the vast majority of which were nonviolent things. But some people got pulled into the other world and made mistakes."

St. Paul's Republican mayor, Norm Coleman (no relation to Brendan or Chris Coleman) offered a different opinion. He had once been described as a 1960s bullhorn-toting activist who had grown his hair down his back as the head of the Student Mobilization Committee at Hofstra University in New York. "To try to use the passion of the times to somehow justify acts of violence is terribly irresponsible," he said. "We haven't heard one ounce of contrition, not one statement of 'I did something wrong,'" he added. "Very few of us in the movement crossed the line from nonviolence to join the SLA or the Weathermen, and she clearly was way over the line."

Minnesota Governor Jesse Ventura ridiculed statements made by Dawkins, and particularly, Sandy Pappas. "Her quote just knocks, slays me right now," he stated on his radio talk show. "She says, 'Don't they have any real crimes to fight?' I think pipe bombs under squad cars is a real crime. I'm going on record with that. That, to me, is a real, real crime. What would [Pappas] suggest is a real crime?" He said that her comments were "beyond belief." Ventura vowed to sign extradition papers for Sara Jane.

"This is California's business, and I will not stand in the way of due process."

Sara Jane's extradition was scheduled for July 15, which would be almost four weeks after her arrest. Fred wrote a letter to the court, pleading that she not continue to be jailed. "Her absence will be as a winter storm to us, leaving us in cold, deadening numbness," he said. Her parents reported that Fred knew Sara Jane's real name and that she was a fugitive. Fred denied that charge.

While Sara Jane waited for her extradition in the Ramsey County jail, her fellow church members at Minnehaha United Methodist in South Minneapolis opened their doors to interviews with *Dateline NBC, 60 Minutes,* and the *Washington Post.* They wanted everyone to know the good deeds that Sara Jane had performed over the last twenty-three years: running soup kitchens, teaching disadvantaged children in summer camp, reading during Lenten services, and narrating the Christmas pageant. Some of them were in tears on the Sunday after her arrest, trying to find answers, wondering how Sara Jane Olson could be Kathy Soliah. Sara Jane's daughter, a high-school arts student, bravely sang in front of the congregation, "Smile, though your heart is breaking," to her dad. Then she said, "I love you, Dad." She joined the choir in the chorus for "Lean On Me" and Bob Marley's "One Love." Fred refrained from playing his trumpet for the 10:30 A.M. contemporary worship service, as had usually been his practice since his family began attending Minnehaha United Methodist five years ago, but he said, "I am overwhelmed by the love and support of this congregation."

Sandy Pappas attended the service too. After Ventura's scolding, she had toned down her rhetoric. "I'm sure that if there is a trial, a modern jury will consider her life since then. Most people are not black or white," she said. "She's innocent until proven guilty."

Another friend, Brendan Coleman, brother of St. Paul City

Councilman Chris Coleman, had been best man at the Olson/ Peterson small civil marriage ceremony. He was a musician and music director for the church. He'd known Fred and Sara Jane since the late seventies, when the three were active in South African politics, sending clothes, books, and medical supplies to South Africa and publicizing the injustices of apartheid. Outside the church, he told the *Star Tribune* that Sara had volunteered at the Center for Victims of Torture, along with her other services to the community. In his mind, everything she had done in the past two decades should have redeemed her from any crime she may have committed. His brother Chris opined, "It was a different era. It's not a reflection of who we are now."

To the congregation, Fred quipped: "There was a story in the paper today with information about me, and I didn't know a lot of it myself." He wore hiking shorts and a T-shirt that read, "YOU LET UP, YOU LOSE."

"Please understand," he said, "I really was not a hippie. I was a medical student and medical intern. I met Sara Jane in 1978. Our relationship was strong and deep, and it continued that way, and today we have a family. I predict," he added, "that within three to six months, we'll be together again as a family!" The congregation let out a collective sigh and smiled with relief.

Pastor Darlington had visited Sara Jane where she was being held at the Ramsey County Detention Facility, and he asked her if she wanted anything. She replied, "Can you find someone to read newspapers to the blind while I'm away?"

On July 6, five weeks after her arrest, Governor Ventura signed the extradition papers, and arrangements were made for Sara Jane to return to California where it had begun.

Three days later, Sara Jane walked into the courtroom, wearing baggy orange jail pants and a shirt, smiling and waving to Fred and her daughters. In a five-minute court proceeding, she signed an extradition waiver, using both names, "Kathleen Ann Soliah/Sara Jane Olson," acknowledging that she was the Symbionese Liberation Army fugitive whom federal authorities had been looking for since 1975. Governor Jesse Ventura signed the extradition warrant. Sara Jane would appear before the court in Los Angeles for a bail hearing on July 15. When the hearing was over, she blew a kiss to her family before leaving the courtroom.

The first lawyer she hired, Howard Bass, told Twin Cities television station, WCCO, "I think she is relieved to be going back to California and to be closing this chapter of her life." He assured a reporter that Sara Jane Olson did not pose a risk of flight, nor was she a danger to the community. However, Sandi Gibbons, a spokeswoman for the Los Angeles District Attorney's office said that the recommended bail in California for conspiracy to commit murder was $1 million. It would be up to the judge.

Judge Larry Paul Fidler had been on the bench in Los Angeles for nearly twenty years, and in that time, he'd heard his share of controversial, high-profile cases. Judge Fidler was a no-nonsense jurist and had little patience for lawyers who were unprepared or insincere. This slender, balding man was about to be put to the test.

On July 13, wearing a purple pants outfit, hands clasped in front of her with a scarf covering her handcuffs, Sara Jane was flown to Los Angeles to face her past. Her new identity was "Case #A325036, The People of the State of California vs. Kathleen Soliah." She was accompanied by her husband and one of her daughters along with Andy Dawkins, Steve Yanisch (investment banker), husband of Rebecca Yanisch (who was running in the Democratic primary for United States Senator), Wendy Knox, a Twin Cities artistic theater director, and other supporters. They planned to tell Judge Fidler that Sara Jane Olson was not a threat to society. Also with her were Officers Reyes, Fanning, Denny, and Hogan.

Several people on the flight asked for Sara Jane's autograph. Katie Couric, Jane Pauley, and producers for *60 Minutes* had already contacted her for interviews. If she had ever dreamed of being a star, this must have felt like her fifteen minutes of fame. As she crossed the tarmac, the woman who had grown up as

Kathy Soliah tilted her face toward the sky, smiled, and with an actress' sense of timing, briefly closed her eyes. She carried the book *Ingrid Bergman: My Story*. David Reyes walked behind her, carrying her personal belongings in a plastic bag. When they landed in Los Angeles, the authorities led her down a boarding-ramp staircase.

Although the bail guidelines in cases involving conspiracy to commit murder were $1 million, Dawkins hoped the bail would be set at $150,000, "so we can take her home." Another supporter, Stephen Cooper, a Minneapolis attorney who was leading the fundraising effort, stated, "Obviously, a million dollars would be hard to raise this quickly, but something in the $200,000 range would be far more obtainable." Rather than use a bail bondsman, where they would have to forfeit ten percent of the total, the contributors wanted to come up with the cash, so they could get a full refund, assuming that Sara Jane attended all of her court appearances. Dawkins told a reporter for the *Star Tribune*, "I will tell the judge that whatever abhorrent behavior may have occurred was a momentary lapse in judgment and has no chance of repeating itself now." Knox, who had directed Sara Jane in *Macbeth*, said that her friend did not belong in jail. Yanisch said that the couple had always supported him in difficult times, so he wanted to speak in her behalf: "I will tell the judge that I am a pretty good judge of people, and based on twenty-one years of firsthand knowledge, she is neither a danger to the community, nor a threat to run."

On July 15, 1999, Sara Jane was transported from the prison to the courthouse, shackled at the ankles and chained at the waist. Two families who barely knew each other sat in the front row of the courtroom to attend her hearing. Steve Soliah, who had flown down from Berkeley, sat with his parents, Marty and Elsie, their granddaughters, and Fred. Judge Fidler patiently listened to voluminous testimony from Sara Jane's supporters and her own plea of "not guilty" to attempted murder. He also heard new details about the prosecution's evidence.

Sara Jane's attorney, Susan Jordan, urged the judge to view her client "through the lens of history when the fabric of the country was torn asunder" by Vietnam, Kent State, and Watergate.

Prosecutor Michael Latin, who had been fifteen years old when the SLA kidnapped Patty Hearst and had now been an attorney for fifteen years, stated that the bombs had been "designed to kill." He explained to the judge that if the bombs had exploded, they would have killed not only the police officers but as many as twenty patrons in the IHOP restaurant as well. He stated that Kathleen Soliah could also be prosecuted for the bank robbery in Carmichael.

As this drama was unfolding in Los Angeles, the Sacramento County Sheriff's Department was pondering whether or not to reopen that case. Their main evidence, at this point, was Patty Hearst's biography, *Every Secret Thing*. Myrna Opsahl's grown children wanted their mother's murderer to be held accountable.

Another fact that came up during the hearing was that in 1986, Soliah had tried to work out a plea bargain agreement, but when prosecutors would not guarantee that there would be no jail time, it fell through. If Kathy Soliah was innocent of the charges, Latin wondered, why didn't she turn herself in? He also added that she had used a friend's passport to travel to Zimbabwe.

Latin admitted that he didn't have a "slam-dunk" case. Kathy's 1976 grand jury indictment had yellowed with age and two of its star witnesses, James Marshall and Arleigh McCree, had died. James Marshall, the only eyewitness, the store owner who had sold the cap and galvanized pipes to Kathy, had died in 1994. Stuart Hanlon claimed, "Since the witness who made the tentative identification of her is dead, there is no way to make a case."

Arleigh McCree, the most compelling witness in the 1976 indictment, had been widely recognized as one of the top explosive experts in the world; he had even been put in charge of the bomb squad for the 1984 Olympics. His reputation was so great that Libyan leader Moammar Khadafy once offered him $140,000 to train terrorists. He was the man his department always called in whenever there was a bomb threat.

On February 8, 1986, Arleigh McCree was called to the home of a Hollywood makeup artist who was a suspect in an earlier shooting. Police were there to search for the gun used in that crime. They found a gun, but they also found two pipe bombs in the man's garage. That is when they summoned Detective McCree to the house. He and his partner, another member of the bomb squad, examined the bombs and determined that they were live. They also came to another alarming conclusion—the bombs were booby-trapped.

Detective McCree warned his fellow officers of the danger and everyone but himself and his partner backed away. The officers then began to defuse the bombs by hand. Nobody knows exactly how it happened. McCree may have been preparing to cut a wire when the bomb blew up, killing him and his partner. Detective Arleigh McCree was killed in the line of duty ten years after he testified at Kathy Soliah's 1976 indictment.

Over Ground

After five hours of testimony, Judge Fidler responded, "She has strong community support, and I'm impressed with the people coming out from Minnesota. But I find this a particularly abhorrent crime in which police officers likely could have and would have been killed and, most likely, there would have been unintended victims. The bomb is the terrorists' weapon of choice." With that, he set bail at the recommended $1 million.

Judge Fidler ordered the defense attorneys to return to court later that week with a plan for a private Twin Cities firm to set up an electronic monitoring system if Sara Jane was able to obtain the bail and be released. The defense attorneys proposed Minnesota Monitoring, Inc. The company would install a piece of photography equipment in Sara Jane's house. At various times during the day or night, a computer program would phone her home. A message would ask her to put her face in front of the equipment, with additional directions such as putting her finger on her nose or grabbing her ear. This technique would prevent her from using a still photograph of herself. After hitting a "send" button, her image would appear within seconds on a computer screen at the office. When a confirmation message was heard, she could hang up and go about her business. The image would be compared to one taken earlier that would pop onto the computer screen during the call. If they wanted to, they could ask for her picture as often as ten times a day. Also, she would be visited monthly by employees of the monitoring company, and the judge would get weekly reports. If she missed a phone call, another would come fifteen minutes later. If she didn't pick up that call, there would be a third call in fifteen minutes. Then, if calls to some relatives couldn't locate her, law-enforcement officials would be notified. All of this would take place within one hour.

Sara Jane's family and supporters were shocked at Judge Fidler's decision. They had not made it over the first hurdle. As Fred escorted their daughter out of the courtroom, she shouted, "I don't want to go." He told her that she couldn't stay with her mom. She had no choice.

Prosecutor Latin, disappointed that Sara Jane was granted bail at all, told a reporter that "Soliah's ability to assume a new identity, blend like a chameleon in a new environment, and then flourish undiscovered under this fraudulent existence" proved that she was a flight risk.

It was about this time that a committee of Sara Jane's friends set up a website, www.saraolsondefense.com, to compete with the websites that had opposing views and to act as a vehicle to raise funds for her defense. The website was updated regularly with information coming from her defense attorneys, letters from friends and family members, and even statements from Sara Jane.

Supporters claimed to have raised $250,000 with T-shirt sales, bumper stickers that said "Free Sara," and buttons, reminiscent of Patty Hearst's supporters before President Carter commuted her sentence. These items were all available on the website and listed as "tax deductible" donations. Sara Jane and her supporters also put together a cookbook full of recipes that Sara Jane had used for her parties. They titled it, *Serving Time, America's Most Wanted Recipes.* A smiling Sara Jane was on the cover, standing in the center of a target wearing a striped apron, one leg kicked back and arms out as if taking a bow for a winning performance. In one hand was a spatula, and in the other, handcuffs. Her cookbook cover was reminiscent of the famed sixties poster of Huey Newton sitting on his wicker throne—spear in one hand, shotgun in the other.

Included with her recipes were family photos and a copy of her 1983–84 certificate from the Baltimore Culinary Arts Institute. The signature on the certificate read, "Sara Olson." Every chapter of the cookbook began with a picture of her, and a target in the background. In the "Salads and Vegetables" chapter, she was peering through a picture frame, her hands up as if to protect herself from vegetables that were tumbling down around her. Under "Rice, Pasta and Breads," the photo depicts her standing defiantly, holding up a tray in one hand, her other hand full of twenty dollar bills, the same denominations that had been stolen from the Crocker National Bank. Her supporters hoped to defray legal expenses with sales from this cookbook, but more than that, it seemed to be a political statement that made light of the serious charges against her as well as the judicial system itself.

While Sara Jane's supporters busied themselves with cookbook sales, soliciting for bail money, and monitoring the defense website, Sara Jane sat in the Los Angeles County jail, which was harder on her than the five weeks she had been imprisoned in St. Paul. She said that the guards taunted her and called her "bomber" and "cop killer." She was alone in a cell. Some inmates smuggled toothpaste and a comb to her. While she waited to be body-searched, another woman inmate warned her not to say anything to anybody and to cooperate.

The $1 million figure jolted Sara Jane's family members who had been in the courtroom, as well as her fundraisers. Kathy Cima, a Minneapolis lawyer who had coordinated the bail fund, said, "It's a devastating and ridiculous amount of money." Steve Yanisch, who had put up $20,000 of his own money, thought that $1 million would be a "significant hurdle".

He was proved wrong. Fundraisers were held at the Peterson-Olson home in St. Paul. Fred's friends and coworkers contributed to her cause. The money poured in. At least 250 people believed that Sara Jane was being wrongly accused, or if not, they thought that she had redeemed herself since those turbulent years and should be forgiven. Fred was grateful and astounded at the out-pouring of affection and loyalty toward his wife.

In less than one week, Fred and Sara Jane's friends and family came up with the $1 million bail money. The money was raised entirely from individuals. One of the fundraisers told the *Star Tribune*: "I remember Sara and Fred had a nice graduation party for their daughter the weekend before all this happened. All her friends were there. A few days later, the same circle of friends was at the jail trying to help her out. The whole thing has been so amazing."

On July 21, Sara Jane bounded down the stairs of the Los Angeles County jail into the arms of her husband. She spoke to about fifty reporters and a dozen TV cameras before heading to San Francisco to confer with her lawyers. She thanked her supporters "for putting up their houses and retirement funds to get me out of jail." She also thanked her family, friends, attorneys, and even the news media. She sent a "special greeting" to her dog, Emma.

"Hey you guys, how ya doing?" she said with a grin. "Needless to say, I'm extremely glad to be out of jail; and although I've per-sonally been rather isolated the last five weeks, I've heard that there has been some media scrutiny of this case, and I want to thank you all for keeping my friends informed of my situation." Wearing the same purple pants suit in which she had arrived, she expressed confidence that her attorneys would successfully de-fend her when the case went to trial.

"The last five weeks in jail have been a real education for me, something I never would have gotten from reading in a book or an article in the newspaper," she told reporters. "I'm looking for-ward to going home and being with my family again and experi-ence with my daughters the trauma of everyday teenage life."

Before flying home to Minnesota, she visited with her family in Palmdale. Elsie, Josephine, and Martha Jane, her youngest sis-ter, the defense lawyers, and some of the fundraising committee met in a hotel room because they wanted privacy. They stayed up late; they had about twenty-four years to catch up on. Sara Jane met a *Los Angeles Times* reporter for lunch in Pasadena, where she stated, "I just want my life back." Wearing a flowery, red sleeveless shift, she was tan and sported a stylish haircut. Her words were measured and she refused to talk about her years on the lam, or whether or not Fred knew about her past. She said, "I have to be careful. I have to assume the possibility that anything I say can be seized upon by the district attorney." When the reporter asked her about her choice of Sara Jane for a name, she denied that it had anything to do with Sara Jane Moore. "There's nothing really glamorous, romantic, or juicy about it," she said. "It was just a name." The reporter from the *Los Angeles Times* said that unlike her press conferences, where she drew on her theatrical abilities, on a one-on-one basis, she was nervous and laughed too often.

In the interview, Sara Jane claimed that her three girls were handling the situation by ignoring it. She blamed the media for exposing her before she had told them herself. They had not asked their mother for an explanation. "They just think everybody else is crazy," added Sara Jane. She said that it helped that, as teenagers, her daughters were totally self-absorbed. To them, she said, the family's situation is "a real bummer, but it's peripheral."

In the introduction to Sara Jane's cookbook, she said that two of her daughters had suffered from eating disorders. Sara Jane said that they eventually realized that food was not the problem, but the sign of the problem(s). She added that both daughters were doing well.

Judi Hollis, Ph.D. wrote in her book *Fat and Furious* that where there are children with eating disorders, there are often family problems. "Illness preserves the family system. We sometimes see parents appearing as a loving couple, upwardly mobile, middle-class, psychologically aware, with 'very little wrong' in THEIR relationship.

"The mothers are often immaculate, well groomed, fashionably thin. Despite their gracious smiles, they often speak in a controlled, deliberate manner that sometimes sounds like ice cubes clicking in the veins."

In *The Secret Life of Families*, Evan Imber-Black wrote, "When families have dreadful and incommunicable secrets, one member's behavior can sometimes serve as an effective distraction, providing everyone with a safe, albeit upsetting topic of conversation. As is true in many families where children create enormously upsetting diversions from core family secrets, the family fixes on their behavior as further proof that the secret should remain buried." She added that "the anxiety of guarding a secret spills over onto those who do not know."

Sara Jane admitted to the *Los Angeles Times* reporter that she was scared because she'd read a lot of books about women in prison. She said that she was going to keep a low profile, except to help her attorneys. To pass the time, she would work in her garden and run sometimes, eleven miles at a time. "If I find myself getting into some kind of reverie about it, I just stop," she said. "Just let it go. A lot of my stability comes from my friends."

After visiting with her parents, Sara Jane and Fred flew up to Berkeley to visit with Steve and confer with her attorneys. On the flight back to Minneapolis, Fred expressed optimism for their situation to a *Star Tribune* reporter: "Reconnecting means that I get to spend a lot of good family time with my wife and kids," he said. "The heartbreak is lifted when you get yourself out of jail and back in the family fold—and you see that coming as a probability and then an inevitability."

This trip had been the first significant time that he had spent with his in-laws. "We had an excellent time. Sara's parents are under maximal stress, and they're getting along in years. They're particularly relieved that Sara is out of jail and to see that she has a huge amount of community support and trust in her upcoming behavior. It's a very emotional time now for her parents to get to know their grandchildren. Lots of tears and lots of hugs." He added that his wife was in good spirits.

When asked if he and his wife and friends would work to improve prison conditions, he replied, "The growth of the prison industry is not an unknown topic for us but to be an activist around that right now is inappropriate." He was anxious to get through the court proceedings and back to his family life. The financial burdens were difficult for his family, as were the emotional strains. He would have to raise at least $500,000 for his wife's legal defense. A pretrial hearing was scheduled for August 21, and if everything went according to schedule, the supporters who had contributed to her bail would get their money back, assuming Sara Jane showed up for trial. He was concerned that if there were delays, it might be difficult to tap her supporters for more money. Hopefully, they could quickly put an end to this and get back to normal.

Fred admitted that he had met Steven Soliah before, briefly, and said that Steven was a good rock-and-roll singer and a guitarist: "He can play anything with six strings." With Fred in a reggae band, the two brothers-in-law had a lot in common.

Fred was concerned when he read that a psychologist had predicted that his wife's arrest would destroy their marriage and cause permanent emotional damage to the children. Psychotherapist Pauline Boss, who wrote *Ambiguous Loss*, had told a reporter from *People* magazine that Sara Jane's "husband and children may no longer know what they can believe. They don't know what is true and what isn't," she said. She added that, "A secret screws up intimate relations between parent and child and certainly between spouses."

In *Ambiguous Loss*, she wrote, "If the uncertainty continues, families often respond with absolutes, either acting as if the person is completely gone, or denying that anything has changed. If they have not already closed out the person who is missing physically or psychologically, they hang on to the hope that things will return to the way they used to be. Fred claimed that the family had emerged stronger than ever. The children completely supported their mother. "To get to be a normal family again would be ideal," he said.

Normality would be a long time in coming. Questions had yet to be answered about Fred himself. Following Sara Jane's arrest, Marty Soliah had told reporters that Fred had known his wife's true identity. Yet Fred denied it. If he had met the Soliah family earlier, wouldn't he have wondered why Sara Jane called herself "Olson"? Wouldn't he have had to know about the previous plea negotiations with her family as mediators? Since the law prohibits spouses from testifying against each other in criminal matters, the truth on this issue would not come out at a trial. However, the prosecution could still accuse Fred of harboring a fugitive.

Evan Imber-Black wrote, "Toxic secrets poison our relationships with each other. A toxic secret may have been formed three generations ago or last month. In either case, key family stories remain untold and unavailable. These are the secrets that take a powerful toll on relationships, disorient our identity, and disable our lives. They handicap our capacity to make clear choices, use resources effectively, and participate in authentic relationships. Even when no one is in immediate physical or emotional danger, toxic secrets nonetheless sap energy, promote anxiety, burden those who know, and mystify those who don't know. Living a toxic secret can feel like living in a pressure cooker." Ironically, "Pressure Cooker" was the name of Fred's reggae band.

Back in St. Paul, a "Welcome Home Sara" sign greeted them in their entryway. Sara Jane stayed up most of the night with her family and supporters. The next afternoon, following a trip to her beauty parlor to get her gray roots colored, she met with reporters in her front yard. Wearing a wide-brimmed straw hat, dark sunglasses, denim shorts, a T-shirt, and a button with the image of a butterfly and the words, "Free Sara," she said, "I'm thrilled to be home. I have a lot of confidence in a positive outcome. I look at every opportunity—even if it starts out bad—as an education. It's hard to be humble. Everybody in Minnesota has people behind them like this. . . . I'm glad to be from Minnesota considering how things have gone for me."

That month, Sara Jane decided to make her name change legal. All she needed was $132, a referee, and two witnesses to vouch for her. In court documents that were filed before her release on the $1 million bail, her attorneys tried to explain why she changed her name from Kathleen Soliah in the first place: "Her name change was a response to fear of government reprisal for association with SLA members. By the time Sara Jane Olson learned of the pending charges, she was well established in a life away from the turmoil and fear generated by the pursuit of the SLA. Surrender would have meant reopening a chapter in her life she tried to put behind her; this she was unable to do."

She used her real birth date on her name-change application, January 16, 1947. On her marriage and driver's licenses, she had claimed April 25, 1949. She was almost two and a half years older than anyone had thought. She explained the reason for making the name change permanent: "Because I've been Sara Jane Olson privately and professionally the last twenty years. I was married as Sara Jane Olson, and I plan to continue living under that name for the rest of my life."

She walked out of the courthouse with Fred, their twelve-year-old daughter, one of her attorneys, and two friends who served as witnesses. One of the witnesses, Mary Jane Kaluza, joked about adopting the Soliah name, and Sara laughingly responded, "Let's all change our names."

Soon after the name-change proceeding, a lawyer from her neighborhood wrote the St. Paul Ramsey county attorney, asking for her to investigate "violations arising out of her [Sara Jane's] blatant use of a false and fictitious name" at the voting booth, on her driver's license, and on her tax returns. An FBI agent later said that although she broke the law, there were so many other things that she could be prosecuted for that there was no good reason to pursue this complaint. For the time being, that charge would not be pursued. Sara Jane Olson was now her legal name.

When asked by reporters to discuss her pending case, she declined on the advice of her attorneys. However, she did say, "I'm on trial for my life. I think it's a chance to try cases that were never indicted because people who could have been indicted are dead," apparently referring to the SLA members who were killed in the fire, inferring that she was getting blamed for their deeds. Ironically, Sara Jane's arrest and cookbook fundraising had provided her with the public forum she never really achieved as Kathy Soliah—a new stage and a fresh audience for her monologues and her new role "over ground."

In October, the Los Angeles district attorney, Gil Garcetti, outlined almost the entire history of the SLA [in a twenty-six-page brief]. He said, "Olson's role in the attempted Los Angeles bombings reflected the extent of her dedication to the path of terrorism embraced by the SLA 'comrades.'" He continued, "Her active participation in other bombings, planned thefts, and two bank robberies—one in which a mother of four was killed—demonstrates her commitment, along with her co-conspirators, to effect revolutionary changes through terrorist acts against innocent victims."

The prosecutors announced that Patty Hearst Shaw had been ordered to testify at Sara Jane Olson's trial, now scheduled for January 10, 2000. Attorney George Martinez, who had seen Hearst Shaw through her last days in jail and also her commutation by President Jimmy Carter, still represented her. He said his client was not happy about the order to testify. She was seeking a presidential pardon from President Bill Clinton for her bank-robbery conviction. Yet from the prosecution's perspective, a pardon would erase her record as a felon, and presumably give her more credibility when she was called to testify.

Patty Hearst Shaw said that she felt sorry for "Kathy's" daughters—she also had teenage daughters—and she did not want to help with the prosecution to convict Kathy. In her book, Hearst said that she liked Kathy. She had no animosity toward her at all. Still, she didn't want to help Soliah either. "Kathy had had a great twenty-five years as a soccer mom. What about me? I've had to live with this nightmare. Kathy has got a lot of explaining to do."

The next month, Olson's defense attorneys filed to have the 1976 indictment charges dismissed, saying that prosecutors lacked convincing evidence and that they were trying to smear Sara Jane's name. Judge Ideman refused to throw out her indictment, but he granted the defense's request to delay the trial until February 7, 2000, in order to accommodate her attorney's request to analyze explosives, evidence that would be used by the prosecution. In the meantime, the defense had received a witness list from the prosecution that included at least 300 people, including Patty Hearst Shaw, Bill and Emily Harris, Steven Soliah, Michael Bortin, and Wendy Yoshimura.

On December 12, 1999, Sara Jane Olson and her defense fundraising committee arranged a cookbook signing at the May Day Café, a small coffeehouse in South Minneapolis. It was a mild day, for a Minnesota winter, almost like fall, with no wind and no snow. In spite of good weather, and in spite of announcements of the signing in the local papers, there were ample parking places on the street.

Fred hugged their youngest daughter and beamed at Sara Jane, as if this were a "coming out" for her new book, as opposed to a fundraiser for her conspiracy and attempted murder trial defense fund. At the same time, the small, bearded man looked vulnerable and seemed to be uncomfortable in the spotlight. There had been much scrutiny about this private man in the newspapers. Even so, he seemed eternally optimistic about his wife's predicament.

Sara Jane was receptive and approachable; however, her group of supporters surrounded her like the secret service, as if everyone in the room were a potential enemy. Sara Jane smiled graciously as she signed books for the few people who attended. Dressed in pants and an oversized gray sweater, she read excerpts from the introduction of her cookbook to the television cameras and onlookers. She read with a practiced dramatic flair.

Later Sara Jane and her attorneys again requested that her February trial be televised, citing that it was the only way she could get a fair trial. Court TV wanted to air the trial, as did CNN. The prosecutors, Michael Latin and Eleanor Hunter, opposed this request on the grounds that the trial would be dangerous to televise since much of the testimony would cover how to make bombs, dissemble bombs, and how the law enforcement agencies tracked those individuals or groups, such as the SLA terrorists, who planted bombs in the first place. Judge James Ideman who had been assigned to the case, agreed with the prosecutors that divulging this information to the general public would be detrimental to public safety. There would be no cameras in his courtroom.

The New Millennium

The year 2000 did not start out well for Sara Jane Olson. In the middle of January, Stuart Hanlon withdrew from the case, citing family conflicts. This was a blow since Hanlon seemed to be her most loyal defender. In addition to that, money was running out, and it was predicted that a trial could cost as much as $600,000. Fred was working "killer night shifts." He hoped to attend the trial, but he needed to keep working to pay the bills.

In light of the family's financial hardship, Judge Ideman assigned a public defender, Henry Hall, also from California, to replace Hanlon. Hall's former clients included the Night Stalker, Richard Ramirez, and Mikhail Markhasev, the man convicted of killing Ennis Cosby, the son of comedian Bill Cosby. Now, Sara Jane and Fred Peterson would have some financial relief.

Not everyone thought this was fair. The courts were overwhelmed with cases for truly needy people and Sara Jane's defense would take money out of the pot. John Stuart, Minnesota's chief public defender, told a reporter from the *St. Paul Pioneer Press* that the "vast majority of people we represent are unemployed or working at minimum-wage jobs. Many of them are on food stamps or some comparable benefit." He added, "Public defense was created so that everybody would have the opportunity to get equal justice." Stuart acknowledged that Sara Jane's case could cost as much as half a million dollars with an out-of-state trial where evidence and witnesses had to be tracked down.

Olson's attorneys filed a motion in Los Angeles County Superior Court to ask the judge to refund half of her $1 million bail money. The Olson-Petersons had borrowed the maximum against their retirement savings and exhausted all their assets except the equity in their home and cars. Sara Jane complained that the legal fees would bankrupt her family and if her bail could not be reduced, she wanted the California taxpayers to pay for her expert witnesses. She stated, "I can't fight this out-of-control conspiracy case that is funded by unlimited government money."

Minnesota's Rules of Court stated that a defendant with higher income or assets should have a public defender if hiring a private lawyer would cause substantial hardship to the person or family. The courts could consider the defendant responsibilities, such as child support, debts, and the projected cost of the defense. In California, if the judge decided that the defendant could not afford an attorney, the state would provide one as well. This case promised to be high profile, and the costs would be astronomical. Judge Ideman may have assigned her a public defender so that the case would not be delayed again if, for some reason, Jordan, Sara Jane's remaining attorney, decided to pull out.

On the other hand, Judge Ideman also ruled that the SLA history could be admitted as evidence. This was a huge blow to the defense and opened up a whole new problem. Stuart Hanlon, who was no longer on the case, called the judge's decision an "attempt of desperate prosecution." Hanlon was furious. "The indictment against Olson is really clear—a conspiracy to blow up two police cars. That's the case, and I think they've determined that they have no evidence of that and so now they are blackening her name." He added, "More than ninety percent of that trial brief is based on Patty Hearst and her book. All these things are being connected by Patty Hearst."

Despite the fact that Judge Ideman had issued gag orders for the defendant, her attorneys, and all witnesses, Olson gave a press conference in Minneapolis stating, "I'm an ordinary American woman. And that's why it's rather a surprise that I am the target of a determined conspiracy prosecution by the Los Angeles District Attorney's office." She continued, "I have a case pending against me that is frightening in its scope. Anything I say can be taken out of context and used against me. I believe that I am being prosecuted for the last twenty-three years of my life as much as for those that preceded them." She called the case a "witch hunt."

Steve Soliah had something to say as well. As his sister prepared for her trial in Los Angeles, he stayed at his parents' home in Palmdale. Bart Weitzel of the *Antelope Valley Press* visited them at their home. He described Steve as a bit thick around the middle, with a receding hairline and gray hair. Because of the upcoming trial, Steve couldn't comment on the case. Marty heard them talking and yelled from the other room, "Stop calling her Kathy Soliah. Sara Jane Olson has been her name for twenty years," explaining that it was her "stage name." He said, "She's a really good actress."

In February, Olson's defense committee held a rally at Lake Harriet Community Church in South Minneapolis. The night was clear with several inches of fresh snow on the ground. Christmas lights still glistened on the surrounding homes. The church was warm with anticipation. Sara Jane's friends hugged her and Fred as they came in from the cold to offer their support. Posters lined the walls featuring the slogan "Ungagged" in a black circle with a red cross through it like a no-smoking sign.

When asked by a reporter from the *St. Paul Pioneer Press* about Judge Ideman's gag order, Mary Ellen Kaluza, who had cosponsored this event with the Minnesota chapter of the National Lawyers Guild, responded, "We are not under a gag order as friends and supporters of Sara. We wanted to provide historical information and demonstrate how the criminal justice system is used in this country, and how it is abused, and how far the government will go to silence dissidents."

When the Vietnam War ended in the seventies, many activists turned their attention to "political prisoners," a principle introduced by Amnesty International (AI), which had been founded in 1961. AI called for the release of people in many countries who were in prison for expressing their beliefs. It had begun as a prison adoption group through which volunteers would write letters to authorities, seeking humane conditions and release for the "prisoners of conscience."

At this rally, about seventy-five people sat in the front pews, some appearing to be former 1960s activists now in their sixties, with long, gray ponytails, various styles of wool hats, baggy clothes, big boots, and no make-up. Tables in the church basement were filled with nacho dishes, brownies, cookies, and soft drinks. An auction was held with memorabilia donated by Sara Jane's supporters—posters, pictures, Guatemalan fabric, and a flea market of goods to aid the fundraising effort. Piano lessons were offered as well as astrological readings. Of course, the cookbook *Serving Time, America's Most Wanted Recipes* was for sale.

The highlight of the evening was Bernardine Dohrn, who had flown to Minneapolis to be the keynote speaker. Bernardine Dohrn had surfaced from the underground in 1980 along with her husband, Billy Ayers, and their two children. In 1982, she served seven months in jail after she refused to cooperate with a grand jury that was investigating the robbery of a Brink's truck in New York. A guard had been shot and killed during the robbery, and two police officers had been killed at a roadblock.

After her release, she passed the New York bar exam and joined the New York office of a Chicago law firm. But the state bar refused to admit her, because they challenged her commitment to the rule of law. A sixty-three-year-old New York police officer, Lt. Terence McTigue, had spoken against her at a character hearing, calling her a "violent terrorist leader." McTigue had been on a bomb squad and told a reporter from the *Star Tribune* that he had been disfigured in the face and hands and lost an eye and most of his hearing when a bomb planted by Croation terrorists had exploded in New York in 1976 as he and another man tried to remove it from Grand Central Station. The other man had been killed.

At fifty-seven, Bernardine's "chorus-line looks" may have

faded, but she had aged well. Tanned, in fitted jeans and a wool blazer, she took her place on the platform with the other speakers. She was now director of the Children and Family Justice Center at Northwestern University in Chicago. Her husband, Billy Ayers, taught in the College of Education at the University of Illinois at Chicago.

Sitting among a panel of other speakers, she stood to thundering applause and took her place at the microphone behind a podium. Her speech centered on the inequities of the prison system and discrimination against women and other minorities in the prison system. She called criminal justice an "oxymoron" and offered that the United States should immediately stop incarcerating people. Referring to Sara Jane Olson, she said, "Women, I think, take a certain unique brunt of the anger of the establishment and the criminal-justice system—particularly women not caught."

She used herself as a comparison: "How did a good girl from Milwaukee like me with a bachelor's degree, with honors, with a law degree from the University of Chicago, now teaching at a law school, end up on the FBI's 'Ten Most Wanted List,' a long time ago?" She replied to the microphone, "I can't answer that," and then she changed the subject.

Any camaraderie between these two women appeared to be perfunctory. Neither Sara Jane nor Bernardine explained to the audience why she was there or what the connection was between them. Bernardine's agenda was prison reform. She wanted to talk about the inequities in U.S. prisons, as did Sara Jane Olson at her cookbook signings.

Stuart Hanlon, balding, bearded, and wearing wrinkled, khaki-colored pants with a wrinkled, beige shirt and colorful patterned tie, was there to support her. He spoke about media bias and overzealous prosecutors.

A man from an Internet network corporation, who was obviously hostile to Bernardine, Sara Jane, and the entire group of supporters, pointed his tape-recorder's microphone at the panel like an accusation and demanded why Sara Jane should be above the law. The speakers on the panel and most of the audience glared at him for his remarks. One woman in the audience walked up to his pew and asked him to leave. Bernardine challenged him to get up on the stage if he wanted the attention so badly. The group, it seemed, had not expected dissenters among them.

When the speeches were over, Sara Jane stood up at the podium and thanked the audience for their financial assistance. Then in a strong, theatrical voice, she read a story about police misconduct and received a loud ovation. Next, her daughter, who had obviously inherited her mother's talent, sang a smooth lyrical rendition of, "Amazing Grace." She was self-assured, mature, and lovely. The audience thanked her with tears and a standing ovation.

One supporter said Sara Jane was "being railroaded. How much is the government spending our money to do this? She'll be acquitted when it finally comes to trial. Then it'll be all [about] the tons of money spent by the government and her family and friends for nothing."

When Judge Ideman heard about the rally and the fact that Sara Jane had defied his gag order, he was furious. He told Susan Jordan that he wouldn't tolerate such violations, but did nothing other than to enforce the gag order more strictly.

He told a reporter from the *St. Paul Pioneer Press,* "Both Stuart Hanlon and your client state or imply that this is some sort of political prosecution of dissidents left over from the 1970s," he said. "The only issue in this case is a very powerful bomb was placed under a car in front of a crowded restaurant. We are not talking about any prosecution of dissidents. This was a very real crime and whoever is responsible should be brought to justice."

That month, Henry Hall withdrew from Sara Jane's case citing office conflicts. Two defense attorneys were now gone. Judge Ideman then appointed Shawn Chapman to replace Hall. In 1995, Chapman had helped her boss, Attorney Johnnie Cochran Jr., convince a jury that O.J. Simpson was innocent of murdering his wife and her friend. Chapman had been in grade school when the SLA members died in the fire. Now she was a partner in a Beverly Hills law firm on Wilshire Boulevard. On the judge's insistence, she promised that even though it would be difficult to get up to speed, she would be ready for an August trial date.

Shawn Chapman hoped to get Jack Scott, the self-described "Human Switzerland," to testify for the defense. He was fifty-seven now, and lived in Berkeley, where he ran a sports medicine clinic. The defense team wanted to use Scott to discredit Patty Hearst Shaw's testimony. Chapman expected him to say that after plotting with SLA members to arrange her abduction, Hearst became the most zealous member of the SLA. He would claim that Hearst had refused opportunities to leave the group. According to Scott, Hearst had orchestrated her kidnapping as a way to break her wedding plans with Steve Weed without having to admit to her parents that they were right to oppose the relationship.

Jack Scott was now very ill with throat cancer. He and his wife, Micki Scott, had one son and two teenage daughters. Although they lived apart, he had moved into her home in Eugene, Oregon, so that she could care for him while he underwent radiation therapy. Years before, when the *Los Angeles Times* had been writing a profile about members connected to the SLA, he had told the reporter that Kathy Soliah helped him gain access to the SLA because he had wanted to write a book. He said, "It became clear to me that the SLA was my generation gone crazy. . . . This wasn't your normal red-blooded American criminal. This was some kind of weird new criminal."

Jack Scott died on February 6, 2000. Commenting on Scott's death, Bill Harris credited Scott with saving their lives at a time when they were the most hunted fugitives in the nation. "I can't say he stood and took a bullet for me, but he did the next best thing," Harris commented. "Jack wasn't afraid to take a risk. He felt it was important that we not die. And he was a journalist. He wanted the story."

Bill Harris, fifty-six years old, was remarried to a lawyer, and was now the father of two young children who he drove to school every day in his Honda Passport S.U.V. He worked as a private investigator in San Francisco. Emily and he were still close, and his children called her "Aunt Emily." She had altered her name and lived a quiet life as a computer-network designer in Southern California.

Bill said that when he met people who remembered him by name, they were surprised that he was not a big, mean, black man. (Many people assumed, at the time, that most members of the SLA were black.) Or crazy, he added. He told a reporter from the *New York Times* that he had never been manic. The reporter claimed that she liked his smile and the fact that when he made a point, "his hazel eyes would peer over wire-framed glasses, suggesting a simmering intensity behind his laid-back veneer." He explained to her that everyone was interested in how they had changed or hadn't changed. He said, "I'm older, no longer self-destructive, and unwilling to go to jail."

He and Emily had not been in trouble with the law since their release from prison. Sara Jane's upcoming trial was a huge disruption in their lives. Bill said that he believed that her prosecution was not as much about planting the bombs, as it was about the events surrounding the bank robbery in Carmichael and Myrna Opsahl's murder. "They want to get me and Emily," he said. "There are people in government who must feel that Emily and I have not paid enough for the crimes they think we've committed." He added that he had seen cops pick on women with children to pressure them to cooperate, and that was why they were going after Sara Jane. "All she has to do is flip, and it's over," Harris said about the prosecutors' strategy. "But she won't do that, because it's not right and it's not true. And now it's a battle of wills," he said. "Who can hang longest?"

If Sara Jane cried at all, she did it in private. In public, she came out swinging. At book signings and press conferences, there was no sign of fear or remorse, not even for what her family was going through. In fact, she was vitriolic, and the more she spoke out, the more negative press she received. To many, it did not seem appropriate at this junction of her life to be touting prison reform and spurning the Los Angeles Police Department and the FBI.

Twin Cities' residents saw "Jail Kathleen" and "Boom! If It Ticks, You Must Convict Soliah" bumper stickers on fenders all over town. One Minnesotan who had lived in the Bay Area during the SLA's reign of terror remembered it first-hand. Describing himself as a "liberal democrat," Larry Larson told a reporter from the *Star Tribune*: "I find all the Minnesota sympathy for Sara Jane Olson perplexing because these people don't realize the depth of sheer terror people out there felt day in and day out. The Bay Area was literally being held hostage by a small group of terrorists who were hunkering down in armed camps with the most serious of intent. This was not some garden-variety left-wing group. This was probably the most violent social-political group in the history of that eccentric area."

Don Olson (another Olson in the Twin Cities phone book) was a former war protester of the 1970s who had served twenty months of a five-year sentence for breaking into draft board offices, "Interfering with the Selective Service," in Minnesota. He told the *Star Tribune:* "living underground was common in those days. Everybody knew people who were hiding from the military or the government. Looking over your shoulder," he added, "was a tough way to live." At fifty-six, he was an alternative radio show host, book distributor, and he helped to sell Sara Jane's cookbook for her defense fund. He supported nonviolence and believed that whatever Sara Jane did twenty-three years ago should be wiped out by the exemplary life she had lived since. "She told me that she has never even met Patty Hearst," he said.

Sara and Serra

In April, Sara Jane headed back to Palmdale for a cookbook sign-ing at St. Stephen's Lutheran Church. She became reacquainted with people she had not seen in thirty years—people who had known her as Kathy Soliah, a top student and the Palmdale High spirit champ. In the Sunday school room of the church, she told a reporter from the *Antelope Valley Press*, "This place has changed so much I don't recognize it. I don't even think I could find my way around."

Sitting in a folding chair, she answered to the name "Kathy" as she signed copies of her cookbook. Elsie sat with her and reintro-duced her to former teachers and old family friends. She said that she could barely remember her childhood. "My life is so different now, and I've changed so much. I don't really remember how I felt then, and it doesn't really matter. All that matters is where it is now. That's sort of fatalistic, but it's also realistic, too," she said.

Reality hit the next month when Sara Jane lost her third de-fense lawyer, Susan Jordan. Jordan told Judge Ideman that she had an ailment known as trigeminal neuralgia, which causes ex-treme pain in the face. She wouldn't be able to hold up to a long trial, she said. She had a backup plan, however. Another attorney, Tony Serra, had agreed to take her place and work with Shawn Chapman for Sara Jane's defense. Serra would be a colorful addi-tion to the team. He had a gold tooth, a gray ponytail, and a ward-robe of secondhand suits. Serra described himself as a "healer."

In a 1993 interview in the *Sacramento Bee*, Serra was reported to have said: "I open cages, I heal, I give freedom." He had repre-

sented drug dealers, Hell's Angels, and Black Panthers. He helped
Stuart Hanlon free former SLA leader Russell Little in the Marcus Foster murder case. One prosecutor who had lost a Black
Panther murder case to Serra in 1979 said, "His pony tail, the long
hair, the old suits, that's what everybody focuses on at first. But
eventually the appearance disappears as a factor. Tony Serra is a
very effective trial attorney—smart, charming, entertaining, impassioned, likeable, and delightful to listen to. He uses his voice
like a musical instrument."

After graduating from the University of California at Berkeley's Boalt School of Law, Serra started his law career in 1962 as a
deputy district attorney for Alameda County. He lasted one year
as a prosecutor. "Imagine spending a career, thirty or forty years,
putting your fellow human beings in cages," Serra said. "It's not
wholesome. It's not mentally healthy. Prosecutors become sado-
masochistic. They become numb. They withdraw. And most of
them eventually develop a physical manifestation of their illness.
They get twitches, or their eyes start to cross. Career prosecutors
are a mental disease category."

Serra once convinced a jury to acquit a member of a seventies
radical group on post-office bombing charges, arguing that his
client had First Amendment protections because he was acting as
a reporter issuing the group's communiqués. He was also an outspoken advocate of marijuana use, saying he works harder than
any lawyer but gets inspired by "cannabis consultation." In the
1989 movie, *True Believer*, actor James Woods portrayed Serra as
a pot-smoking, counterculture idealist.

Serra was a sixties creation. He enjoyed sitting in front of a
fireplace smoking hash. "I do that as much as I can," he said. For
hobbies, he liked taking long walks and bicycle rides around his
neighborhood and reading English authors. "The greatest influence on my life was the ideology of the sixties: anti-materialism,
brotherhood, nonracism, love. Those are the things I believe in."

He and his ex-wife named their children Shelter, Ivory, Chime,
Wonder, and Lilac. He stressed that money was not important to

him. If that was true, it was lucky that one of his brothers, a world-famous sculptor, made enough money to put Serra's children through school. Serra hoped that they would get good grades.

Stuart Hanlon said, "Tony Serra is not going to back down from anybody, including the judge if he thinks the judge is wrong. Judge Ideman appears to always think he's right, so I think there's going to be some tense times in court. He is the most unique, and probably the best trial lawyer in the United States. There's nobody like him."

Sara Jane's friend Mary Sutton told a reporter from the *Associated Press* that she was impressed with Serra as well. She said, "It's terribly unfortunate for Susan, but Sara once again is fortunate to have someone else step up to the plate for her. He's very dynamic, a true humanist," she said.

According the *St. Paul Pioneer Press*, Susan Jordan commented that since the judge had decided to allow the history of the SLA as evidence, the case had become overwhelmingly complicated. According to her, the amount of evidence that had been collected exceeded that of the Oklahoma City bombing trial of Timothy McVeigh. Serra needed more time to prepare. In favor of the new defense team, Judge Ideman delayed the trial once again until January 8, 2001.

Each delay meant that much more time before Sara Jane's supporters would get their bail money returned. Andy Dawkins claimed that one family had borrowed money from their child's college fund and now they were getting worried. Mary Sutton assured members of the press that bail refunds were not a problem.

"It's unfortunate," she said, "for the people that donated, but if they're paying attention, they have to realize this is all completely out of Sara's control and hopefully people will be able to manage." According to her, the delays were the fault of the Los Angeles District Attorney's office for expanding the scope of the trial to include the history of the SLA. Another supporter said that this was the reason attorneys were being driven away.

In May, Patricia Hearst Shaw, angry at having to relive her kidnapping and to once again be in the media spotlight, defied Judge Ideman's gag order and interviewed with a reporter from *Talk* magazine. "I'm at the end of my rope," she said. "I keep trying to forget these people. And they keep dragging me back into it! It's really not Kathy Soliah's trial. It has turned into my trial. And I'm not going to play dead anymore." Hearst added that she did not feel sorry for Sara Jane Olson and that "she was just getting a good dollop of it." There were consequences to actions, and she admonished Sara Jane for not going to the police right away. She added that she wished they'd never found Sara Jane Olson.

Olson's supporters were angry that she was being compared to Hearst. One of her most ardent allies, Macalester College Professor Peter Rachleff, said, "Comparing Sara to Patty Hearst because they're middle-aged mothers raising kids shows how flat the media tries to make issues. They are from the same generation, but one is a multimillionaire who built a life out of privilege to feather her own nest while Sara came from a lower middle-class family, and she and Fred have worked for everything they have."

The defense lawyers were furious with Hearst Shaw and also with Los Angeles District Attorney Gil Garcetti who had also talked to the press and defied the gag order. They wanted both of them to be fined. The defense team seemed to have forgotten the "ungagged" rally with Bernardine Dohrn. The situation was getting out of control. Judge Ideman accepted Garcetti's excuse that when he had spoken to the press, he had forgotten that there was a gag order. The judge denounced Hearst Shaw but stated that he was powerless to punish her because she lived in another state. In what seemed like complete frustration, he lifted the gag order. Now all parties were unleashed. Olson, who stated that she had nothing to say anyway ("That's why I have lawyers."), went on the radio talk-show circuit.

In a Los Angeles radio interview, she said, "I was one of . . .

perhaps tens of thousands of people who felt the same way, and acted the same way. I never underwent any kind of redemption. . . . I never really changed. I just got older."

At a fundraiser at the Women's Center in San Francisco's Mission District, she slammed Hearst Shaw and the Los Angeles Police Department. According to her, Patty's version of events had gone unchallenged for more than thirty years. Referring to *Every Secret Thing*, Olson told a group of supporters, "Someone did a little writing about a group called the Symbionese Liberation Army and her version has been enshrined as the undisputed truth . . . until my trial," where she said that she would dispute Patty's testimony. "How much was self-serving, and how much was melodrama?" she asked during an hour-long speech. "Most of the SLA members were killed in 1974. Others have gone on to lead quiet and productive lives. I guess the LAPD tries to write its version of the SLA's history through Ms. Hearst's crystal-clear memory. She should remember that she was a member of the SLA."

She added, "I don't think she would come to court if she wasn't forced to. This isn't a fight between Patricia Hearst and me. We're both pawns. We're both being used for somebody else's ends." To a *Star Tribune* reporter she stated that the trial would be a credibility contest between her and Patty Hearst Shaw.

Another fundraiser, billed "Ungagged," was held a year after Sara Jane's arrest, again at the Lake Harriet Community Church in Minneapolis. It was a hot, humid afternoon in July, and the church basement was stifling and the lights were kept off to keep the room cooler. A few dozen people had paid about fifteen dollars to attend. Television crews were there, laying cords on the floor, pinning them down with electrical tape, and searching for working outlets. Volunteers served refreshments as Sara Jane, wearing black capri pants, a sleeveless, gauzy shirt, and gray clogs, leaned against a wall near the kitchen. Her daughter prepared to play the piano and sing: "I call this one, 'A Tribute to Gil Garcetti,'" she said. She sat down at the piano, opened a song-book, and played a tune from "The Wizard of Oz" for the Los Angeles District Attorney:

If I could while away the hours, conferring with the flowers, consulting with the rain, then my head I'd be scratchin, while my thoughts were busy hatchin, If I Only Had a Brain. The crowd in the church basement laughed as Fred danced to the music, and the party went on as if life in prison were not even an option. Sara stepped up to the microphone:

"I am Sara Jane Olson," she said in a determined voice. "And I am ungagged." She then launched into the injustice of American prisons. "I'm walking dread-first into the American justice system. But there are people far worse off, those lacking support and publicity in the American gulag we call prisons." She scanned the crowd with her piercing, small blue eyes, and paused at the perfect moments to stress her points. Rachael Hanel from an Internet news source described Sara Jane's speech as "well-rehearsed, eloquent, and passionate." The television lights did not seem to intimidate her. "I'm not fighting the battle just for myself anymore. It's to drain the American prison system of the human blood that feeds it, nourishes it, and keeps it growing every day."

She called the conspiracy charge "a piece of magic," dreamed up by the Los Angeles police prosecutors. "It's a struggle enough against an actual case, but when they throw in ghosts, well. . . . It's a shame to have the ability to ruin someone's life, simply because you can." She said that she was facing this conspiracy charge solely for political reasons. "Why this? Why now, twenty-five years later?"

Toward the end of the year, in another discovery motion, Chapman wanted the confidential background information on James Bryan, John Hall, and Arleigh McCree. Information on these officers was supposedly sealed, not public information. One month after Shawn Chapman's request, Bryan's and Hall's names, phone numbers, and addresses appeared on Sara Jane's website. Officer Hall stated that his family has "lived in fear since that information became public. My wife, my children, my grandchildren live in terror," he told the court. "My family is in fear for their lives; I am in fear for them, and I am angry."

The defense team denied knowing that the information was "sealed" until after it had been posted. Chapman said it was "an accident." Judge Ideman admonished Sara Jane, saying, "I would say to the defendant that this is a dangerous game," warning her that her case had been "gravely harmed" by the disclosure of the officers' addresses. He called this act "witness intimidation." Now not only would cameras be banned from the courtroom, but he also threatened to impanel an anonymous jury. "This is the cost of misconduct. When you violate the law and attempt to intimidate witnesses, consequences will flow. I think you've damaged your client."

James Bryan sued Sara Jane. He had suffered emotional distress and had taken a stress-related leave after the bomb was discovered, saying that he required medical treatment and had to leave the force because he was so severely disabled "he couldn't function as a police officer." He remembered seeing Kathy Soliah outside the IHOP restaurant where the bomb was found and he said that she had a look of "absolute contempt and hatred" on her face. The problem was, he had not put that in his report at the time, nor had he mentioned that to the grand jury in 1976. Judge Ideman cautioned the prosecution that if they called Bryan as a witness, they could be opening up another can of worms because the defense could bring out his entire mental health history.

The defense asked for yet another delay due to the discovery of "mounds of new SLA evidence." Judge Ideman replied, "There will be no more delays. Ready or not, we will start January 8, 2000, unless any of the parties are in trial, in the hospital, or in jail." Shawn Chapman was not deterred by the judge's declaration that his courtroom was a camera-free zone, and continued to lobby to have the trial televised, which seemed to contradict Sara Jane's comments to a Los Angeles reporter: "I'm thinking about where I'm going to be in fifteen years. I'm not interested in any celebrity status, and media is to me a distraction. I don't want anyone to know anything about me."

On this note, she embarked on a book tour up and down the California coast. The events were marked by low attendance, but her mission was not to discuss her recipes. Like Bernardine Dohrn, and Sara Jane Moore as well, she continued her criticisms of the American prison system.

In San Diego, she called for a stronger grassroots movement to slow the growth of the prison industry. At the California Coalition for Women Prisoners, she recalled hearing stories of women being sexually assaulted by guards.

"Conditions for women in U.S. prisons are condemned by Amnesty International who cited sex abuse, lack of proper medical treatment. A new civil rights movement is needed in this state and country . . . to halt and roll back the high imprisonment rates. Perhaps we can inject some humanity in the prison system where rehabilitation and redemption and not recidivism are our goals," she said. She compared government oppression in the United States to that of South Africa, citing racial profiling and the growth of the prison industry while funding for education lags behind. When someone in the audience asked her if she knew who tipped off *America's Most Wanted*, she answered, "I quit worrying about that because it really doesn't matter anymore."

In December, the defense made yet another motion to delay Sara Jane's trial. This strategy had worked for Emily and Bill Harris back in 1976, and perhaps it would work for Sara Jane as well. The reasons for the motion included the withdrawals of Stuart Hanlon, Henry Hall, and Susan Jordan. They stated that Tony Serra was engaged in various trials throughout the state and unable to devote much time to Sara Jane's case. Shawn Chapman pleaded that she was "virtually alone."

This time, the motion did not have to be answered. In December, Judge Ideman was transferred to another jurisdiction. The defense team—what remained of them—was thrilled. In their minds, Judge Ideman had been partial to the prosecution. In fact, they accused him of working for the prosecution. The new judge assigned to the case would be Larry Fidler, the same judge who had ordered the $1 million bail. He would be in appeals court for the first three months of the year. The trial was rescheduled for April 30, 2001.

Randolph and Catherine had divorced in 1982, seven years after Patty's capture. Though Randolph married two more times, a good friend said that Hearst was never the same after Patty's kidnapping.

In December 1999 Catherine Hearst died of a stroke. One year later, in December 2000, Randolph Hearst died at a New York City hospital after a massive stroke. He was eighty-five.

Act Six

> *"The consequences of our actions take hold of us quite indifferent to our claim that meanwhile we have 'improved.'"*
>
> ✐ NEITZSCHE, *BEYOND GOOD AND EVIL* (1886), 179, TR. WALTER KAUFMANN

Turning Point

On January 20, 2001, one day before President Bill Clinton left office, he pardoned forty-six-year-old Patty Hearst Shaw for her role in the Hibernia Bank robbery. Her attorney, George Martinez, expressed Hearst Shaw's profound gratitude to the president. He added that although her parents had both died, the pardon would have been extremely meaningful to them.

A presidential pardon differs from a "commutation of sentence," which she had received in 1979, twenty-two years earlier. A presidential pardon is the official forgiveness for a crime. It would reinstate certain civil rights, such as to vote or to run for election.

Hearst Shaw had enjoyed a twenty-year marriage to Bernard Shaw, who had been her bodyguard after her release from prison. She had also written her autobiography, *Every Secret Thing*, with Alvin Moscow, which became a 1988 movie titled *Patty Hearst*, starring Natasha Richardson. She'd performed charitable work and appeared in several movies directed by John Waters, as well as in several television sitcoms.

Stuart Hanlon was not pleased with Clinton's pardon. "I think it's outrageous that the rich white people should get pardoned and the nonwhite people who don't have power do not get pardoned," he stated on Sara Jane's defense website. "At a time like this, when Patty Hearst's credibility is at issue in this trial, this is just not fair. She has admitted being involved in a bank robbery. She pleaded guilty to shooting at the sporting goods store, and her family paid off victims of a murder" (referring to a settlement that the Hearsts reportedly paid to the Opsahls). He continued, "And she gets a pardon. It's a really sad comment on justice."

Sara Jane posted this commentary on her website in regard to Hearst Shaw's pardon: "President Clinton's pardon of Patricia Hearst Shaw is an indication to the Los Angeles County District Attorney that he should cease my prosecution. It is ironic that Ms. Hearst-Shaw, in the year of her pardon, will face the most intense cross-examination about her SLA escapades since her original court entanglements over a quarter of a century ago.

"Former President Carter commuted her sentence in the late 1970s and now President Clinton, at the urging of Carter, has laid Ms. Hearst Shaw's saga to rest. I do not believe this pardon should be construed as a gauge of her story's truthfulness. Ms. Hearst Shaw's fiction was dictated by the political/social philosophy of her family in the 1970s who were, after all, paying for her defense.

"While I do not begrudge her the pardon, it is unfortunate that Clinton did not pardon Leonard Peltier (convicted of killing two FBI agents). Peltier has, and has had for years, both national and international backing from people with influential social and political status, as well as support from many ordinary people like myself.

"Money, access to power, and friends in high places have, once again as with her earlier commutation, influenced Presidential prerogative in favor of Patricia Hearst. I think my prosecution should stop now. Just because Clinton pardoned Patty Hearst does not mean that her story is true."

Up until now, Sara Jane and her defense team may have thought that all of the trial delays were in their favor. (Those same tactics had certainly worked for the Harrises back in the seventies.) Things were different now. The prosecutors wanted to solve Myrna Opsahl's murder. Her family was pressing the issue. At first, the Sacramento authorities did not want to pursue the case, claiming that they could not win for lack of evidence. The FBI had given away some crucial evidence such as ski masks and wigs, but they had kept a number of SLA weapons and many boxes of ammunition. Each new trial delay gave the investigators more time to uncover additional evidence. With advances in metallurgical science, detectives were able to get a close match between the pellets taken from Myrna Opsahl's body and the pellets found in shotgun shells seized by federal agents when SLA members were arrested. The prosecutors shared new evidence with the Sacramento authorities.

The FBI, spurred by all the press coverage, decided to join forces with investigators from the Sacramento County sheriff's office to see whether there was a way to prosecute the robbers of the Crocker National Bank in federal court. If the state wouldn't go after them, the federal government would. Steven Soliah had already been acquitted of the bank robbery, so it was unlikely that they would go after him. Patty Hearst would probably be given immunity from prosecution if she testified against the other perpetrators.

Anyone involved with the robbery could possibly face charges in connection with Myrna Opsahl's death. All they needed was someone to "flip," as Bill Harris had put it. Jon Opsahl said, "I think they are all equally guilty of murdering my mom."

Ever since Olson had been arrested, Jon Opsahl had been looking for the closure he and his family had never found. It was reported in the *St. Paul Pioneer Press* that Opsahl said, "My mom was a lot like Kathleen Soliah is pretending to be now. She volunteered in the community. She was a doctor's wife. She had four kids." He added that at the time his mother was murdered, he had been told that there was no evidence to charge anyone. "I accepted that," he said. "I lived with it. That's the way things were."

Of Olson, he said, "I thought she might want to set things right, express remorse. Instead, she puts on her soccer mom and amateur gourmet act and hides behind a bunch of stonewalling lawyers, showing no remorse."

Prosecutors stated that Patty Hearst Shaw would be a key witness against Sara Jane Olson in the newly reopened bank-robbery case. At a hearing in February, Sara Jane expressed outrage about these latest developments. Shaken, with tears in her eyes, she lashed out at prosecutors, saying that they, along with the Los Angeles Police Department, had politicized her case: "They're trying to take away my freedom forever and destroy me and destroy my family." As to the charges against her, she said, "I was not in Los Angeles. I did not place those bombs under those cars. I was not in the Carmichael Bank in Sacramento [sic]. I am innocent." She also said that her family had been ruined financially.

That month, Sara Jane Olson sat down for an interview on ABC's *Prime Time Thursday* with Tavis Smiley of Black Entertainment Television. Sara Jane looked strong and handled herself well, again denying that she had any involvement with the SLA.

However, Mary Ellen Kaluza, Sara Jane's friend and witness to her name change, was not pleased with ABC's interview. She posted her comments on the defense website: "For those of you who missed 'Prime Time' on ABC, you missed a stunning piece of biased journalism," she wrote. She was angry that the show viewed the fire where the SLA died, and aired Tom King's account of the incident. She was furious that Officer John Bryan was interviewed, when in her mind, he had no credibility. She was angry that Jon Opsahl got airtime, and accused him of omitting Patty Hearst's name because her family had contributed to the cost of a wrongful death suit to his family after his mother's murder. She said that Sara Jane's attorneys and members of her defense committee had all been interviewed, but ABC had cut them from the broadcast.

Sara Jane also responded on her defense website: "At my home, in Minnesota, as I go about my daily life, it is easy to forget that I am being transformed by the Los Angeles District Attorney's Office into a model of Anti-Americanism and thuggery. That office's representatives schlep up and down the state, relentlessly prodding a D.A. in Sacramento, tinting my reputation with a slight stain of pale yellow because [the district attorney] hasn't indicted me. There are sudden zapped reports of fingerprints miraculously discovered in a vehicle, or was it a bank? Or on a wall? Down the street? Or anywhere? EVERYWHERE!! As my husband says, it doesn't matter if it's true. The subliminal message gets through—"Oh yeah, she MUST be guilty of something"—and, really, that's the important message. It taints a jury pool with an all-pervasive notion of guilt."

After the segment was broadcast in March, Sara Jane was interviewed for the 10:00 P.M. news on local stations in Minneapolis and St. Paul. The composure she had shown in the previous interview was gone. Until now, she had seemed to love the attention, being featured in major newspapers nationwide, on radio and TV talk shows, and appearing on the covers of magazines. She'd even been included in *People* magazine's "Most Intriguing People" section—she was finally the star she had dreamed about becoming when she was in high school. But this interview by a local station following the viewing of ABC's *Primetime Thursday* was a turning point.

She answered reporters' questions with anger—some viewers said that they could imagine her placing bombs under police cars after that interview. Laurie Levinson, a professor of law and director of the Center for Ethical Advocacy at Loyola Law School, told Bob von Sternberg from the *Star Tribune*: "It sounds like she's losing her cool, sounding like the radical the prosecutor says she is." Even Olson's loyal friend Andy Dawkins told the same reporter, "I don't know how well she's handled the public relations of this, because she's looked to be an angry person, instead of a sympathetic person."

Indeed, sympathizers who had spent almost two years wondering why Los Angeles prosecutors would bother going after a "soccer mom" with an impeccable reputation now stepped back and began to wonder if there were more to the charges than they had assumed.

The circumstances of Sara Jane's upcoming trial changed almost daily. Judge Fidler decided to allow cameras in his courtroom, saying that the public interest in viewing and studying the instant proceedings outweighed any adverse effect that may result due to the coverage.

Tony Serra had a reputation for failing to keep court dates, and he failed to show up for three hearings regarding his newest client, pleading that he was busy with other cases. When the prosecutors complained about his behavior, he called it a personal attack on his character and availability: "I am aggrieved by it," he told Linda Deutsch of the *Associated Press*. He blamed the prosecutors for all of the delays, saying that they had been hiding discovery material. Judge Fidler ordered Serra to come to court and tell him why he should not be removed from the case. Serra promised him that he would be available and ready for the trial. He also pleaded with the judge not to "let them [the prosecution] turn the trial into a circus." He said, that "I relish the chance to go after Patty Hearst's credibility. We're going to show that Patty Hearst speaks with false tongue and bears false witness."

Law experts thought that the timing of the trial was fortuitous for Sara Jane Olson because police credibility in Los Angeles had been undercut by cases in which the LAPD had exaggerated, lied, or planted evidence. People did not trust them. Ron Rosenbaum, a lawyer who had followed the case, said that the whole thing was nuts and that nobody would have heard of the case had it not been for Patty Hearst. He said that Sara Jane's supporters raised the profile by making her a cause célèbre and attempting to put the FBI and LAPD on trial. "They forced the government to make it a much bigger case than it ever needed to be," he said. Sara Jane's supporters said that they needed to keep the events in the news in order to raise consciousness so that people would contribute to the defense fund.

In hopes of finding Jim Kilgore, the FBI offered a $20,000 re-
ward to anyone with information on him. The FBI agent in
charge of Kilgore's case unveiled a bust created by renowned
forensic sculptor Frank Bender of Philadelphia, depicting what a
fifty-three-year-old, gray-haired Kilgore might look like. "He
could very well be somebody's neighbor, a productive member of
the community," Bender said. At this point, the authorities knew
only that Kilgore was a sports fanatic and had been traced to
Seattle about the same time that Sara Jane was there acting under
the name of Nancy Bennett. They thought that he probably lived
in America and had worked as a house painter and a cook.

In April, before the trial was to begin, Trygve Opsahl, Myrna's
husband, gave an interview to Kermit Pattison for the *St. Paul Pioneer Press*, remembering the day his wife was murdered. He and
four members of his family drove through the Sacramento area,
visiting sites connected to the crime. The Crocker National Bank
was now a Presbyterian church. "The front door is right there,"
he said. "That's where they came in."

Describing her murder, the seventy-five-year-old man raised
his wrinkled hands and put his forefingers and thumbs together
in a grapefruit-size circle. "She had a hole about this big in the
left flank," he said. And then he recalled the frantic ride from the
bank to the hospital and back again. When he finally reached her,
he remembered, "No pulse. Dilated pupils," ticking off details in
his native Norwegian accent. . . . "maybe an occasional blip on the
EKG machine, but that was about it."

A New Kind of Terrorist

By now, the prosecution had an estimated 30,000 pages of evidence and 25,000 items. The trial was expected to last at least six months. Sara Jane's defense bill to California taxpayers had already exceeded $500,000. No one knew what the prosecution had spent, but estimates were at least $1,500,000. The trial hadn't even started yet. A reporter for the *St. Paul Pioneer Press* wrote, "Olson finds herself rocked by multiple aftershocks of two bombs disarmed more than a quarter-century ago. A case that took decades in coming may take years to resolve."

Just when it looked as though this last trial date was locked in and Court TV would air the trial, another snag occurred. Tony Serra and Shawn Chapman were arraigned on misdemeanor offenses as a result of the November website postings of the names and addresses of the police officers, the intended victims of the car bombs. Now Sara Jane's attorneys might be defendants in their own trial. Serra hired Hanlon to represent him and Chapman hired Johnnie Cochran, who she had assisted on the O. J. Simpson case. Serra told a reporter from the *Los Angeles Times* that they were "prodded into a position where there's a conflict of interest between us and our client." Serra entered an "innocent" plea, but Chapman did not enter a plea because a previous judge had already determined that she was not responsible for posting the information. Both attorneys claimed that this was a ploy by the prosecution to separate them from Sara Jane's case. They said that both prosecutors should be removed from the case because they could be called as potential witnesses as well as their client

Sara Jane Olson and Judge Ideman. Serra and Chapman now stated that they wanted out as well. (Two months later, charges against both attorneys would be dropped. Serra, who blamed postings on his secretary, agreed to pay $5,000 to the Police Memorial Foundation, which supports widows and children of slain police officers.)

The defense asked that the trial be delayed until September 2001 because of all the new evidence. Judge Fidler denied their request. Tony Serra said that they requested the delay, "Not because we fear the evidence. We need the resources and time to absorb the material the prosecution has dumped on us. . . . This is trial by ambush and we're peeved," he said. He added that the defense was handicapped by expenses that included four attorneys, two paralegals, three private investigators, and expert witnesses. Fidler said that Sara Jane was not entitled to the same level of defense as O. J. Simpson because he had paid his own bills. "We're not cutting Ms. Olson off," Fidler said, but "you are not entitled to a dream team."

According to Sara Jane's lawyers, the Los Angeles Police Department harbored a twenty-five-year grudge against the SLA. They proclaimed that their client was a political prisoner who was being persecuted for her humanitarian, left-wing ideals. Her supporters compared Sara Jane to Mumia Abu-Jamal, who was convicted of killing a police officer, and Leonard Peltier. According to them, these two men were political victims and had been denied fair trials, and they feared that the same thing would happen to Sara Jane. Shawn Chapman expressed concern over the people that Olson aligned herself with politically.

If there were a trial, the public would go back to the sixties and the jury would see that Sara Jane Olson had supported civil rights. Tony Serra said, "The Olson case is the last criminal trial of the sixties." As Laurie Levenson, the Loyola Law School professor, told the *Los Angeles Times*, it was to be the case where Serra would finally prove that America's capitalist legal system is flawed and that the alleged evil of SLA radicals was minor compared to law enforcement's abuse of power.

In May, the appeals court granted a trial delay for a fifth time so that the defense team could prepare themselves. The new trial date was scheduled for September 4, 2001. Fred said that the news was "excellent" and now his wife would have a better chance of getting a fair trial.

The prosecutors tried to get the delay reversed, but to no avail. However, Judge Fidler ruled that they would be able to take testimony from three women—eyewitnesses from the Carmichael bank robbery—who were in their eighties and not well. They might be too ill or they could die before the September trial date.

On May 10, the *Chicago Tribune* reported that the prosecution possessed correspondence, allegedly in Sara Jane's handwriting, which tied her to fuses purchased two weeks before the pipe bombs were discovered underneath the Los Angeles police cars. According to transcripts made by attorneys during a discussion in Judge Fidler's chambers in March, the FBI had found the return address on a package of fuses leading them to an Ohio company that manufactured them. Agents from the FBI had gone to the factory and obtained the original letter ordering the fuses, and concluded that the handwriting in the letter matched Sara Jane Olson's handwriting.

Stuart Hanlon said that the defense would have to change their strategy in light of this new evidence. They would have to fight any admission of handwriting evidence at the trial. Hanlon also admitted that the defense team had recently learned that in 1975, the FBI had been led to a post office box after its search of the SLA house in San Francisco. In the box, agents had found 200 feet of fuse, which could be used for bombs. The prosecution had the letter ordering the fuses and the FBI had the fuses. It didn't look good for Sara Jane.

Sara Jane spoke at another gathering at the May Day Café in Minneapolis. This event was a very different presentation from her cookbook signing in December 1999, when she had read from her introduction and happily signed books for her supporters. Although she had not been contrite at that event, she had been softer and calmer. Now, two years after her arrest, she railed against all the authorities. She accused police, prosecutors, witnesses, and judges of framing her with "mysterious evidence." She said, "Perhaps the fact that some persons have even questioned police tactics in a massacre [of the SLA members] in 1974—six people barbecued and a community terrorized—is enough of an incentive for an institution to think it needs to set the record straight," she said. "Throw in a couple of young, ambitious D.A.'s and the shadowy but always helpful FBI and, voila! A case of mammoth proportions has evolved. And it's being done over my very-alive body." She said that she was never anything more than a sympathizer with the SLA and that she never tried to kill anyone. Those who called her a "criminal," she said were "liars."

To some, this rhetoric did not seem appropriate considering the nature of the charges against her. Those who had sympathized with Sara Jane when she had been first arrested mused that perhaps she was right when she had reiterated that she was the same person now that she had always been. Friends from her years of growing up in Palmdale said that she had been a promising actress who could step outside her own skin with ease and become someone else. Perhaps the stress of her predicament was causing her roles to cross.

In August, Sara Jane's trial was rescheduled, once again for September 24, but that date was short-lived. Shawn Chapman pleaded a health problem—a non–life-threatening issue that she would deal with in a "few weeks." Judge Fidler postponed the trial until October 15, 2000.

Unfortunately for Sara Jane, this last delay proved to be one too many. Sara Jane and her good friend Mary Sutton had moved to Southern California, where they planned to stay for the duration of the trial. Sutton was going to organize people to attend the trial and oversee demonstrations.

The defense team had planned to elect a jury dominated by inner-city African-American women who they thought would acquit Sara Jane because they despised the LAPD, which had been plagued by corruption and race scandals. Sara Jane told a reporter from *The San Francisco Weekly*: "We are all inter-connected, but not in control of our destiny."

Those words were proven true on September 11, 2001, when radical fundamental Islamic terrorists hijacked four airplanes and turned them into flying bombs, two of them crashing into the Twin World Trade Towers in New York City. Another plane crashed into the Pentagon in Washington, D.C. In the fourth plane, passengers overtook the terrorist hijackers and brought the plane down in a field in Pennsylvania. Over 3,000 civilians were killed on that day. America was at war.

Suddenly, "terrorist" was a buzzword, a sound byte, a person or a group to be hated and feared. The Symbionese Liberation Army had been a terrorist group. Sara Jane was an alleged con-spirator in terrorist bombings. Her carefully choreographed legal battle, the seven trial delays over the past two and one-half years, and her attorneys' posturing had suddenly backfired. In hindsight, perhaps she should have taken the plea agreement was offered long before she'd ever been arrested. Stuart Hanlon said, now, that the Los Angeles District Attorney had promised back then that if Sara Jane cooperated, they would have backed off. Instead, she had made the decision to take her chances with a jury.

On September 17, her defense fund committee issued this statement on her website: "Sara Jane Olson and the Sara Jane Olson Defense Fund Committee abhor the violence and destruc-tion that took place on September 11. Our hearts go out to the victims and their families. We sincerely hope that the answer to this disaster will not involve further violence against innocent people."

Stuart Hanlon told a reporter for the *San Francisco Weekly*: "The catastrophe has affected my own view of the world. I, myself, would have been the best possible juror for Sara—but I cannot get those images of the World Trade Center out of my head."

On September 11, Americans saw hundreds of firefighters and police sacrifice their lives in the line of duty. Like the O.J. Simpson strategy to play the "race card," Sara Jane's defense strategy had been to put the LAPD on trial. That didn't look like such a good idea now. Police officers were heroes. The horrible tragedy on September 11 had created a new wave of patriotism, and it was hard for Olson's defense to imagine that any juror would want to hear about police corruption. Arthur H. Patterson, a jury selection consultant with DecisionQuest, commented, "When your country is being attacked, it's not time to attack your government. People don't want to hear that."

Sara Jane's lawyers asked for yet another trial delay. Shawn Chapman said, "In light of these concerns [not possible to get a fair trial], and because we believe that the passage of time and the diversions created by the holiday season will lessen the impact of the events of September 11, 2001, we are respectfully requesting that jury selection begin on January 3, 2002." Stuart Hanlon said, "We got serious after September 11."

Prosecutors argued, "There is no valid reason that the turn of international events should cause the judicial system, or any single case within it, to come to a grinding halt." Judge Fidler agreed with them.

The trial would go on as scheduled. He said that there was no proof that prospective jurors might be biased against Olson because of the terrorist attacks. It would be up to the lawyers to question potential jurors about their views. After he made his decision, Sara Jane, wearing a shiny silver suit and a hot pink shirt, told Harriet Ryan from Court TV, "I'm prepared for it now."

"Kathy's Comedy Courthouse"
Patty Hearst

On Halloween Sara Jane Olson, who had declared the case against her a "witch hunt in the guise of a conspiracy case," decided to plead guilty. She shocked not only her supporters, but her family as well. After all of her legal maneuvering, her public bravado and indignation for being wrongly accused, no one expected a guilty plea.

Judge Fidler asked her a series of questions to ensure that she understood what she was doing and that she was doing it of her own free will. The *New York Times* reported that she appeared off-handed, chatting amiably with her lawyers even while being addressed by the judge or the prosecutors. When she was asked a routine question about whether she had taken drugs or alcohol, which could have clouded her judgment, she quipped, "I wish."

By pleading guilty, she waved the right to appeal her plea, but reserved the right to challenge sentencing decisions of the state parole board. Her attorneys acknowledged that the board could extend her sentence if it deemed her a danger to society. The prosecutor, Eleanor Hunter, asked her whether she was "pleading guilty, freely and voluntarily." Sara Jane replied, "I am."

In a one-hour meeting in Judge Fidler's chambers, Sara Jane's attorneys advised her that she would probably have to serve about five years in prison. The prosecution recommended that she would be allowed to serve her time at Shakopee prison in Minnesota so that she be able to see her family. With that in mind, Judge Fidler warned her that there was no guarantee, and she could still be sentenced to life behind bars. She was informed that she would have to appear in court on December 7 for sentencing and her prison term would begin on January 18, 2002.

Sara Jane's plea confused and angered her family and her supporters. Fred, Elsie, and her tearful, nineteen-year-old daughter sat in the front row of the courtroom as Sara Jane entered her guilty plea. Then Sara Jane hugged her own mother, Elsie.

Peter Rachleff, a history professor at Macalester College in St. Paul, who had spoken two years earlier at the Bernardine Dohrn rally on Sara Jane's behalf, said, "I've been trying to make sense of it since I heard. I can only assume this was probably the result of a great deal of pressure on her, her family, and her defense team, even more so since September 11." He continued, "As a historian, I am aware of many, many cases in which the plea in court did not reflect guilt or innocence, but had to do with power and pressure. Hopefully, her good work in the last twenty-five years in St. Paul will carry some weight at sentencing."

Mary Sutton said, "There was not a choice. There's absolutely no way she could get a fair trial. It stinks."

As they walked out of the courtroom, Fred hugged his wife and his daughter. "I'm proud of my wife and stand by my wife as a dedicated husband should," he said.

For a few minutes, it appeared that the long saga had finally come to an end. But not so. Seconds after she walked out of the courthouse, Sara Jane was greeted by a swarm of reporters. Flashing cameras, and pointing their tape recorder microphones at her, they wanted to know what had happened in the courtroom. Her responses were viewed on national television.

Changing character, her demeanor became tense and serious. On the steps of the Los Angeles Criminal Court Building, Sara Jane emoted, "I pleaded to something of which I am *not* guilty. The East Coast terrorist attacks," she stated, "were going to have a negative effect on my trial."

She told reporters that the police had gained "esteem" since the events of September 11, and she had to accept the possibility of being convicted and sentenced to life in prison. Fred stood behind her, a grim look on his face, as his wife talked to reporters. Sara Jane seemed proud, not a woman who had just committed herself to at least five years in prison. Rather than repenting or being conciliatory, if only for her family's sake, this middle-aged housewife repeated her 1960s political agenda. She stated defiantly, "I'm still the same person I was then. I believe in democracy for all people." It was as if thirty years had not gone by. She added, "I don't have any regrets."

Gerald Parker, the student of Marty Soliah who had been so shamed by his teaching methods, saw Olson on the nightly news from his home in North Dakota. He noted: "Sara Jane exhibits the same sneering look that I remember so well in her father in those junior-high days. It was that same sneer that I would see when I would hear him holler at me and tell me that his young boy at home could catch a ball better than I could. I remember that boy was Steve and I think that he had a most interesting escape from the judicial system concerning a bank robbery and shooting?"

At the same time, Parker expressed some sympathy for Steve, Kathy, and Jo Soliah. "I know that they turned out as they did because of their family. I cannot imagine how it must have been to live under his roof and have to put up with the badgering and sneering humiliation that he was capable of! If one didn't live up to his expectations, it was not easy to be around him.

"Most of a human's personality is formed by early grade school days, and it is interesting to note that Soliah is indeed the same person that she was back in those 'turbulent' seventies. Give her a piece of pipe, some gunpowder, and a few nails and tape, and she would be at it again and be proud of her efforts."

Prosecutors were not impressed with Sara Jane's latest performance. Attorney Eleanor Hunter said, "Then she was either lying in court, or she is lying to the press just to save face. If she thought she was not guilty, she should have gone to trial."

Sandi Gibbons, a spokeswoman for the Los Angeles County District Attorney's office, said that Olson's court admission outweighed two years of defense posturing. "We knew we had over-whelming evidence against her," she stated. "The words that are important are the words said in a courtroom. What they said outside court was posturing, and we expected it."

In Highland Park, neighbors took their kids trick-or-treating that night as they did every year. It was a beautiful evening, a gift for Minnesotan's in late October. There was a Post-it note on the Olson-Peterson door that said, "NO CANDY." Reactions to her plea were mixed from neighbors who lived nearby. "They're just wonderful people, and unfortunately we all have to be held ac-countable for our actions," said John Fabie. "We don't think that she had very good legal counsel. There should've been some sort of plea bargain that would've prevented this."

Another neighbor, Jim Odeen, who was going door-to-door with his son said, "If she would have come clean right away, she would have been more sympathetic. This has gone on so long, it made her look like she was hiding something. She could have been out [of prison] by now."

Laurie Levenson discussed the implications of the guilty plea in the *Los Angeles Times*. She explained that many defendants wanted to have it both ways, getting the benefits of pleading guilty without admitting responsibility for their actions. She called it a "moral sidestep." By California law, defendants could plead *nolo contendere* (no contest), where the defendant does not actually admit she is guilty, but only states that she will not con-test the prosecution's allegations. In other instances, defendants might assert their innocence to a particular charge without chal-lenging the prosecution's overall case. Levinson asserted that it had been Judge Fidler's responsibility to ensure that Sara Jane's guilty plea was truthful. Sara Jane knew the script. The answer for the court was "guilty," and the answer for the reporters was, "not really." This incongruity must have made it very clear to the court that she had not pled guilty because of outside pressures, such as improper coercion.

Sara Jane's impromptu comments on the steps of the Los

Angeles Criminal Courts Building sent shockwaves, not only to her family and supporters, but more importantly, to Judge Fidler. The next day, November 1, he ordered her to appear in his courtroom the following week, on Tuesday, November 6, to explain why he shouldn't set aside her guilty plea and resume her trial. Was she guilty or wasn't she? There would be a meeting in his chambers with her defense attorneys, the prosecutors, and then a courtroom hearing. If Judge Fidler decided to void her guilty plea, the trial could go forward as previously planned with the attorneys scheduled to deliver opening statements in December. According to courtroom personnel, this was a new precedent. Legal experts could not recall when a judge had taken such a step.

Michael Latin said, "I've never been in a situation like this before. I've been in situations where a defendant comes back and asks to withdraw a plea, but that is not what's happening here." It seemed that Olson had even stunned her attorneys this time. Shawn Chapman said that she didn't know what to expect at Tuesday's court session. In defense of her client, Chapman said that Sara Jane had only admitted in her plea that she had acted to "encourage, endorse or incite the bombing attempt." Chapman went on to say that "the prisons are filled with people proclaiming their innocence."

That excuse didn't ring true with Jack Golan, who ran the Internet site critical of Sara Jane Olson and her defense team. He said that Sara Jane's earlier claims of innocence should now be looked at as lies: "They [the defense] know a losing case when they see one. They were up against a massive amount of incriminating evidence that not only indicted Kathleen Soliah but their other SLA clients as well. There was no upside in going to trial. Keeping this out of court was like cutting off oxygen to a fire."

Sara Jane's friend Mary Ellen Kaluza said, "Everyone is sad, because she does not deserve to go to jail."

Another friend, Kathy Cima, the lawyer who had been instrumental in raising the $1 million bail money, could not figure out why Sara Jane had entered a guilty plea: "If this was going to be the outcome, I think she should have done this two years ago." She said that she would have had a better chance then because the prosecution would have had less evidence. On top of that, she could have spared her family and friends the monetary and emotional hardships. "There was a lot of money that has been invested. . . . Admittedly, [this was] not going to be a slam-dunk win, but you wonder why she chose not to keep fighting," she said.

Michael Bortin said, "I think she made the right decision. As a brother-in-law, and as a friend of hers, I'm always sad when someone's going to go to jail. On the other hand, I'm happy it has been resolved." This was a surprising switch from someone who had told reporters earlier that Kathy had nothing to do with the pipe bombs placed underneath the police cars and that the whole case was a joke. This was the same man who had asked why anyone would care about "a bunch of people running around with bombs twenty-five years ago." He had vowed that his sister-in-law and Jim Kilgore, if they ever found him, would not be convicted. Perhaps Bortin, because of his possible involvement, was relieved that there would not be a trial.

By avoiding a trial, Olson may have been trying to protect Michael Bortin from testimony she might have had to give regarding the Crocker National Bank robbery. She may have felt protective of her sister Josephine, who had married him in 1988. She may have wanted to protect her brother Steve, who had been acquitted in 1976 for the bank robbery in which Myrna Opsahl was killed. She may have wanted to protect her old boyfriend, Jim Kilgore, who was still underground. She may have wanted to protect Emily Harris, her former lover, who, according to Patty Hearst, had shot Myrna Opsahl to death during the bank robbery. Or it may have been simpler than that. If all of the evidence against her was presented in trial, on Court TV, her family, her supporters, her community, and the nation would certainly have cause to doubt her innocence.

Her family was visibly shaken. A reporter called her brother

Lance in Iowa, who said, "I'm surprised. I thought she was planning on going through with it." Elsie said, "I'm sad. It was a complete surprise to me that she pleaded guilty. I always believed she was not guilty."

Marty was sitting at home alone in his living room watching TV when he got the news that his oldest daughter had pleaded guilty. He told Bart Weitzel of the *Antelope Valley Press*, "Well, if she did, they must've worked out some kind of deal where she didn't have to go through six months of trial," he said. Then he buried his face in his hands. "I don't understand," he continued. He told the reporter that Kathy never discussed her legal situations with him. "They talk to their mother, but they don't talk to 'Grandpa' about that stuff."

He blamed Patty Hearst for his daughter's predicament. He said, "The one that stirred up the whole thing was the bigmouth, Patty Hearst. Back then the FBI told me that they weren't looking for her [Kathy] anymore and that she was not wanted." Then he relived what he remembered about the shootout in which the SLA members were killed. "I talked to a photographer who was there and said that those two girls came out of the house with their hands up, and the police shot at them and forced them back into the fire."

Marty thought that a trial might have explained how the country was divided in those years, the law-and-order forces against the protesters and radical outlaws. "I would have liked [Sara Jane's trial] to have gone on longer just to expose those guys," he said. "The ones who should have pleaded guilty was those guys," indicating the officers who had laid siege to the SLA safehouse.

One of Sara Jane's staunchest supporters from the very beginning seemed to be having second thoughts. After her comments to reporters on the courthouse steps, State Representative Andy Dawkins stated, "You can't do both." He said that he was "as surprised as anyone could be" and added, "I hope this is an example that someone can have bad judgment—very bad judgment—

and reform and rehabilitate and not always be a bad person. It's shocking, disturbing, and surprising. The woman I knew for twenty years was a wonderful, great, outstanding woman. They asked for one continuance [trial delay] too many."

He also said, "There's so much to this, it's so layered. It goes back to the kind of politics and government violence of the time, shootings at Kent State, civil rights marchers in the South—a whole different mind-set. . . . But if you really, truly intended to harm in any way another person, then I think five years is understandable. Maybe, in the interest of her family, she had to do this.

"I always thought she had made friends with people who had done terrible deeds," he said, "but I did not expect a plea that she was guilty of aiding and abetting in any way making bombs to kill people."

Minneapolis gun shop owner Mark Koscielski, who was still selling anti-Olson bumper stickers, told the *Star Tribune* that he saw things differently. He said he hopes "she gets life. It was a terrorist act."

By now, the United States had launched massive air strikes against terrorist camps in Taliban-controlled Afghanistan. United States ground forces had moved in to rid Afghanistan of the Taliban leader Mullah Omar and the Al-Qaida leader Osama Bin Laden, who was thought to be responsible for the attacks on the World Trade Towers and the Pentagon. Every night, viewers watched the devastation of bombs on their televisions. There was talk of biological warfare and nuclear warfare, and many Americans were purchasing gas masks. In addition, letters containing anthrax—a white, granular, bacterium that could cause death if inhaled—had been sent to NBC, ABC, American Media, Inc., and various offices of the Unites States Senate. Postal workers nationwide were on alert. The word *terrorist* filled the newspapers every day. It was not a good time to be labeled one.

One week after Sara Jane's plea, local newspapers detailed some of the evidence that the prosecution had against her. All of this evidence would be explicated in a hearing held in the beginning of December. It looked as though Sara Jane's remarks to the press on Halloween would come back to haunt her.

Deputy District Attorney Michael Latin had asked the judge to review the agreement with Olson. He was not comfortable with "the plea as it stands." If Sara Jane had pled guilty because her attorneys had told her it would get her a lesser sentence, Latin did not want her plea based on "false assurances." Under California state law, the Board of Prison Terms could extend the sentence to up to life in prison if it was determined that she was a danger to the community. Tony Serra said that was unlikely.

On Tuesday, November 6, Sara Jane had no choice but to face the wrath of Judge Larry Fidler and explain why she flip-flopped on her guilty plea to the press. (It was, coincidentally, the twenty-eighth anniversary of the Marcus Foster assassination.) Judge Fidler read her a brief explanation of the law of conspiracy and aiding and abetting. Since the SLA testimony was going to be allowed, the prosecutors could link her to their criminal activity even if she had not participated directly in their crimes. Aiding and abetting was enough. If they could prove their case, she risked life in prison.

He asked her if, based upon that information, she was guilty of the charges to which she pleaded last week. When she didn't answer immediately, Fidler told her she could meet with her attorneys privately. During that meeting, Serra persuaded her that Judge Fidler was not trying to publicly humiliate her. He said later, "She didn't want to go through the whole thing like she was a child."

After about five minutes, she returned to the jammed courtroom and flashed her characteristic defiance. Olson listened as Judge Fidler reprimanded her. When he asked her a question about the possibility of her spending life in prison, she hesitated again. He ordered her to respond.

He explained that the law clearly states that people cannot enter guilty pleas if they are, in fact, innocent. He asked her lawyers if Sara Jane wanted to reaffirm her plea or continue to declare her innocence outside the court. "Ms. Olson publicly disavowed her guilt and proclaimed her innocence. A guilty plea is not a way-station on the way to a press conference to declare your innocence." He added, "She must make a choice. She cannot have it both ways." He said to Sara Jane, "If you are innocent, I won't accept your plea. You can go to trial."

Olson stood before the judge and declared in a shaking voice, "I want to make it clear, Your Honor, that I did not make those bombs, possess those bombs, or place those bombs. Under the concept of aiding and abetting, I plead guilty."

He asked her, "And you want your plea to stand?"

After about fifteen seconds, she sighed heavily and mumbled, "All right."

"Is that a yes?" asked Judge Fidler.

"Yes." Her jaw set in defiance and frustration, she promptly sat down, defeated.

This time, Olson's restatement of guilt was viewed on national television. Thanks to the judge, she was still in the spotlight. Perhaps this wasn't what she had in mind because now even her staunchest supporters knew she had lied at least once.

And she had shaken the confidence of her lawyers. She had gone too far when she pled guilty, under oath, to a federal judge and then recanted her plea to the press on the courthouse steps. It was like an encore performance when there hadn't even been an ovation calling for one. She didn't follow the script. The directors had lost control of their star. Above all, when she made those statements to the press following her guilty plea, she seemed to have forgotten that she had not yet been sentenced.

Tony Serra expressed his concern. He said that a plea deal was fraught with risk for their client because it set forth no maximum sentence. Now her release date was in the hands of California's Parole Board, which, under Governor Gray Davis, had become one of the toughest in the nation. "They don't parole people in California," Serra said. "They have to be sued to parole people in California." He said that he was in "deep depression," over Sara Jane's plea. "Is it scary? I don't like ever pleading anyone, and this was a defensible case. This was a once-in-a-lifetime opportunity to cross-examine Patty Hearst, who has large vulnerable zones.

"But September 11 sure as hell didn't bode well for our client, and therefore I'm satisfied we made the right decision," he said. "If she gets life, I think I'll commit suicide, for Christ's sake. It'll be the worst thing ever. When the parole board sits, I sure as hell will be holding my breath."

Legal experts agreed. One high-profile Los Angeles attorney, Harland Braun, said, "Anything that leaves it up to the California parole board right now and with police officers as the victims, she's never going to get out. I'd be afraid." He reiterated Serra's point and said that the plea was "terrible" for Olson because "no maximum sentence was set and because it did not resolve the northern California charges, and added that her proclamation of innocence afterward was no help." He added, "That was very bad PR. One of the things judges would like you to say is that it happened many years ago and you regret doing it. But if you go out there and flaunt it, you're just asking for it. That's called stupid."

It was important to Judge Fidler to make it clear that Sara Jane's plea and her reiteration of that plea were of her own free will and that she had not been coerced in any way. The judge had the right to withdraw her guilty plea and call a trial as originally planned. He could choose to let a jury decide whether or not she was innocent or guilty. That had been her choice. She'd chosen to restate her guilty plea.

Sixty-four-year-old Hadessa Gilbert had joined Sara Jane's defense committee the previous year after attending a reception on her behalf. Gilbert had given speeches about the case and appeared on talk shows. She had also hosted consciousness-raising groups at her home in Los Angeles. She described herself as a left-wing Democrat and said that she felt a duty to work on Sara Jane's behalf. She said that she thought that Fidler was annoyed about her friend's behavior on October 31 and was punishing her for saying she couldn't get a fair trial. Gilbert told a reporter from the *Los Angeles Times*: "I think the judge was exacting his pound of flesh."

Portraying Sara Jane Olson as a victim of September 11 did not sit well with many people who had followed her saga.

Back in Minnesota, headlines in the local papers read, "Is She Guilty or Innocent?" She had become a caricature. Political cartoonists illustrated her as the head of the SLA's seven cobra symbol, vacillating, "I'm innocent, I'm guilty, I'm innocent. . . ." One radio commentator said he hoped he'd never have to hear her name again because it was like poking pins in his eyeballs. Another local reporter and radio talk show host, Joe Soucheray, had developed a segment called "Our Little Terrorist" (OLT), where callers-in could vent their opinions on Sara Jane.

Newspapers were inundated with editorial comments from their readers. Mike McGee wrote to the *Star Tribune*, stating in part, "Her defense attorney's statement that she is 'truly a victim of September 11 is nauseating and defames the true victims and heroes of that day. She's a victim all right, but apparently only of his poor legal counsel." He added, "Go serve your time, Olson, so the newspaper can report stories about real victims."

Mike Bierscheid wrote, "It is a shame that it took the tragic events of September 11 for Sara Jane Olson and her supporters to finally realize that a terrorist is a terrorist is a terrorist." These opinions echoed the views of the "average person on the street."

After Sara Jane's second guilty plea, she exited the courtroom to a crowd of reporters. This time, she said, "I don't want to talk. I'm done talkin' [sic]."

Hadessa Gilbert's comment was, "I can't believe all of these reporters are here just to witness someone else's misery."

Sandi Gibbons, spokesperson for the prosecution, would not comment, except to say, "It's a wrap, people."

Cowardice or Coercion?

On November 12, Sara Jane wrote this declaration to Judge Fidler:

> *I implore you, Judge Fidler, to allow me to withdraw my guilty pleas to Counts IV and V of my Indictment. While I cannot claim to have misunderstood your admonitions that I answer "guilty" only if I was fully aware of the import of your queries at the November 6th hearing, at the time I felt I had no choice.*
>
> *After deeper reflection, I realize I cannot plead guilty when I know I am not. I understand, given the uncertainty of any jury verdict in any trial, that I may be found guilty. The attacks on our country created genuine fear in the public and, consequently, the jury pool. I understand that a jury trial is a profound risk. I have always been willing, until recently to put my fate in the hands of twelve peers because I am innocent and because I am represented by two brilliant attorneys.*
>
> *I was prepared to go to trial after I was informed of your order for a second hearing regarding my guilty plea. Cowardice prevented me from doing what I knew I should: Throw caution aside and move forward to trial. I am not second-guessing my decision as much as I have found the courage to take what I know is the honest course. Please, Judge Fidler, grant my request to go to trial on all of the charges for which I was indicted in 1976.*

This motion added another twist to this bizarre tale. Most legal experts believed that her plea would stand. She had pleaded guilty two times. It would be difficult for her to claim that she hadn't understood what she was doing. According to a board spokeswoman, the California Board of Prison Terms, which conducted about 2,000 parole hearings every year, had freed only about one percent of those prisoners. Sara Jane's attorneys told her that if she had accepted her original plea bargain, twenty years to life in prison, she would be paroled after serving just five years and three months. Andy Dawkins said that she couldn't sleep after she pleaded guilty. "After she couldn't sleep for a week, her family said, 'If you can't live with yourself, then you've got to see what you can do about proving it to a jury.'"

Mary Sutton said that Sara Jane gave the plea under a lot of pressure, and that she didn't feel good about it. Minnesota Attorney Ron Rosenbaum, a longtime follower of the case, stated, "I hate to tell you, you're not supposed to feel good about it. This seems to be a woman who has difficulty coming to grips and taking responsibility for what she did. I don't think her argument will wash and don't see the basis for the judge to allow it."

In California, to withdraw a guilty plea, "good cause" is required. Good cause could rely on such grounds as a plea made without a lawyer, a bad defense lawyer, or ignorance of the direct consequences of the plea. Sara Jane had publicly stated that her lawyers were "brilliant." Judge Fidler had asked her before she pled guilty, "Do you knowingly, intelligently and voluntarily waive your right to a trial by jury and waive your rights to appeal?" She had answered, "Yes."

Sandi Gibbons said, "Ms. Soliah-Olson appears to hold the American justice system in the same contempt as she did thirty years ago when she was running with the SLA. What part of guilty doesn't she understand?"

As to Sara Jane's latest plea, Laura Billings from the *St. Paul Pioneer Press* wrote, "It was not one of her better performances. When the judge had asked Sara Jane if she wished her plea to stand, there was a long pause as if she didn't know her lines. Her syntax seemed awkward and out of place, as the suggestion that she, too, was a victim of September 11. A victim of her own bad choices, certainly. A victim of bad legal counsel, possibly. But hardly a victim. And hardly as victimized as the friends in St. Paul who believed her claims of innocence." The reporter quoted F. Scott Fitzgerald, who once claimed that there were no second acts in American life, "but Olson defied that rule, just as surely as her generation defied the conventions."

Sara Jane was interviewed the following Thursday on *Democracy Now*, a syndicated radio show in Los Angeles. She likened her pleading guilty to, going in and doing penance for having publicly disavowed her original guilty plea. "It irked me, but my attorneys were correct," she said. "It was the right thing to do." She complained that she was powerless and called her case "Just another American soap opera." Since her October 31 guilty plea, she had been described in the media as "defiant." On the radio talk show, she had an answer for that. She said she was "trying to retain a shred of one's dignity. It simply sounds better [in the media] if I'm described as a defiant bitch."

A reporter for the Twin Cities publication *City Pages* e-mailed Sara Jane's defense fund committee hoping that they might elaborate on her reasons for reiterating her guilty plea. They wanted to follow up on a story they'd published the previous winter. The reporter was surprised when the answer came from Sara Jane herself:

"The mainstream media, of which *City Pages* is a part, finds it nearly impossible to present 'my side of the story' clearly and fairly. Many of my 'supporters' (not personal friends who are rarely quoted) in the Twin Cities have backpedaled furiously in their support since I made the plea. Many have done so, I assume, due to the rightwing political fallout after the events of September 11 where even a whiff of liberalness is a political death knell." She added, "While you may be sincere in your request, the inevitable plethora of nasty, 'name withheld' letters to the editor that will follow and that will ALL be printed is not worth it to me."

City Pages published her letter and in response wrote that only one of the six letters to the editor (letters that offered a variety of opinions) regarding their previous story withheld the writer's name. They welcomed letters from Sara Jane's supporters who would like to be quoted.

Words of repentance were still not in her vocabulary. According to her the Los Angeles District Attorney's office "negotiated in bad faith through the whole thing and, repeatedly dumped an enormous amount of evidence on us and basically said good luck." As to the September 11 attacks, she said that she "immediately realized, uh, oh, this is probably going to affect the public tremendously." That's when friends and supporters convinced her that she should reassess her situation. She decided, finally, "I had to accept doing time to ensure that I had a future. . . . Going before a jury is a dangerous proposition. I had no choice." Reflecting on the past two years, she called it "a big juicy story—it's just whatever sells papers. . . . It's a dead story now. Who cares?" As to her guilty plea, she said, "They got what they wanted, and I gave it to them."

The next week, Tony Serra spoke. In a carefully worded statement, he said, "At no time has Ms. Olson ever conceded to me her factual guilt with respect to any of the charges; in fact, she has always asserted the contrary—that she is innocent of the charges," he wrote. "It was clear to me and to anyone who witnessed Ms. Olson's demeanor during the plea and heard the intonations of her voice during the plea, that she was equivocal, hesitant, confused, ambivalent, and pressured during her plea. I, in part, take responsibility for creating conditions in her mind that mounted to psychological duress, in regard to pleading guilty," Serra added. "I sincerely believe that Ms. Olson was in a psychological condition of coercion during the course of her pleas."

Legal experts surmised that Serra appeared to be making an attempt to give the court some basis for dismissing the pleas. It was clumsy and it was transparent. "He's falling a little bit on his sword to try to give her better grounds for her motion," said Laurie Levinson. "It may be too little, too late."

A woman wrote to the *Los Angeles Times*, "Whether she's Kathleen Soliah, Sara Jane Olson, or now, apparently, an actress playing in *Hamlet*, "the lady doth protest too much, methinks."

The morning of December 3, 2001, did not begin well for Sara Jane. Fred, her three daughters, her parents, and her supporters were in the packed courtroom waiting to hear the judge's decision. The hearing, scheduled for 9:30 A.M. was expected to last about thirty minutes. However, as had become typical in this case, there was a snag. Tony Serra did not show up.

Now, the burden was on Chapman to fill in for him and explain to Judge Fidler how her client had been "coerced" by Serra. "We can't go forward with the motion without him because he intends to testify as to the things that he did and said to coerce Ms. Olson into the plea." Was this a ploy to get yet another continuance? Judge Fidler called Serra's absence "absolutely unprofessional and inexcusable." He acknowledged the affidavit that Serra had filed but contended that there was no support in his declaration that he had coerced Ms. Olson. Furthermore, in her own declaration, asking to withdraw her guilty plea, she never mentioned that Serra had coerced her. The judge called her declaration inadequate in its face and insufficient as a matter of law.

"If those declarations stand," he said, "Ms. Olson and Mr. Serra are subject to cross-examination to the degree that the matters in contention are put into dispute." He explained that the prosecutors could fully cross-examine Ms. Olson on her declaration of innocence, which in essence would be a small court trial.

Ms. Chapman said that the cross-examination should be limited to her client's "state of mind" when she made her guilty plea, and if the judge was going to allow limitless cross-examination then they would withdraw their declaration. The judge said that in this case, her state of mind, was, "I am innocent." Jurors had not yet been voir dired (sworn to tell the truth in order to ascertain their competence), and therefore there was no factual support when she claimed she could not get a fair trial due to the September 11 attacks. Now that they knew that Sara Jane could be cross-examined, and that the judge would explain the parameters to prove that she was innocent of the charges, Chapman withdrew her client's declaration.

The judge said, "Fine." He also made it clear that judges do not accept guilty pleas from innocent people. He said, "I took that guilty plea in effect twice from Ms. Olson after full advisement of counsel, after explaining to her all the nuance of the laws and aiding and abetting and conspiracy." He said, "It is basically were you lying to me then or are you lying to me now? That's what it comes down to. She cannot have it both ways, and she will not have it both ways in this court."

Now, without Tony Serra there, Chapman was on her own. She told the judge that Sara Jane had been presented a "Hobson's Choice," which is "if you're innocent go to trial, only plead guilty if you are guilty, and that left her in a very tenuous and difficult position," she said. She went on to explain that her client was innocent but had an attorney, Tony Serra, whose powers of persuasion, and presence were overwhelming, and Ms. Olson was not a lawyer and had placed a great deal of faith and confidence and reliance upon Mr. Serra. Because she had been coerced, Chapman explained, "cowardice" caused her to go along with Serra's recommendation.

Judge Fidler was losing patience. "Are you claiming that Mr. Serra as some sort of Svengali somehow overpowered a very intelligent woman's free will? I thought we were out of the dark ages, that somehow this powerful man will overcome this woman who can't think for herself? That's ridiculous. That's actually insulting. I think that's an absolutely absurd statement."

Chapman tried to explain to the judge that Serra was working pro bono and that Ms. Olson did not have funds to retain another attorney. Because he was doing them this favor, working for free, it was not possible to put demands on him, such as showing up at the hearings. They needed Serra.

She said that the district attorney's office had misrepresented the facts in regard to the prison time that Sara Jane would have to face. She was afraid that they would lobby the parole board to give her client a stiffer sentence, although they assured her that they would not do that. Sara Jane had always wanted to go to trial until Tony Serra got to her, Chapman stated.

According to her, he flew in to Los Angeles the morning of October 31 and screamed and yelled at Sara Jane, saying that she would be a "fucking idiot" if she did not take the deal that the district attorney's office had offered her. If she pled guilty to Counts IV and V she would get four years if it were a concurrent sentence and five and a quarter years if it were a consecutive sentence. According to Chapman, when they got to court, the prosecutors then said that it was not their position to promise how much time Sara Jane would serve, it was up to the parole board. She could get life. Chapman said she was stunned. She felt "defeated as a lawyer."

Judge Fidler asked, "Are you saying that you never stood up to Mr. Serra, that you didn't tell him about your professional concerns about what was going on?"

"It's difficult if not impossible to have a conversation with Mr. Serra," she replied. "He doesn't return my calls. I don't have a relationship with him. I can't communicate with him. Ms. Olson has more of a relationship with him than I do and I think she looks to him as her lead attorney." She added, "I don't know why he's not here, but this is really just the most agonizing argument I've ever had to make to any court and frankly my faith in the system has been shaken. . . ."

Judge Fidler interrupted: "What's the system done as opposed to what your side has done? What has the system done in this case except present you an opportunity to go to trial if you wanted to go to trial? I made the options clear. The system gave you an opportunity to litigate if you had chosen to take it at the time when it was appropriate. Don't blame the system."

Chapman tried to explain that she didn't really blame the system, but she blamed the district attorney's office. "The court knows that innocent people are convicted all the time and guilty people are acquitted all the time. Going to trial is a risk. Placing your faith, particularly when your fate is life in this case, in the hands of twelve people particularly in a climate which, I appreciate that there was going to be a voir dire process and a questionnaire, but it's still a sensitive climate and if it wasn't placing your life in the hands of twelve people is dangerous and risky." Just the same, she said over and over in this hearing that her client had wanted to go to trial.

Judge Fidler reminded her that after the guilty plea, the prosecution and the defense laid out their entire case to the *Los Angeles Times*. He said, "I was taken by one of the comments attributed to you where you were talking about the strengths and weaknesses of the case. There was a portion of the case where you said, 'I can't explain that. We can't explain that.' Now are you telling me the relative strengths of the People's case have no bearing whatsoever on Ms. Olson's decision to plea?"

"I am absolutely telling you that. Ms. Olson has remained steadfast in her desire to want to go to trial. You're right that members of the defense team had tried to impress upon her that there were certain strengths of the prosecution's case and that she was facing life if convicted, and she has always been willing to take that risk. Always."

She then told the judge that she had advised her client to stand by the comments she made to the press because that was the truth. "She's innocent, she pled guilty because she felt it was in her best interest to do so." Tony Serra had disagreed and convinced her to stick with her guilty plea under the aiding and abetting theory because that was what the court wanted to hear.

Judge Fidler said, "So if I understand correctly, when Mr.

Serra was lying to the court, in essence misrepresenting to the court, you stood or sat right next to him and didn't say a word. Don't you have some professional responsibility to let me know that something wrong is going on?" Like a father speaking to an unruly child, he explained, "Your responsibility is to your client and to your profession, not to Mr. Serra, and I think you know that."

Chapman responded that Sara Jane did not want her to jeopardize her relationship with Serra. Now it was the People's turn to present their side.

The Girl Defense

Prosecutor Eleanor Hunter opened: "When counsel gets up there and says Ms. Olson has been willing to go to trial, we have to remember that she also fled and was a fugitive for twenty-four years. She lived under an assumed name, she used other people's passports to flee the country, coincidentally when Patty Hearst's book came out. She's had an opportunity to go to trial on two different occasions.

"Council's argument basically is insulting on many levels specifically she's giving the 'Girl Defense.' I'm just a girl, I couldn't stand up to Mr. Serra. . . . well the county is paying Ms. Chapman a lot of money to stand up and represent her client and obviously she's been able to represent her client because she's been the one who's been here in court for motions or hearings. And so for her to come into court and say, 'Gosh, I just couldn't stand up. He was just a big strong man and I couldn't do it' is pretty insulting. We all know Ms. Chapman is obviously professional, she represented that at the very beginning in order to get the county funds to be paid by the county that she was uniquely familiar with this case and that's why she should be appointed and the county should be paying for her services.

"Now the defendant is using the 'Girl Defense.' She goes into court, we go back and there were discussions, and every time that we were coming close to trial the defense would approach us and say, 'We want a deal.' They would get a continuance, then we would go forward and discuss the negotiations." She explained that she and Michael Latin had thought that if Sara Jane had pled guilty to Counts IV and V, she would get the term of ten years and would receive one-third of that time. That term was never offered, however, because the defense kept asking to continue the case. She said that when it looked like the court would not grant another continuance, the defense team sent them a letter stipulating what Sara Jane would or would not agree to. There was no deal. She said that Tony Serra was never in on any of the discussions, but Ms. Chapman had asked, "What would you accept? Would you commit yourself to not taking a position before the board?" The answer was no. If she was innocent then she should go to trial.

"We are not dealing with a child here," Prosecutor Hunter continued. "We are dealing with a woman, educated, who is in her fifties who has a lifetime of experience and she's. . . . she's not going to be just sitting there and be browbeaten by some man."

Hunter reminded Judge Fidler that he had asked Sara Jane about the concept of "aiding and abetting and conspiracy." "There was no ambiguity," continued Hunter. "There was no hesitation. Yes, she is an actress and she can hem and haw and be theatrical and all, but she looked you in the eye and said, 'I am guilty.'

"What I think is most telling, Your Honor, if you take a look at the declaration submitted by the defendant in connection with this motion to withdraw, you don't hear anything in there that she was coerced. You don't hear Tony Serra was screaming at her using bad language and forced her to do anything. In fact, I think she said he was brilliant. There is no implication that this woman was coerced into doing anything. I don't believe she could be coerced into doing anything. She pled guilty in this case because she knew what the evidence was against her and the court had indicated that you wouldn't accept a plea from an innocent person. Well, accepting Ms. Olson's plea would not violate that rule."

After a recess in the hearing, Judge Fidler asked Eleanor Hunter and Michael Latin to continue their case. Michael Latin was the first to speak:

"The very first negotiations in this case took place in 1986 when our office received a communication from a former law partner of Susan Jordan who ultimately became the initial trial counsel in this case. We met in November of that year. They offered to surrender the defendant and have her plead guilty on the condition that we guarantee that she would serve no time in custody. We sent a letter back rejecting that offer and that is why she remained a fugitive. She was offering to surrender but essentially was holding our office hostage and requiring us to make a guarantee of no time in exchange for her surrender. We did not take advantage of that and she remained a fugitive until June of 1999.

"Ms. Hunter and I have observed a very clear pattern: We never discussed negotiations unless and until the case was coming up for trial and the tactics that were being used to stop the trial from going forward were not succeeding. And as soon as we were on the eve of trial and it appeared that the evidence would be presented in short order, they would come and approach us about the possibility of settlement. We never contacted the defense about settling this case. It was always the reverse; they would contact us and try to have discussions.

"Ms. Hunter and I had a similar discussion in December 1999 with Stuart Hanlon and Susan Jordan. Again, we offered ten years. This was just before we were to go to trial in January 2000. Next, Mr. Hanlon withdrew from the case. In February, we received a message from Susan Jordan, which went something like this: 'We've talked to our client and she will take three years in state prison. If you're prepared to do it, let's do it now. Call me back.'"

Mr. Latin and Ms. Hunter played the tape to the district attorney at the time, Gil Garcetti, and they all agreed that their offer was not sufficient, and they did not accept the offer. Latin explained to Judge Fidler that on April 27, 2000, Ms. Jordan sent them another letter and one to Judge Ideman who was the presiding judge of the case at that time. She wanted to discuss a settlement. The meeting, which included Judge Ideman, Michael

Latin, Eleanor Hunter, Susan Jordan, and Sara Jane Olson, was held on May 1. The defense team was hoping to cut a better deal than they were going to get from the prosecutors. They also discussed Myrna Opsahl's murder at the Crocker National Bank in Carmichael. As they approached the next trial date that month, Mr. Hanlon requested a meeting in chambers to discuss a settlement again.

"Much has been made about the fact that she wasn't interested in pleading guilty until after the September 11 attacks. We received a letter in August of 2000 before any of those things came into the issue. In the letter, Ms. Chapman indicated that her client would be willing to plead to counts two through five, more of the counts than we required as part of our disposition and it was that letter to which we replied indicating that we appreciated her willingness to accept responsibility for the attempted murders. However, the offer that she was making was not commensurate with the gravity of the offense and we would reject the offer.

"The defense team, whoever that is, has not included Mr. Serra. That is the chronology of events relating to the plea discussions."

Judge Fidler asked him if he and Ms. Hunter were prepared to make an offer of proof* as to what evidence they had concerning Ms. Olson's guilt. They said that they were. Mr. Latin explained that their most significant witness would have been Patricia Hearst.

She would testify that Sara Jane was a member of the Second Team who planned other bombings, including a similar bombing up at the Marin County Civic Center. "They were supposed to take place on the same day. Ultimately, the two plantings of the bombs took place one day apart but the team that came to Los Angeles came down here with the intent of committing these

---

*A presentation of evidence for the record, outside the presence of a jury. Usually made after the judge has said that evidence is not admissible but will be preserved on record for an appeal.

murders on the same day as the bombs were planted in Marin County and three separate people were up in Marin County."

He talked about the witness James Marshall who was now deceased, but had identified Kathy Soliah, from a photo lineup at the time of the grand jury. He explained that they could trace the piece of pipe back to that sale, made by Marshal, the day before the bombings. Latin said, "What many people don't know about the bombings in this case is that the pipe bombs are *two of the largest pipe bombs ever planted in the history of the United States.*" As he said that, he was holding up a replica of the pipe bomb.

As noted in the grand jury indictment, he said that the evidence relating to the Los Angeles bombings was based upon a cross-comparison of the components of the two devices with materials that were found at the apartment at 288 Precita Street in San Francisco. Steve Soliah had testified in his own trial that he had moved Kathy into this apartment.

Latin continued. "It's been reported many times in the press that it was an attempt to blow up police cars, and that's not true. It was a bomb that was designed to blow up people, to take human lives. It would have taken more lives than the ones that were in the cars and this is why." He described how he had more information about how the bombs were assembled than had been in the 1976 indictment testimony.

"It's been reported that the bomb fell off the car; that's not true." Latin explained that the bomb was never *on* the car; but actually on the ground, underneath the front seat of the vehicle where the officers would be sitting. The horseshoe magnet, attached by a wire to the shim, which separated the contacts, was placed on the undercarriage of the car. The bomb was designed so that when the car moved, the wire attached to the magnet would pull out the shim and allow the contacts to touch each other, causing the bomb to explode. But something unforeseen happened.

Since Officers Bryant and Hall had parked with the front end of their vehicle up against the wall of the restaurant, the bomb was placed approximately five to seven feet away from the wall of the restaurant, and that wall contained a large plate-glass window.) A photograph of the restaurant was exhibited for the judge to see. While the officers were in the restaurant, the car to the right of the police car had left the parking lot. It would have been expected that the officers would have pulled straight out, once they got back to their car. But since the space next to them had opened up, they turned the wheel. That caused the shim, which was made of wood, to move in an angular direction as opposed to straight, and when it did, it dragged the round head screw with it as it pulled. The clothespin came completely out of joint. It closed, but the two screws came within approximately a sixteenth of an inch of touching each other.

"Now these bombs were filled with powder and loaded with shrapnel. Each bomb had approximately 144 screws, designed to go through people. A bomb of this power would have set each of these screws off in different directions at approximately four times the speed of a bullet from an army rifle.

"Officers Hall and Bryan had no idea when they pulled out of that spot how lucky they were. They continued driving down Sunset Boulevard, responding to a call with the horseshoe magnet on the undercarriage of their car. As they were driving, they heard the call that someone had found a bomb in the parking lot at the IHOP. They drove back to the scene and saw that the bomb was in the spot that they had been parked. Then they discovered the triggering mechanism attached to the undercarriage of their car, and it was then that they realized that they had been the targets."

Latin explained that Marvin Morales, who had found the bomb, told him that he came "this close to kicking the bomb." Luckily he didn't, and he and his friends went into the restaurant as well as the hotel across the street and reported the bomb. Latin called them heroes. He said that the bomb squad was so concerned that the two screws might inadvertently touch each other that they had no choice but to try to disarm the bomb before the area was evacuated. The bomb could have blown up at any second. He showed some still photographs on the screen of what happened when the police and FBI did a re-creation of what would have happened to the police car if the bomb had exploded.

He said, "We believe that the defendant and her friends knew that the bomb, because it would have gone off underneath a moving vehicle with the gas lines full and gas pumping from the gas tank, that it would have not only caused one explosion but there would have been a secondary explosion in the gas tanks. We ran this experiment to see if this would indeed occur and it did. That's what those flames are in the photograph. There's no doubt that the officers would have been killed. There lives were decided by a sixteenth of an inch."

During Latin's presentation, Olson continued her inappropriate behavior. Instead of showing concern, fear, or remorse, instead of looking at the screens of evidence, she sat in her chair laughing and smirking with Shawn Chapman as if this were a social event. Policemen from the LAPD bomb squad, who had transported the replica of the bomb, observed the proceedings from the gallery.

"This is the largest pipe bomb ever recovered in the city of Los Angeles, in the history of this city. It is one of the largest pipe bombs recovered in the history of the United States of America, and probably the most powerful; this is only one of two that were planted." (And only one of three that were intended.)

Latin went on to explain Patricia Hearst's version of when Jim Kilgore and Bill Harris had attended the VFW convention at the Holiday Inn in downtown Los Angeles and how they chickened out. That bomb was later recovered in that same Precita Street closet where all the other bomb components were found. Latin showed a photograph of the bomb on the screen.

Next, he described the second bomb at the Hollenbeck Station that was found by the young officer, Marty Feinmark, who had just finished a tour of Vietnam. He said that Feinmark did not know about the horseshoe magnet attached to his car's undercarriage and when he saw the bomb, he was moving his hands around. "But for the grace of God, he would have set the thing off too."

Latin talked about the Precita Street apartment. "It had two bedrooms; one was resided in by the defendant, the other was resided in by two of the FBI's most wanted at the time: Bill and Emily Harris." He displayed a photograph of the closet that separated the two bedrooms where they found a number of sawed-off shotguns, handguns, manuals for guns, and bomb components. "That briefcase that was intended for the VFW bomb was recovered there." That bomb was a complete, active bomb that was found in the closet. He described all of the components for the bombs and added that the 144 concrete nails were the hardest nails manufactured, that they had the highest melting point, meaning that it would take more heat to melt them than any other kind of nail. Once he finished explaining the workings of the bombs, Latin turned the proceedings over to Hunter who said, "We can safely say that the bombs that were found in Los Angeles were made from the people who occupied the location at 288 Precita."

She showed the court a copy of the rental agreement, which had been signed by Emily Harris, using another name. Harris had told the landlord that she would be living there with her husband and her sister, who was later identified as Kathy Soliah. "We have her personal belongings from that apartment. We have some old checks of Ms. Soliah," (which she pronounced So Ly ah).

At this point, Sara Jane let out an outburst with, "It's SOH lee ah!"

She seemed to have lost all control and, at the same time, forgotten that Soliah was the name she had denied for all of those years. Judge Fidler, who had shown the patience of Job, was furious. He admonished her that she could end up in jail with another outburst like that. He warned, "If you do it again, I'll remand you." Even then, she protested his admonishment, like an insolent child. She rolled her eyes, shook her head, and muttered to Chapman. Finally, Sara Jane settled back in to her chair, looking defeated and completely worn down.

The judge told Hunter to proceed, and she explained that they found Ms. Soliah's writing, which had been identified, as well as her fingerprints, forty-seven of them on items in the closet. They were found not only on writings, but on a manual for 9-mm guns, the doorjamb of the closet, and on the inside closet wall. "So we have proof that Ms. Soliah was actually inside that closet. We have her fingerprint in the bedroom; we have fourteen in the kitchen. One of them was on a *Joy of Cooking* cookbook."

Hunter also explained that Kathy Soliah had been under surveillance for a couple of days before the arrests at Precita. The FBI had seen her arrive at the apartment at the end of the evening, stay overnight, and then leave the following morning. A picture of Kathy Soliah appeared on the screen, as she was walking out of the apartment with her brother Steve and her sister Josephine. There was no doubt that she lived in the apartment where the bomb making materials, connected with the Los Angeles bombs, were stored.

The remaining members of the SLA had been underground and were on America's Ten Most Wanted list at the time. Since the SLA never threw anything away, the FBI was able to recover their writings, which included a "Declaration of War." This was found in the Precita apartment closet. One of the goals was to stage a People's War. One of the documents stated that they would mobilize and initiate guerrilla warfare in the United States in order to start a revolutionary war that would culminate in the total annihilation of the capitalist ruling class. Hunter admitted that the document had been drafted before Kathy Soliah joined the group. Another document stated that if you were an informant, you would be sentenced to death without trial. "That was their philosophy," she said, adding that this was seen as having a bearing on Patricia Hearst's mindset. The SLA were not mere protesters; they took actions against society and then broadcast their ideals through their writings, many of which were found in that same closet.

Hunter pointed out that although Soliah joined the group later, Marcus Foster's assassination on November 6, 1973, had been well publicized through radio, television, and newspapers, as had Patricia Hearst's kidnapping on February 4, 1974. These points were important, she said, because "It tells us what type of group the defendant voluntarily joined when she gave her speech in June 1974."

The SLA went underground after the shootout with Kathy Soliah's help. Hunter explained how they obtained their false IDs, which now appeared on the presentation screen. "They got birth certificates of deceased infants, and several of those cards that we see in the upper left-hand corner we were able to link to Ms. Soliah's fingerprints and handwriting. We also have her having an I.D. right there in the middle. That is Ms. Soliah using the name, 'Catherine Beggs.' Underneath that one is also Ms. Soliah and that's using the name 'Michal Ann Mora.' So at this point, she was using false IDs." Next on the screen were two letters that had been written to Kathy Soliah when the SLA was planning to abandon their farmhouse in Pennsylvania and Soliah was renting them apartments in Sacramento.

Hunter pointed to the screen, which showed some little pieces of paper, which she referred to as the "paint brush list." "In a wallet that contained Kathy Soliah's fake I.D. of Michal Ann Mora, there was a little piece of paper with phone numbers." Each member of the SLA—Wendy Yoshimura, Patricia Hearst, Steve Soliah, Bill Harris, and Emily Harris—had a similar piece of paper in each of their wallets. The list was who to call in an emergency. "So basically, that's [their] card carrying member of being part of this group, because again only the people that were in this group had access to this information."

The Crocker Bank robbery in Carmichael was next on Hunter's list. She reiterated Patty Hearst's version from *Every Secret*

Thing of what occurred that day. But she could corroborate Hearst's story. "Patty Hearst said that the defendant had a .9-millimeter gun and that's a gun that she used. And while she was in the bank, she dropped some of the casings on the ground and we were able to analyze those casings with casings that were found in a .9-millimeter that was found in her dresser or night stand in the bedroom that she occupied at Precita, along with some ammunition that was found in the ground, and it matched the bait stamp and also the type and caliber make."

The cars that were used in the bank robbery also tied Kathy Soliah to the SLA. One of the cars was a blue Ford Mustang that had been stolen on April 7, 1975. The other one was a 1967 Pontiac Firebird, which had been stolen on April 12, 1975. Hunter said that Soliah had attended the party along with Kilgore and Bortin, where the keys to the Firebird had been stolen.

The garage Emily Harris rented to hide the Firebird had Kathy Soliah's palm print on the wall. Wendy Yoshimura had testified to a grand jury that she had driven one of these cars and Patty Hearst had driven the other as getaway cars after the robbery. Patty Hearst's account of this robbery was true. The Mustang had been rented between the dates of April 17 to April 22, a day after the robbery. Another false identification that had been used to rent this car was found at the Precita apartment where Kathy Soliah lived. The keys to that car were found there as well. False identifications to rent the switch cars were also found in the closet along with a "bakery list," which stated how to go about a bank robbery.

If that wasn't enough evidence, Hunter stated, there had been a confession by Michael Bortin, not to a police officer, but to a friend of his, that he had been involved in the bank robbery, "that it was himself, Kathy Soliah, Jim Kilgore, and Emily Harris who went inside, and it was Emily Harris who pulled the trigger." Hunter said that he confessed this information to two different people, both of whom testified in front of a grand jury.

Next in the presentation was a photograph of a 9-mm handgun sitting on a dressing table in Kathy Soliah's bedroom on Precita. The manual for that handgun was in the closet, and her fingerprints were on it.

In summary, Hunter said that Kathy Soliah had been an active member of the SLA. After the shootout, she had participated in the Guild Savings and Loan robbery as well as the Crocker National Bank robbery. "There were several other bombings in this case: It will be the Mission Street, Taraval, Emeryville, and Marin County. Patty Hearst would have testified that the defendant was involved in the planning for these bombings. She would have told of their surveillance of the areas and also explained their mission to try to incite something within the government.

Hunter showed another document on the screen, the rental application for a post office box. The name on the rental identification was Linda Bernasconi. The handwriting on the application was proved to be Kathy Soliah's handwriting. Her fingerprint was also on the document. In addition, another document shown in the middle of the screen was a letter to Western Reserve asking for explosive fuse to be sent to the P.O. Box that the defendant had rented. "That request had been made about a week before the bombing here in Los Angeles," Hunter said. "That handwriting was also matched to the defendant.

"In addition, a cousin of either Joe Remiro or Russ Little had met Kathy Soliah at the rally where she defended the SLA. The cousin was prepared to testify that Soliah had passed her notes to try to help Remiro and Little escape from jail."

Now that Hunter had outlined for Judge Fidler the evidence against Sara Jane Olson and how it would have been presented in court, it was Shawn Chapman's turn. Did she have an offer of proof to counter the prosecution's stance as to the timelines of the plea negotiations or any evidence that had been presented? She said that Patricia Hearst was a convicted felon and had been proved a liar time and time again. She said that they could impeach Ms. Hearst. Then she asked, "What does this have to do with anything?"

Judge Fidler replied, "It has a lot to do with it because the linchpin of the motion that your client has filed is her factual innocence. And if her factual innocence is not apparent at this point, the burden is no longer on the People: The burden is on you to show good cause to withdrawing the plea by clear and convincing evidence. The burden has shifted to you. The People made an offer of proof of what they're capable of presenting. One of the things I have to decide is whether this claim of 'innocent' has any merit whatsoever. It has a lot to do with it."

Chapman answered, "Well, excuse me."

The judge reiterated that Olson's motion to withdraw her plea failed to mention coercion by Tony Serra. All it said was that she felt she was a coward. He said, "You show me where it says psychological coercion by Mr. Serra, which is what you claim."

Chapman said, "It obviously doesn't say that."

Judge Fidler replied, "Yes, obviously it does not."

As for Chapman's offer of proof, she stated that Bill Harris would testify that Ms. Olson was innocent. Joe Remiro would also testify on her behalf. Russ Little would say that she was never a member of the SLA. Wendy Yoshimura would say that she was not in Los Angeles at the time the bombs were planted, that she was in Mendocino County. Marty Soliah would testify for her. Then she said, "And having been a member of the O. J. Simpson defense team, as I sit here, it's just reminiscent of the mountain of evidence that those district attorneys spoke of in that case, and we all know the result there. This reminds me very much of that, really much ado about nothing when it comes down to what this case is all about."

Fidler interrupted, "You think blowing up police officers and bystanders is nothing?"

Chapman said that, no, she thought that was horrible but her client had nothing to do with it. She said there was no direct evidence. It was circumstantial. She said their most reliable testimony would have been from James Marshall, who claimed to have sold her the bomb parts, but he was dead, so he wouldn't be able to testify. Again she called Patty Hearst a liar.

Judge Fidler said, "Correct me if I'm wrong. All the witnesses you stated on behalf of the defense are all convicted felons, are they not?"

"Yes, they are. Not all of them, not all of them."

"What is your response to the fingerprint and handwriting evidence that links your client to the crime here in Los Angeles, whether she actively planted or made a bomb or whether she merely assisted by ordering parts or being aware and storing parts? What is your response to that?"

Chapman told the judge to correct her if she was wrong, but she didn't find that those documents connected her client to the bombs in Los Angeles.

Fidler said, "If you have the exact same kind of bombs, and the bombs are similar and some end up in Los Angeles and some apparently are meant for somewhere else, you believe that's exculpatory [tending to clear from a charge of guilt]?

Chapman continued saying that the only handwriting she found suspect was that contained in the letter with the name Linda Bernasconi ordering the bomb fuses. With this, she concluded her defense. Now it was the prosecutors' turn again; however, Judge Fidler had promised Chapman that she would have the last word.

Michael Latin reminded the court, "Russell Little is a convicted felon; Joe Remiro is a convicted felon; Wendy Yoshimura is a convicted felon; and Bill Harris is a convicted felon. Furthermore, all of those names were missing from the witness list. He said that they had gotten a letter from the defense team stating that Wendy Yoshimura would not be called as a witness. Ms. Chapman, who had stated that fuses were not even used in the pipe bombs, was correct. But those fuses were part of the evidence that proved that Kathy Soliah was involved in the makings of other bombs. She participated in the making of the SLA bombs for the purpose of committing murder of innocent people." He added that the fuse that had been ordered was solely for the purpose of bomb making. It was an order for two hundred feet of it. "In all that time," he said," there were nine different identities that Kathy Soliah had taken on."

He explained again how these false IDs had been obtained. "That's what the defendant did when she changed her name to Sara Jane Olson. She used a false date of birth, she used a false prior place of birth, she used all kinds of false information using the same general M.O. that all of the SLA members did.

"The data that was recorded on those index cards in handwriting that was shown on one of the slides contained a number of deceased infants whose identities were subsequently used by each of the members of the SLA and those cards were found in the closet on Precita along with identification cards with the SLA members' photographs with the names of the deceased infants. Those things were done in the defendant's handwriting."

Chapman got in her last word: "I neglected to mention the testimony of Josephine Soliah who is not a convicted felon." She admitted that her client may have done some illegal things but that they did not rise to the level of conspiring to murder. Soliah gave a eulogy for her dear friend Angela Atwood. She wanted to help the fugitives because she was afraid they might be killed as her friend was. Chapman reminded the court of the "context of the times." The public was questioning authority "more than they do today."

When she finished, Judge Fidler said, "I have one question and I have something to read and then I will go ahead and rule.

"Again, I understand she's withdrawing her declaration because to leave her declaration in will subject her to cross-examination. Is she willing to be cross-examined on her involvement in this case as part of this motion?"

Chapman asked, "Her involvement in the case?"

"Yes, as to her guilt or innocence. What she says is she is

moving to withdraw her plea because she is in fact innocent. I am saying, is she willing to subject herself to cross-examination?"

"No."

"All right. Let me read a fax I just got. Thank you. This is from Mr. Serra:

> "*Dear Judge Fidler:*
>
> *I apologize profusely for not making the appearance today; but I attribute it to my karma, not to my volition.*
>
> *I got up at 3:50 A.M., arrived at the Oakland Airport for my 7:00 A.M. flight at approximately 5:30 A.M. This has always been adequate time since September 11th for security check, et cetera. Oakland Airport this morning was an extraordinary mess. It turns out it was a two-hour-plus security line. At five minutes past 7:00 I was about twenty minutes from the metal detector and my flight had left. I know from past experience the 8:30 flight is booked completely, and I figured there were others ahead of me who had also missed the 7:00 A.M. flight who will be on standby before me. Therefore, in a state of mind of dank frustration, I went home and went back to bed.*
>
> *However, as you know, I am in jury trial in Redding, California, which is a four-hour drive from San Francisco and had arranged for a 1:00 P.M. flight back to San Francisco from Los Angeles. I did not know there would be an afternoon session and figured this hearing will [sic] be finished by 10:30 A.M. given a 9:30 appearance.*
>
> *I won't ever let this happen again. I will fly the night before. Please accept my heartfelt apology.*
>
> *Mr. Serra'* "

Judge Fidler said, "Now I am prepared to rule. Let's talk about the burden of proof and the nature of the motion. This is a motion to withdraw a guilty plea that has actually been entered once and then we've all tried to come up with the terminology for what took place on November 6. I will call it reaffirming the plea in open court before me.

"The standard of proof and burden of proof and the standard to withdraw a guilty plea.... first of all, the burden is on the person making the motion, which is the defendant. She must show good cause and she must show that by clear and convincing evidence." He then said that Serra's motion would be stricken because although Serra may have been telling the truth in his note, "That is not an excuse for failing to show up, and to not call the court is the bigger joke of all, with all due respect.

"I honestly wonder sometimes, Ms. Chapman (and not necessarily directed to you), I wonder if the defense thinks that I drive a car to work or I take a turnip truck. Seriously, think about that because some of the events and some of the actions in this case suggest that the defense believes the latter."

He went over Olson's declaration to withdraw her plea and Serra's declaration that he had coerced her. He reminded her that he had been with her in chambers on the day that she had pled guilty, and there had been verbal as well as written communications regarding her plea and her pending prison term. There were no promises made by the district attorney as to what representations they would make to the parole board in that meeting, he said.

Next he went into Serra's declaration that the "events of September 11 have created a climate of opinion based on the surge of patriotism that precludes the defendant from having a fair trial; that Sara Jane Olson had been labeled by the prosecution as a domestic terrorist and a jury panel might be biased and a conviction on the conspiracy charge was great."

The judge said that there was no support of that. He said, "I think it's fine to be concerned that an act that absolutely rocked this country might in some way affect this trial." However, there were no specific facts, as a jury had not yet been selected. He added, "I think this constant trying to link this trial to the tragedy of September 11 is just abhorrent. It is just not there, and I am so tired of it and it is so unfair not only to all those who died on September 11 but to the jurors of this county that they somehow cannot separate what took place on September 11, 2001, from the date of the crimes in this matter is absolutely ridiculous, not supported by any fact, and it's just that. It's just an allegation to attempt to get another continuance in this case, so every time that the defendant was forced to actually look at going to trial, there was always something that came up. There has been every attempt to keep this case from going to trial.

"The fact that Ms. Olson has withdrawn her declaration, she does not have to be cross-examined and Mr. Serra is not here to present anything more, and the fact that there's all these inherent inconsistencies within the declaration, they don't at all support each other nor do they support your version of the events.

"The burden of proof in a criminal trial as it should and always must resides with the People. And they have to prove it beyond a reasonable doubt and the defendant doesn't have to say a word. That privilege against self-incrimination is one of the most important that we have in the United States; once a person pleads guilty, that's gone. The burden of proof has shifted; the burden of proof is on the defendant. And I think it just speaks volumes without a word being spoken that Ms. Olson will not submit to cross-examination on her guilt or innocence.

"You have yet to really explain the fingerprint evidence. You can say he said, she said, each side has its convicted felons. Your witnesses are either convicted felons or one family member, but you have yet to adequately explain fingerprint evidence and handwriting evidence and to say 'well, it wasn't these fuses, that may have been some other bomb.' Please. It just doesn't add up.

"I don't believe for a minute that Ms. Olson is seeking to withdraw her plea because she is in fact innocent. I believe that she has a tremendously difficult time admitting to what she did. I don't think she likes having to tell her supporters that she pled guilty and that she *is* guilty because she had a whole community that not only posted bail for her, they bought her story, lock, stock, and barrel, and that guilty plea had to come as a shock to them. Not once but twice! Then she goes out and attempts to gain the benefit of the bargain but at the same time be able to say I'm really innocent—it's the system that's making me do it.'

"And I say to that, that's nonsense. Okay, she pled guilty because she *is* guilty. The facts show she is guilty. She admitted she is guilty, and everything I heard since then I just do not accept. You have not convinced me. You have not carried your burden and therefore the motion is denied. The plea stands.

"I couldn't for a minute accept a guilty plea from a person that I believed was innocent, nor would I. I could not sleep. I intend to sleep very well tonight."

Justice

Judge Fidler informed Sara Jane that she could spend the holidays with her family as had been arranged at her first guilty plea. He decided to delay her sentencing until the very day she was to be incarcerated, January 18, 2002, which meant that her supporters would have another month to wait before getting their money back, assuming that Sara Jane Olson did not decide to flee.

On the first week of January, Sara Jane wrote a letter to her bail donors thanking them for allowing her to have the past two and one-half years with Fred and her daughters. She realized their generosity had been extremely difficult due to the long delays. "Like many journeys, it slipped from my control at certain junctures and I made mistakes."

She reiterated her innocence and said that she had pled guilty so that her family, who were exhausted and broke, could get on with their lives. She had relied on Tony Serra's expertise. "I would no more face a monstrously huge criminal trial (one of the largest, most complicated in American legal history against a lone citizen) without trained legal advice than I would have a gardener remove an inflamed strawberry gall bladder. Maybe someone else would but not this 'girl.'"

She explained that the conspiracy charge was difficult to defend and said that it would thrive in a courtroom culture of "circumstantial innuendo." Her withdrawal motion had resulted in a display of Napoleonic law when the defendant was presumed guilty until proven innocent.

///

On December 13, Olson granted an interview, at Shawn Chapman's Beverly Hill office, with *Los Angeles Times* and *New York Times* reporters. Her demeanor was cheerful if not relieved. Resigning herself to years in prison, she said she knew she was breaking the law when she had decided to help the remaining SLA members. In her mind, she had been morally obligated to help the SLA. "I thought I was doing society a favor by preventing more deaths, and it was in honor of my friend Angela," she said. "It doesn't mean there are no regrets. There were just not bad intentions." She said that she had only had a mild interest in politics and that she rejected the SLA's violent agenda. She continued to deny involvement in the bombings or in participating in any bank robberies.

If she was truly motivated by compassion, she was asked, why had she chosen to assist a group that killed the first black school superintendent in Oakland? She replied that she had told the other members that the killing was politically inept. She said it had alienated the people the group claimed to be representing, minorities. Then she was asked why had it not alienated her?

"I really just thought I was trying to help them to survive. Does it help if more people are dying?"

She thought Judge Fidler had acted inappropriately as had the prosecutors who, she said, had lied about their intentions with the State Board of Prison Terms to impose a life sentence. Also Sara Jane was not impressed with Tony Serra's "bad Karma," and she was angry with him for not showing up at her hearing, even if he was working the case pro bono.

She admitted that the prosecution had a "circumstantial case" against her and that a jury might have found her guilty for conspiring with the SLA. She called that a "downfall," and added that the biggest "mystery" was a letter that appeared to be sent in her handwriting ordering fuses before the bombing attempt. She said that it looked like her handwriting, but she didn't remember writing the letter.

She hoped that she wouldn't be harassed in prison and said

that she would use the time constructively. "I don't expect it will be a lot of fun, but it will be educational in many ways." She added that she would use the time to learn Spanish and to teach other inmates English.

Sara Jane said that her family did not know about her previous life. She had told Fred that she had had a falling out with her parents and he could not ask her about it. "Why would I have told them? Would it have made my life better? No. Would it make it worse? Probably."

She reflected on the past few months and agreed that her case had become a circus. She compared her story to a modern-day fable, with the moral being: "Be careful what you do—it may come back to haunt you." Her closing statement to the reporter was, "I'd rather not go down in history at all. I'm going down because of history."

Olson admitted that the prosecution had offered her more lenient treatment if she would agree to cooperate in the prosecution of other members of the SLA in particular in the case of the Sacramento bank robbery. She refused because of the harm it might inflict on those who might end up in jail, she said. "I know they have lives like me and I don't want to destroy other peoples' lives the way my life is being destroyed."

Sara Jane Olson's guilty plea prompted Jon Opsahl to step his pressure on the Sacramento prosecutors to solve his mother's murder. He had waited twenty-five years. He launched a website, *www.myrnaopsahl.com* that detailed the evidence against the SLA at the Crocker National Bank in Carmichael. In his mind, it was unfathomable that with all that evidence, the case had not been pursued. The Los Angeles prosecutors agreed with him and continued their pressure in Sacramento as well.

With the help of her investigator, Jan Skully, the Sacramento District Attorney decided there was enough evidence to make the arrests. New forensic techniques connected some of the lead pellets that were in Mrs. Opsahl's body to a shotgun found at the

SLA safehouses in San Francisco, at the time of the Harris's and Hearst's arrest, tying the SLA to the crime. Because lead is so impure, each batch of shotgun pellets is unique, and sources close to the investigation said the lead in Mrs. Opsahl's body was a direct match to shells found in San Francisco. "They all came out of the same melt of lead," one source said. "And there's ton of evidence that links them to the safehouses. We have them coming out of there, and their fingerprints are all over there." New fingerprint techniques had been developed as well, which could positively connect them to the robbery case.

Up until now, the strongest evidence the Sacramento District Attorney's office had was from Patty Hearst's testimony and her book, *Every Secret Thing*. Olson's guilty plea had given Hearst more credibility. But the Sacramento authorities also had evidence from Steve Soliah's trial in 1976. Prosecutors had introduced a wealth of physical evidence including testimony in that trial from an FBI expert that pistol shells found at the scene of the robbery matched shells found inside the Precita Avenue house Steve shared with Patty. The 9-mm bullets had carried markings that were made by the same "Bunter tool." In addition, there was the license plate evidence. But in spite of all the evidence, after Steve's acquittal, prosecutors had dropped the case.

After Sara Jane was arrested and the judge allowed the SLA history to be admitted as evidence against her, the Crocker National Bank robbery and Myrna Opsahl's murder came to light again. All of Olson's maneuvering and attorney posturing was a gift, in a way, to the prosecutors. Boxes of evidence appeared. Their case was not just circumstantial. The Sacramento's district attorney had time to reconsider the case and more importantly, media coverage and the extra time gave Jon Opsahl the chance of a public forum to find his mother's killers.

The Sacramento district attorney's office had originally planned to make the charges on the same day as Sara Jane Olson's sentencing. But officials were fearful there might be problems arresting the suspects or that they would flee. Sacramento sheriff's detectives flew to Los Angeles, Oakland, and Portland, Oregon on Monday, January 14, to begin surveillance of Emily Harris, Bill Harris, and Michael Bortin. On Tuesday, Sacramento Sheriff Lou Blanas phoned the Opsahl family to tell them officers planned to make the arrests the next day. On Wednesday morning, January 16, 2002, Sara Jane Olson's fifty-fifth birthday, the officers moved in simultaneously.

At 8:02 A.M., fifty-five-year-old Emily Harris, now using her middle name, Emily Montague, was arrested without incident while driving a green Chrysler Sebring near her home in Altadena, California. She was taken to the Criminal Courts Building in Los Angeles where she was seen by a local magistrate who remanded her into the custody of the Sacramento Sheriff's Department. Unlike her arrest for Patty Hearst's kidnapping in September 1975, she remained stoic throughout the flight on a sheriff's airplane to Sacramento.

After her first conviction, Emily had waged a hunger strike in the women's prison in Frontera to get a coveted slot in the institution's computer training program. Eventually earning parole, she became a computer consultant for the entertainment industry, settling in the upscale section of Altadena, with rambling houses and imported cars. Altadena was home to corporate executives and Pasadena's nearby Jet Propulsion Laboratory. Emily lived with her partner, Noreen Lenay, in a four-bedroom house, which they had bought for $256,500 in 1995. Neighbors were shocked that Emily Montague was Emily Harris. They described the two women as lovers of animals, who hired a gardener to keep the grounds of their Spanish-style home immaculate. Their next-door neighbor said that Harris and Lenay had gone to Kauai before the holidays, and when they returned, they made macadamia nut cookies and shared them with the neighbors. Emily's morning jogs were now morning walks. This same woman who had called Myrna Opsahl a "bourgeois pig" after she shot her, had grieved when she had to put one of her aging dogs to sleep.

At 8:18 A.M., Emily's former husband, fifty-six-year-old, Bill

Harris, driving a green Honda Passport, was arrested in Oakland, California as he was taking his seven and thirteen-year-old sons to their San Francisco school. During the arrest, the boys called their mother from a cell phone and she came to pick them up. They were all extremely upset. Bill was taken to Sacramento and booked into the County Main jail where he made a scene to officers about being arrested in front of his children. He was outraged.

After he'd completed his jail term for kidnapping Patty Hearst, Bill had conducted some investigations for the district attorney's office in San Francisco, but his felony record kept him from obtaining a state license so he had hired on with Stuart Hanlon as a private investigator. That is where he met his current wife, Rebecca S. Young, a San Francisco attorney who worked in Hanlon's firm. They married and had two children. At the time of Harris' second arrest, Rebecca Young Harris was a teacher of law, running a criminal defense clinic. The family lived in a modest, two-story gray house about a mile from Oakland's Lake Merritt, where Bill had given Kathy Soliah the eulogy tape for the six slain SLA members. The Volvo station wagon in the Harris's driveway had license plates reading, "FRDM4U (Freedom For You).

After Sara Jane's arrest in 1999, Bill Harris had given an interview to a reporter from the *Los Angeles Times*. Harris had said, "If you do something and you succeed, then you're a revolutionary of high quality, and you get to be George Washington, the father of the country. But if you challenge power and you're rubbed out, you're in the trash bin of history." During that interview, he described himself as a "soccer dad," and when he was asked if he would ever explain his past to his oldest son, who was eleven at the time, he said, "He knows something's going on. I'll sit down with him when he's eighteen and try to explain it to him."

Also at 8:18, Portland police arrested fifty-three-year-old Michael Bortin at his home. Officers had staked out his house and called him on the phone telling him to come outside and surrender. The call awakened him and his wife, Sara Jane's sister,

Josephine. They got up to find their house surrounded by police. Michael went outside and was arrested in his underwear. The Bortins were raising four children, the youngest just twelve years old. Michael had spent the past twenty years in the hardwood flooring business and called his company Zen Hardwood Floors.

After her husband's arrest, Josephine told reporters, "It was pretty shocking." Police officers in bulletproof vests forced her husband to the ground and pointed guns at his head as they handcuffed him. "All I know is they did a bit of overkill this morning," she said. "We weren't going out with guns ablazing. We're just two middle-aged, middle-class, hard-working people who were not expecting this."

Authorities held Bortin in the Portland jail pending an extradition hearing to be sent to Sacramento. His next-door neighbor, Nick Henderson, told a reporter for the *Sacramento Bee*: "My gut reaction is, this is a big, blind stupid political machine that needs to be fed, and I'm really sad that my relatively nice neighbor here is a part of it." But after a short pause, he added, "Maybe that's an insensitive remark on my part. I don't know anything about the person who was killed. But it's been so many years. The context I'm living with is so different."

He wasn't aware that Bortin had once served eighteen months in prison for the explosives charge at the Berkeley Bomb Factory or that he'd violated parole and spent another eighteen months in prison or that he'd spent almost eight years in hiding before resurfacing because his mother was ill. He did know that Bortin kept a tidy yard, did fine woodworking, and careful refurbishing.

The Bortins lived in a neighborhood of old Victorian houses, with young families. Josephine still worked as a night nurse. A bumper sticker on Bortin's van read, "Visualize whirled peas."

Although the prosecutors had requested that Olson be arrested on Friday when her sentencing for the bomb plot was scheduled, the Sacramento sheriff's office called Shawn Chapman and told her that deputies were not going to allow someone suspected of murder to remain free. They said, "Either you make arrangements for Olson or we'll come and find her." They gave Chapman two hours to surrender her client. She called Sara Jane and at 3:30 P.M., she and Fred and their daughters came to Chapman's office.

At 4:30 P.M. that Wednesday, January 16, after a tearful good-bye to her family, Sara Jane Olson surrendered to authorities and was booked at the Twin Towers jail on suspicion of murder. Her formal arraignment would be the following Tuesday, January 22, in Sacramento.

Steve Soliah, who was reached by phone, had no comment. Marty Soliah said that he was not surprised by the murder charges. "I knew it was coming as long as Patty Hearst keeps shooting her mouth off," he told a CNN producer at his home in Palmdale. "It disgusts me."

Jon Opsahl, a doctor now, expressed his thanks to the prosecutors in Los Angeles and Sacramento for their work. He talked about how his mother's death had haunted him all these years. When he was a boy riding his bike around his neighborhood in Carmichael and he would see a green Oldsmobile station wagon just like his mother's, he wanted above all else for her to be at the wheel. Weeks after she had been murdered, he would still burst out of his bedroom to yell for her, only to catch himself remembering that she was dead.

"It's not a grief issue after twenty-seven years," he said, "It's the injustice of known killers being allowed to get away with murder."

Jon Opsahl said, "My dad, who is seventy-six, is very pleased. He always held out hope that something would break in the case." Jon and his wife, Teresa, had devoted their lives to raising their own three children: Lauren, fourteen, Falon, six, and Jonathon, three. Teresa said that Jon's mom had never had the opportunity to see how great the kids she had brought into the world had turned out. "She'll never be able to know what great grandkids she had."

Jon Opsahl recalled an airplane vacation to Hawaii with his family two years earlier. Falon had never flown before. She looked at the clouds swirling outside of the plane's window and asked her parents, "Is this where Grandma is?"

With the new murder charges pending, the chance that Olson would ever be sent to Shakopee Women's Prison in Minnesota became remote. Now she would be needed in Sacramento for the upcoming trials of her former comrades as well as for her own trial for murder. In return for their testimony, her former comrades, Patty Hearst, Wendy Yoshimura, and her brother Steve Soliah were given immunity from prosecution.

Sara Jane was twenty-seven years old when she had eulogized her friend, Angela Atwood, at Ho Chi Minh Park. On her fifty-fifth birthday, January 16, 2002, she was being held accountable for the decisions made twenty-eight years earlier. Perhaps for the first time in her life, Olson was fully realizing the inevitability of facing legal consequences for her actions. The next day, Judge Fidler would explain to her what those consequences would be.

Sentence

Sara Jane entered the courtroom like she had so many times in the past two-and-one-half years, throwing kisses to her family and supporters who had flown in from the Twin Cities to offer their support. There was one significant difference, however. The quality of her stage presence would have no affect on her future. Her sentence had been determined before she walked into the courtroom and even an Oscar performance could not change that.

Sara Jane looked extremely tense, her smile, strained, her fingers clasped tightly in front of her. Her long strawberry blonde hair was straw-like and streaked with gray. There were new lines on her face, like a map of the past twenty-seven years. Chapman draped one arm around Olson's chair and sometimes placed her hand on her arm for support.

This hearing was merely a formality, a chance for some of her supporters to be heard, and an opportunity to get their statements on the record for the Parole Board. Perhaps it would make a difference down the line. After all they'd been through, collecting the bail money, setting up the web site, organizing the letter campaign, the cookbook, and the press conferences, making the trips back and forth from St. Paul to Los Angeles, it had come to this. It certainly had been an ordeal.

Sara Jane had written a statement to the probation board, where she explained her actions. She spoke of her formative years in the sixties and seventies, the Civil Rights Movement, the Vietnam War, the inequalities and unfairness in the world's population. She included the Watergate scandal and wrote, "With the apparent collapse of democracy due to the criminalization of President Nixon, there were very few anchors left to hold on to for stability." In the midst of all that turmoil, she had gone to Mexico with a girlfriend and come home a month later to find that her best friend, Angela Atwood, had joined a "heretofore unknown urban guerrilla group and had gone 'underground.'" She described Atwood as a "Girl Scout," who was a product of her times—liberal, antiwar, and a lover of movies and Rock and Roll. Sara Jane said that Angela's newfound militancy hadn't meant anything to her but she has since wondered if she should have been more concerned. "At the time, it just seemed to be a part of the "Berkeley Baptism" into progressive politics, one that many embraced and then, after incorporating that point of view, went on with their ordinary lives."

She wrote of the "blooding birthing" of the Symbionese Liberation Army but said that the police and FBI fire was out of proportion to the havoc that the group had been capable of wreaking. She blamed the hysteria of the media and law enforcement for making the SLA, conceding, though, that they had done some destructive things. She averred that Marcus Foster's assassination and Patty Hearst's kidnapping were senseless. But she said she had been confused at the time.

When Emily Harris asked her for money, Sara Jane wrote that she thought it would help save their lives and it was the "Christian thing to do." "At that time, loyalty to one's friend [Atwood] counted for something, even if that friend seemed to be on the path to self-destruction." Olson said that she barely knew Bill and Emily, and "I knew nothing about Hearst other than what I read in the papers. I never really got to know her, but from what I saw, she seemed committed to her cause."

Olson had sought the help of Jack Scott because if the Harrises sought his help, that would eliminate their need for her help, she wrote. She believed that he had connections, money, and ingenuity. She knew they went out "east," but not exactly where.

The reason she helped them after their return, she wrote, was, "There was a certain glamour attached to them. They were just these three people rather small in physical stature who, I thought would be shot to pieces if I didn't do my bit to help. I admit that I rented a car here-and-there, that I borrowed money from my brother, sister, and boyfriend to give to them since I didn't make much extra; I transported them occasionally and helped them find apartments. I did help Emily move into a Precita Avenue apartment. I agreed to take a carload of her things—clothes, books, household goods—to an empty apartment. I donated a box of kitchen utensils and a couple of cookbooks.

"My checks that were found in that apartment could have come in with those utensils. The checks were for an old, defunct account. I remember this because a year before, early 1974, I had been returning home quite late from a theater rehearsal, dressed in a floor-length rehearsal skirt and high-heel boots, when a man began to chase me. I ran, tripped over the hood of a car, and flipped on my back in time to barely deflect a punch, after which he ran off with my purse. I woke up early the next morning, went to the bank to report my checks stolen, and found out that some-one had already tried to cash a check and had been apprehended. I closed the account."

In this letter to the Probation Board, Olson could not defend the letter she allegedly wrote to order fuses. "Even though I am told that law enforcement had the technology to reproduce handwriting and transfer a fingerprint (one of mine was found on the letter), it is hard for me to imagine that they would manu-facture evidence against me," she wrote.

"I had been thinking of going away for a long time in the fall of 1975. I knew that, since I had helped them get birth certificates for IDs, I was probably guilty of something that could earn me a stint in jail if found out. I had gotten a false ID for myself, since aiding the remaining SLA fugitives in their daily survival and using my own name seemed rather naïve. I think I had gotten instructions about how to get false IDs out of *The Berkeley Barb* or some other alternative newspaper. At the time, young men, often accompanied by their girlfriends, were going across the border to Canada to avoid the draft and, accordingly, such knowledge was not considered ill-gotten.

"My 'plans' suddenly were put into play with my brother's arrest. Those of the more famous three, of course, preceded his. Four, that's right. I always forget about Wendy Yoshimura. I never knew her. I saw her, but I didn't really know her. My brother, according to the newspaper, was charged with harboring. I knew that would probably be my fate, as well. Then later, he was charged with bank robbery and murder. I was appalled and frightened. Here was a completely innocent man. I knew my parents couldn't finance legal help for the harboring charge, much less for a bank robbery trial. It was a devastating development. I knew they would never be able to help me or my sister, so we decided to stay away for awhile."

She wrote that like many others of her generation, her zeal led to some bad decisions. But even so, she still participated in helping her community and having three daughters made that even more imperative. She said that she never meant to hurt anyone. "I will continue to live with the agony and sadness that my unknowingly participating in such actions brings. I believed that the only risk was to myself and I felt it was duty, out of loyalty and love for Angela and her memory, to help her friends.

"I was a member of a generation of idealists and I have never lost my desire to care about my country and its people. I know that people can care for other people but still bring them harm and suffering. I am one of those people and for anything I have done to harm others, I am truly sorry and gracefully accept the prison sentence to which I am assigned."

The Probation Report had nineteen letters of reference, written by her supporters. Andy Dawkins staked his "political reputation," that Olson posed no threat to society if she were not incarcerated. "On the contrary," he wrote, "she would most certainly continue her twenty-two-year history of making the world a better place with fuller and happier lives."

Peter Rachleff, a Ph.D. from the Department of History at a private college in Minnesota, also wrote a compelling letter in his friend's behalf. He spoke of the prosecution's "broad-ranging conspiracy case against her" and how he'd watched the mass media vilify her and turn her into a caricature that did not reflect who she really was.

He said that Olson's case had been an interesting learning experience for him. "In twenty years of speaking out on behalf of various 'causes,' I have never received the sorts of hate mail and hostile phone calls that my engagement with Sara's case has provoked. These responses have whetted my interest further, to explore why it is that this story pushed such 'hot buttons' with some elements in our community. I have begun to think more systematically about how our current culture has not allowed us to make peace with the 1960s, to place the behaviors of antiwar activists, anti-racist activists, and even underground political groups in a context that enables us to understand them, to understand ourselves, and to understand the continuing development of our culture and our nation since then. Sara Jane Olson has found herself, unwillingly, I believe, as an icon of that period, and many, many passionate feelings have been projected upon her."

Amy Gardner, a preschool teacher who had know Olson since 1982 when they worked together in a group to oppose apartheid in South Africa noted: "Whether we needed someone to go into an elementary school and educate children about apartheid, contact hospitals for donations of medical supplies, get the neighborhood drug store to donated notebooks and pencils, or cook a fundraising dinner, Sara did it," she wrote. She said that Sara was "selfless."

She had another point to make as well. "If the purpose of putting people in prison is to rehabilitate them, there is no need. Sara is a fine human being just the way she is. If the purpose of prison is to take dangerous people off the streets, there is no need. The Sara we've come to know and love over the past twenty years would hurt no one. If the purpose of prison is to punish or exact amends for wrongdoings, has she not been punished enough by living a life in exile for the past twenty-five years, separated from her parents and siblings, keeping such a huge secret? Have amends not been made through all her good works, the way she has carried herself as a human being for the past one-quarter century? If retribution needs to be made, I hope it will be in a venue where Sara can keep giving. It will be a great loss to the community should she go behind bars. Sara is a giver, not a taker. Please don't take the opportunity for this to continue away from us."

There were letters from her detractors as well. Dr. Trygve Opsahl wrote in part, "She shows no remorse or regret. I feel she is the same person now as she was then." His son, Jon wrote that he believed Sara Jane was in the bank during the robbery and she could give evidence against his mother's killer if she desired. "Her refusal to cooperate shows no remorse for this crime or compassion for the victim's family. She takes no responsibility for any of her crimes. She is a convicted terrorist who refuses to take responsibility. She should do her time."

The shotgun pellets removed from Myrna Opsahl's body had been analyzed in 2001 by what the FBI called "Inductively Coupled Plasma-Atomic Emission Spectroscopy." The tests, with accuracy rates comparable to DNA testing, matched the lead of the pellets in Mrs. Opsahl's torso to the lead found in shotgun shells discovered in an SLA safe house in San Francisco. The palm prints found at the Precita Avenue safe house matched Sara Jane Olson's palm prints—or Kathy Soliah's. Patty Hearst's story had been made credible by hard evidence. Sara Jane knew that her nemesis, Hearst, was not her only potential detractor in the upcoming murder trial. Her brother, Steve, her brother-in-law, Mike, Wendy Yoshimura, and Jim Kilgore if they found him, could also testify against her. No matter what happened in the present courtroom sentencing, her troubles were far from over.

The defiance in Sara Jane's eyes had finally dissolved. Her lips and her chin trembled. From her seat, she faced Fred, dressed in a white shirt and suit, looking like he had lost a war. Their three daughters sat next to him, dressed impeccably, the weight of the world on their young tear-stained faces. Elsie Soliah was there as well, and she would finally be heard after a lifetime of silence. Marty sat next to her, quiet for a change. Steve looked grim. He wouldn't have to worry about being charged with bank robbery again, but he would probably be called to testify against his sister and his brother-in-law. Of course, Josephine could not be there to support her sister. Her husband, Mike, was in a Portland jail.

Two rows back were Jon Opsahl and his wife, Teresa. Members of the police force were also in attendance. The courtroom was packed with friends, relatives, and others who wanted to see Sara Jane Olson sentenced to a term at least as long as the years she'd been free.

Shawn Chapman asked the judge if he had had a chance to review some of the letters that had been sent on Olson's behalf. He said he had. She then informed him that some people had flown in from St. Paul and would like to say a few words on Sara Jane's behalf. Judge Fidler didn't have a problem with that, as long as they realized that Sara Jane's sentencing had already been predetermined. However, if she wanted their statements for the record he would hear what they had to say. Chapman introduced each supporter before they spoke.

Dr. Francisco De La Rosa was an emergency physician at United Hospital in St. Paul and worked with Fred. He was most impressed with Sara Jane's cooking skills and the fact that she had included him in her family. Fred's brother-in-law Kenneth Fischer from Ann Arbor, Michigan, who had known Sara Jane for twenty-three years, spoke of her dedication to the community.

Sara Jane's daughters' teacher, Indranee Sivagnanaguru, lauded what a good parent she had been, how she had taught her children to help and care for other people. Sivagnanaguru expressed her distress at how the case had affected the three young girls. Pastor John Darlington, pastor of Minnehaha United Methodist Church who had supported Olson from the beginning, spoke of her community service, feeding the hungry, helping house the homeless, reading to the blind, helping people learn English as their second language. He said she was the one the church called on when they needed someone to act out a Bible story so that it would come to life for the kids.

Elsie Soliah spoke on her daughter's behalf. To watch her was like watching an older version of Sara Jane, an identical jaw line, similar eyes facial expressions and gestures, with the same determination and defiance. Her hair was brilliant white with short, tight curls. She even wore large round glasses. She defended her daughter expressively in a voice that ranged from high to low as she read from her prepared script.

Elsie spoke of how she had been fooled by FBI Agent Curtis Holt in 1976, thinking that the authorities had lost interest in their daughter. She said when she and Marty had asked him about the "bomb rumor," they were told that it was a "symbolic piece of junk." According to Elsie, they were told that the bomb could not possibly have exploded. Then she talked about the day that Detective Fanning and Detective Reyes had come to their youngest daughter, Martha's, house. They had told her, "This particular bomb had sat on their desk for years in their department as a paper weight," she said, glancing over at Hunter and Latin. She had been appalled at the last hearing when the prosecutors had used their Power Point presentation to show the destruction that would have occurred had the bomb gone off.

In the end, she reiterated that her daughter was never a member of the SLA. "Our daughter has lived an upstanding life and was active in her community affairs, and she was arrested after all these years. We have been harassed for twenty-six years. Our mail tampered, telephone tapped, even film stolen from our camera at our youngest son's wedding. All I can say is this does not begin to tell you what our lives have been, and so I would just like to say will you please know that our daughter is a good person, but you have heard that already."

Then she bent down to hug Olson, who was seated a few feet away. A sheriff's deputy instinctively approached the two women—defendants are not supposed to be hugged—but Judge Larry Fidler unobtrusively waved the deputy off. Elsie hugged her daughter, and Sara Jane burst fully into tears and hugged her mother back saying, over and over, "You're so nice, you're so nice."

Fred was next. "I am not as good a contemporaneous speaker as the preceding people." Reading from a prepared statement, he explained that he had been practicing medicine for twenty-five years and had been happily married to Sara Jane for twenty-two. He talked about their loving marriage and their happy family life. He spoke of their family values. "We are both great believers in the participatory democracy as a way of life that gives equal opportunity to citizens to achieve health, education, welfare, culture, physical strength, and spiritual growth." He looked over at his wife and said, "I am very proud of you."

He glanced back at his three daughters and then explained to the judge that he and Sara Jane had provided their children with love and security, and how they looked up to their mother as a role model. Once again, he looked lovingly at his wife and said, "Good job."

"They have learned firsthand about the U.S. Constitution with this case and the Bill of Rights as it applies to citizens. They have seen adults in authority positions, and their actions and behavior will leave them life-long memories."

He looked lovingly at Olson and in a quivering voice proclaimed, "And to my lovely wife Sara, California now is entrusted to clothe you and feed you and shelter you and correct you and try you; that this family of ours and our dear friends will not be diminished in our love for you and our respect for you, and we will always stand by you until you come home."

When Fred finished, he took his seat, and Shawn Chapman invited any of Sara Jane's daughters to speak. Her youngest daughter, the same girl who had worn butterfly barrettes in her hair just two and one-half years earlier when her mother was taken to jail for the first time, stood looking older than her fifteen years. Her blond hair was swept back, and she wore a black jacket and striped skirt. She had written her statement on white sheets of paper, which trembled in her hands. She said that her mom had brought her up to believe that she could be anything she wanted to be and that she had the right to speak her opinions. Between bouts of weeping, she spoke of a home filled with love and compassion. She lauded her mom's cooking skills. "She would buy me cake mixes every week so I could get better at cooking 'cause I like it and I wanted to take after my mom."

She sobbed as she explained how she would cry when she was alone for fear of losing her mom. "I am so happy she is strong, she is brave, she has been through the triumph. I will try to be just like her, always have a smile light up the room—she always tries to make everybody laugh. She is one of the best mothers anyone would ever want." With a pleading face, she looked at Judge Fidler and cried, "I am sure if you met her you would agree." This broken-hearted fifteen-year-old girl summed up with, "My mom is just like Stevie Wonder's song, 'You Are the Sunshine of My Life.' I will always be on your side, no matter what happens."

And then, she rushed to her mother and wrapped her arms around her. At first, Sara Jane looked panicked, knowing that this was not allowed. Once again, Judge Fidler waived the deputy away and let this sobbing child be held by her mom. Sara Jane broke down and cried and asked for someone to help her daughter, who was then led back to her seat.

Sara Jane spoke from her seat. "I want to say that because I knew a person at one time named Angela Atwood, who, as I knew her, was a lovely girl and a good friend to me. When friends of hers came asking for help, I helped them. I thought I was doing a good deed; I was saving lives. I still maintain that I did not participate in these events in Los Angeles, but in helping people, if I did anything that brought harm to other people, I am truly sorry because I did not mean to, and I apologize to anyone I might have done that to. I am extremely sincere."

She then thanked the people who had stood by her. She asked for their forgiveness for any pain she might have caused them. She thanked her family, naming her parents; Steve and his partner, Laurie; her sisters Martha and Josephine, and her brother Lance. He had written a letter to the judge, stating, "Sara's no criminal. Her life these past twenty years with its selfless charity and social concern and exhausting schedule is an example and a challenge to us all, and a prison term, most especially a long prison term, is simply not called for in this cases.... Show mercy."

Sara Jane expressed gratitude that she had been able to be reunited with her family again. "I do appreciate what a wonderful family they are."

Michael Latin, with graying hair, wearing a blue suit, dark blue shirt and blue tie, asked permission to show the picture of the bomb once again. Chapman objected, but Judge Fidler overruled her. Latin articulately explained how lucky Officers Bryan and Hall were that the bomb didn't go off. "Because the officers pulled out at an angle, the clothespin got slightly twisted out of joint." From the photograph, it was almost impossible to see the one-thirty-second-of an inch space between the screws that should have made contact. (At a previous hearing the space between the screws had been referred to as one-sixteenth of an inch).

Latin then introduced the two intended victims of the car bombs. Sara Jane was dry-eyed now and watched as John Hall appeared with his arm in a sling, approached the table to speak. "I recall how full the restaurant had been that night with men, women, and children waiting in line to be seated to enjoy their dinners. I specifically remember walking to our black-and-white as I had waved to a little girl no older than seven or eight. She was sitting in a booth with her parents and baby brother no more than four or five in front of our vehicle. The little girl was seated in the front of a large window smiling and waving energetically back at us.

"Your Honor, it horrifies me to think that the lives of dozens of innocent people like that child in the window would have ended in an instant had the defendant and her coconspirators successfully carried out their terrorist acts. As for myself, I would have certainly died that evening leaving behind my wife and three-month-old daughter. My other two children would never have been born, nor one of my grandsons.

"When a person aids and conspires with terrorists, is that person as guilty as a terrorist who commits the act? Does the passing of time cause a terrorist sentencing to lesson? Does the life of a terrorist victim and the lives of his family mean less to the courts then the defendant sitting before you?

"For myself and my family, the only fair sentence in our eyes is for Ms. Olson to serve twenty-six-and-a-half years with no possibility of parole." He added that no form of terrorism should ever be tolerated in our nation.

Marty Feinmark, now fiftyish, with mustache, beard and a bald crown, spoke of being a rookie at the time he found the bomb underneath the unmarked police car. From his training, he knew not to touch any suspicious devices, but he was young and when his flashlight illuminated the trash bag under his car, he crawled underneath and pulled the bag back. When he saw the large pipe and a bunch or red wires, he froze. Monofilament was practically invisible at night and if he'd moved his hand just a couple more inches, and accidentally touched the wire, he said he "wouldn't be here today." He said he wanted the world to know that that particular car was not a police car. It was a Community Relations car for the police department. Civilian employees carrying children would have been the ones to be blown up. "Innocent victims."

"Ms. Olson said she's sorry for what she's done. I can only think of Jon Opsahl's mother. That's probably more important than this case. If she's convicted, I hope she can apologize to those people, too."

Next, Michael Latin disputed one of the statements in Olson's Letter to the Probation Board: "The defendant's performance as an engaged citizen over the last twenty-six years has shown only positive actions that benefits society." He took exception with the word, "only."

"We had admissions at the time of the bail hearing that the defendant has engaged in a number of actions in an effort to evade justice that were felonies in and of themselves including using a false social security number, registering for false identifications, exiting the country with a false passport or the passport of another, voter fraud and applications in two different states for false driver's license, using all false birth dates and registration data." He reminded the judge those crimes were felonies and normally prosecuted. "People suffered consequences for those actions, but Ms. Olson has suffered none."

Judge Fidler assured Mr. Latin that his comments would be noted for the record. And then he sentenced Sara Jane Olson to twenty-years–two consecutive terms of ten years–to-life for the conspiracy bomb plot in 1975. She would serve a minimum of five years and three months. He explained that the Board of Prison Terms would decide if and when she will be released, and he warned her again that her sentence could be for life.

Judge Fidler released the $1 million in bail money that had had been raised by her friends and family but imposed a new bail of $1 million for the murder charge in Sacramento. Of course that was only symbolic since she'd be in jail for the bombing charge anyway.

California law required that arraignment must be made within forty-eight hours of an arrest, and so Judge Fidler arraigned Olson for the Sacramento robbery/murder crime immediately after her sentencing. Shawn Chapman entered her "not guilty" plea so Olson would be formally arraigned on January 22 in Sacramento.

Following the sentencing, Olson was quickly escorted from the courtroom, where she changed into her jail garb, a blue jumpsuit. Fidler allowed her to spend about an hour with more than twenty friends and family members who had attended the sentencing. In the locked room, her eighteen-year-old daughter sang, "I'll take you home, Kathleen." It had been one of Marty's favorite songs, and it had inspired him to name his daughter Kathleen. After an emotional farewell, Sara Jane's last words to the crowd were, "Thank you for coming. I love you." She was then flown to Sacramento in a sheriff's plane to await her next court hearing on the following Tuesday on the charge for the murder of Myrna Opsahl.

Jon Opsahl had appeared near tears during the sentencing. He said later that he felt truly sorry for Olson's family and friends. "I am sure they will adjust as we did when we had our mother ripped from our home," he said. He added, "Her apology was too little, too late."

Laurie Levinson, the Loyola Law School professor, said after the testimonies that it was possible that the Sacramento murder charges might provide "the ultimate pressure" for Olson to cooperate by telling authorities what happened inside the Carmichael bank. Although her credibility was certainly questionable ("She never says the same thing twice"), Levinson thought a taste of prison might sway her to cooperate.

Sacramento: A Reunion

On Tuesday, hands shackled at their waists and ankles, dressed in green pullover shirts and orange jail pants, Emily Montague (Harris) and Bill Harris stood before another judge in Sacramento for their own arraignment in Myrna Opsahl's murder. Gone was Bill's long, curly dark hair, replaced by a gray coif, combed straight back, and a neatly trimmed beard. He'd put on pounds over the years, and with his wire-rimmed glasses, he resembled a college professor. Harris informed the judge that he could not afford an attorney so he was appointed a San Francisco lawyer, Charles Bourdon, to represent him.

Emily didn't look any more like the radical either, but she appeared as tense and high-strung as she had been in her youth. Her face was pale, and she constantly rubbed her fingers together, the same nervous habit that Jim Kilgore had accused her of in the Crocker National Bank (playing with her watch band) when according to Patty Hearst, Emily accidentally pulled the trigger. Montague squinted through wire-rims, her short blond hair neatly swept back in a conservative cut, and wrinkles etching her eyes and neck.

Unlike her former husband, Emily could afford her own attorney, and she hired Stuart Hanlon. He said that Bill and Emily were strong members of their communities. "They are not guilty, and we will fight this case." He blasted prosecutors for deciding to bring the evidence to light now—it was "unfair" because of the length of time since the robbery. Now it would be more difficult for the Harrises to defend themselves. "These charges should have been brought back then, but they weren't." He feared that his clients would be portrayed as terrorists because of September 11. When he was asked about the timing of the arrests, he speculated that the prosecutors may have put pressure on Olson to testify against her former comrades, he said, "I don't think that's going to happen."

On the same day, in a Portland courtroom, Mike Bortin appeared before a judge in a blue jail outfit and glasses. He had been charged for being a fugitive and did not enter a plea. "I would like to state for the record that I am not a fugitive and that I have been a legal resident of the state of Oregon for twelve years." The judge informed him that the California governor's office would have to request his extradition from Oregon to face the murder charge and that might take up to five weeks. Until then he would be held without bail.

Shawn Chapman was appointed to defend Sara Jane Olson. Chapman said of the SLA bank robbery plot, "There's nothing Sara Jane could offer them. She has always said she knew these people [SLA] and helped them in small ways but was never admitted to the inner circle, never asked to do big criminal acts, so she doesn't know about the Carmichael bank robbery."

All of the defendants pleaded, "not guilty" and their attorneys requested that the bail be low since none of their clients were flight-risks. That decision would be made in a week on February 1, 2002.

Jim Kilgore was still the missing link. The FBI offered a $20,000 reward for his apprehension. Kilgore probably now looked like the rest of his comrades, middle-aged, gray hair, and probably a bit pudgy. He had been nearsighted when he was young, and it was a good bet that he wore bifocals now. The FBI said that Kilgore had been the SLA's bomb maker and he had been a suspect as the Unabomber before Ted Kaczynski was arrested for the crimes. In the seventies Kilgore had blue eyes and brownish-red hair. He was five-feet-ten, stocky, and weighed 175 pounds. He played golf, basketball, and baseball. Perhaps he, too, was a soccer dad.

Rachel Harp had been a twenty-one-year-old assistant to the loan department manager in the Crocker National Bank in 1975. She had sat about twenty feet from where Myrna Opsahl was shot. She remembered Mrs. Opsahl's moans and the masked woman yelling for everyone to lie down. Patrons and tellers were screaming and crying. When the robbers fled, she had gone to the bank's kitchen for paper towels to try to stop Mrs. Opsahl's bleeding. Now, after the arrests, she said that for all these years, she had suffered a "residue of anger, fear, and wariness. It never faded," she told reporters from the *Los Angeles Times*. "They didn't just shoot her that day, they took part of us away too." She added that at the time, she had tried to tell the authorities what had actually happened in the bank that day, but they only wanted to focus on Steven Soliah. She tried again after *Every Secret Thing* was published because it corroborated her account. No one would listen.

Carolyn Reese's husband had been a doctor with Trygve Opsahl at American River Hospital the day they brought Myrna in on a gurney. "Can you imagine the shock of finding out that this is your friend and, more unfortunately, that this poor soul is your beloved, cherished wife? I have grieved for her for twenty-seven years. Those people were heartless," she said.

The newspapers had a field day with all of the latest developments. Tim Findley at the *New York Times* had covered the SLA for the *San Francisco Chronicle* back in the seventies and he said that it had all been haunting. He had received the SLA's first communiqué in November 1973 claiming the credit for assassinating Marcus Foster. "Nothing if not theatrical," he called them. He referred to Sara Jane Olson as a loose-change wannabee and an amateur thespian.

But now, seeing all of them in the courtroom, he referred to them as "aging revolutionaries, Peter Pan's pirates with sagging jowls and thinning white hair." He speculated, as did many other reporters, that the SLA was more about leading a wild, gangster life rather than instigating social change. If they had not kidnapped Patty Hearst, they would have remained unknown.

After twenty-seven years, they were all drawn together again, this fringe group of revolutionaries that had once declared war on the bourgeois, the very capitalist establishment that they had all eventually joined. They had jobs, mortgages, took vacations, volunteered in their community, and cooked gourmet meals.

Mike Bortin once said, "There's not this dichotomy between what Kathy was and what she is now. She was doing the same things in the early seventies. You can't fake a resumé for twenty-five years." In the *Sacramento Bee,* Marjie Lundstrum seemed to agree with him. "Appearances may change, but people don't. Not what lies beneath."

On January 19, 2002, the *Star Tribune* editorial staff wrote: "Whatever sympathy or ire Olson's story may inspire, a few things must be remembered: First, bomb plots and murderous bank heists don't count as activism. Second, neither cooking skill nor time diminishes culpability. Third, defendants are innocent until they're proven guilty. These are the lessons Olson's case has to teach. Whatever else is wrong with American society, one thing is right: Its people continue to put their hope in the justice system. They believe that peace must be kept, that wrongdoers must be found out, that accusations must be explored, that proven crimes must be punished. These demands of justice should be fulfilled just as readily for a doctor's wife from St. Paul as for a jobless wanderer from Detroit. Surely the activist in Sara Jane Olson would agree."

Timeline

1973

March 5: Donald DeFreeze (Cinque) escapes from Soledad prison.

November 6: Oakland Schools Superintendent Marcus Foster is slain.

1974

January 10: Russell Little and Joseph Remiro are arrested and charged with Foster's murder.

February 4: Patricia Hearst is kidnapped from her Berkeley apartment.

April 15: Patty Hearst is photographed wielding a rifle while robbing the Hibernia Bank in San Francisco. Her new name is "Tania."

May 16: Shooting at Mel's Sporting Goods Store.

May 17: Six members of the SLA die during a shootout with Los Angeles police.

1975

April 21: Myrna Opsahl is killed during the SLA robbery of the Crocker National Bank.

August 21–22: Pipe bombs are placed under two Los Angeles police cars.

September 18: San Francisco police and the FBI find SLA safe-houses on Precita and Morse Streets and arrest Hearst, William and Emily Harris, Wendy Yoshimura, and Steven Soliah.

⌐ *1976*

February 16: A Los Angeles County grand jury indicts Kathleen Soliah on conspiracy charges, accusing her of planting the Los Angeles police car bombs. She has disappeared.

March 20: Hearst is convicted for the Hibernia Bank robbery. She is sentenced to seven years in prison.

April 27: Steven Soliah, the only one charged in the Crocker National Bank robbery, is acquitted in federal court in Sacramento.

⌐ *1977*

April: Patty Hearst names Kathleen Soliah and seven others in the Crocker National Bank holdup where Myrna Opsahl was killed.

⌐ *1979*

February 1: President Jimmy Carter commutes Hearst's sentence, and she is released after serving twenty-one months.

⌐ *1999–2002*

June 16, 1999: Kathleen Soliah, living under the name *Sara Jane Olson*, is arrested in St. Paul, Minnesota.

January 20, 2001: President Bill Clinton pardons Hearst.

October 31, 2001: Olson pleads guilty to two counts of trying to bomb Los Angeles police cars with intent to murder. The court refuses her later attempt to reverse the plea.

December 2001: Jon Opsahl, Myrna Opsahl's son, launches a Web site, myrnaopsahl.com, that details the evidence against the SLA. Pressure mounts on the Sacramento District Attorney to press murder charges against Sara Jane Olson.

January 16, 2002: William Harris, Emily Harris, Michael Bortin, and Olson are arrested and charged with murder in the first-degree for Myrna Opsahl's slaying. James Kilgore, a fugitive, is also charged.

Where Are They Now?

F. Lee Bailey: Bailey practices law in West Palm Beach, Florida. He drew media attention during the O.J. Simpson murder trial with his cross-examination of Los Angeles police detective Mark Fuhrman. The next year, Bailey spent more than six weeks in jail for contempt of court after refusing to turn over $18 million to the government in a drug trafficking case.

H. Rap Brown: In 1991, he was convicted of attempted murder after a shootout in New York City that had occurred twenty years earlier in 1971. He came out of prison five years later with a new name, Jamil Abdullah Al-Amin, and new faith, Islam. He seemed to be a new man, a peaceful man. However, in January 2000, he failed to appear in court on charges of theft by receiving stolen property and impersonating a police officer. When deputies came to serve a warrant on him in that case, they say he opened fire. One of the deputies was killed; another was wounded. Al-Amin was captured in Alabama in an area where he worked as a civil rights organizer. He told reporters after his preliminary hearing in Alabama that the case was "a big government conspiracy." In March 2002, Al Amin was convicted for the crimes, and sentenced to life in prison.

Eldridge Cleaver: Two days after Martin Luther King Jr.'s assassination, Cleaver was shot and wounded. He issued an "executive order" to the Black Panthers to assassinate policemen as a retaliatory measure. Cleaver himself had driven to San Francisco with some other Panthers and personally ambushed a police car, wounding two officers and leaving one with metal fragments permanently in his neck. Cleaver fled to Algeria in 1968 and returned to the United States in 1975 after experiencing a "religious conversion."

Rennie Davis: Davis later became a venture capitalist and lecturer on meditation and self-awareness. One of his workshops was entitled, "Room Without Veils." The workshop promised to "unlock a unique toolbox" that would "allow connection to your own organic intelligence." Topics covered in the workshop included "Navigating Armageddon, "Understanding Your Energy Signature," and "Unlocking Your Innocence." Davis appeared in Chicago for the 1996 Democratic National Convention to appear on a panel with Tom Hayden discussing "a progressive counterbalance to the religious right."

Abbie Hoffman: Years after the 1968 Democratic Convention, Hoffman had plastic surgery and assumed the underground alias of "Barry Freed," a freelance writer-activist, in 1974 to avoid trial on charges of possessing cocaine. He stayed underground in upper New York state until 1980, when he surrendered to authorities. He was sentenced to a work-release program in 1981–82, when he resumed his life of political activism. In 1987, Hoffman was arrested for the forty-second time while protesting CIA recruitment at the University of Massachusetts with Amy Carter and thirteen others. At a 1988 reunion of the Chicago Seven, Hoffman described himself as "an American dissident. I don't think my goals have changed since I was four and I fought schoolyard bullies." On April 12, 1989, Hoffman was found dead at his home in New Hope, Pennsylvania. The death was ruled as a suicide.

William Kunstler: In his autobiography, *My Life as a Radical Lawyer,* Kunstler described his decades of attempting to put the American criminal justice system on trial. His clients over the years included Lenny Bruce, H. Rap Brown, Stokely Carmichael, American Indian Movement leaders, Jack Ruby, Martin Luther King, Malcolm X, and Islamic terrorists. On Labor Day, 1995, William Kunstler died of a heart attack at age 76.

Huey Newton: On August 22, 1989, Newton was gunned down on an Oakland street, in the same neighborhood where he had murdered a police officer twenty years earlier. For the last six years of his life, the former Minister of Defense for the Black Panther Party had been addicted to base cocaine, and he was murdered by a crack dealer who Newton had burned in a drug deal. The funeral program read, "Huey Newton lived just long enough to have been the unknown idealist, a popular and heroic champion of the oppressed." He was "a world hero, our king in shining armor," said one of the eulogists.

Jerry Rubin: Yippie turned Yuppie in the 1980s, as Rubin cut his hair and put on a business suit. He worked on Wall Street and became a business entrepreneur. Rubin was fatally injured in 1994 when he was struck by a car while jaywalking in Los Angeles.

Bobby Seale: Seale now has his own web page in which he describes himself as "the old cripple-footed revolutionary humanist." The web page, entitled "From the Sixties. . . to the Future!", is about getting to the future via the whole syntheses of the quantum, computer and DNA molecular revolutions, and within the cyberspace non-linear range. The web page also includes some of his favorite barbecue recipes.

Bernardine Dohrn and **Billy Ayers:** At fifty-nine years old, Dohrn is director of the Children and Family Justice Center at Northwestern University in Chicago. Ayers teaches at the College of Education at the University of Illinois in Chicago. In 2001, Ayers released his memoirs, *Fugitive Days,* about their life as Weathermen. He was quoted as saying that he did not regret setting bombs as a member of the Weathermen and that he could not rule out doing it again. Some Northwestern alumni threatened to withhold future donations if Dohrn was not fired. They called her an "unrepentant terrorist." The dean defended her.

Joseph Remiro: Remiro is still serving a life sentence at Pelican Bay Prison in California for the Marcus Foster murder.

Russell Little: Little's conviction was overturned due to an error in reading jury instructions. It's reported that he served less than five years in prison and was working as a charter boat captain in Hawaii.

Emily (Harris) Montague: She was released on $1 million bail on February 17, 2002. Her attorney, Stuart Hanlon, commented, "She's feeling great." He added, "She was very thankful there was family and friends who raised this money for her. Her full-time job is now to prove what they have been saying about her for all these years is not true."

William (Bill) Harris: Five days after his former wife was released, Harris posted $1 million bail and left the Sacramento County jail. He reportedly put up property for his bail.

Michael Bortin: On March 15, 2002, he was released from jail after posting $500,000 bail.

James Kilgore: The search for Kilgore had intensified in 1995 when his name came up as a possible Unabomber suspect. He used the same brand of batteries as the Unabomber, although he did not fit the psychological profile. He was also a suspect in the $1 million bombing of the guesthouse at the Hearst Castle in San Simeon and another bombing at the Hearst mountain estate at Wyntoon, Siskiyou County, according to the FBI. There is now a $20,000 reward for his arrest. If anyone has information regarding James Kilgore, please call 1-800-CRIMETV or 415-553-7400.

Selected Bibliography

Alexander, Shana, 1979, *Anyone's Daughter,* Viking

Alpert, Jane, 1981, *Growing up Underground,* Morrow

American Justice, Profiles, Fugitives, Riot

America's Most Wanted

Antelope Valley Press, California

Ayers, William, 2001, *Fugitive Days, A Memoir,* Beacon

Baker, Marilyn, Sally Brompton, 1974, *Exclusive, The Inside Story of Patricia Hearst and the SLA,* MacMillan

Berkeley Barb, California

Boss, Pauline, 1999, *Ambiguous Loss,* Harvard

Boulton, David, 1975, *The Making of Tania Hearst,* New English Library

Bryan, John, 1975, *This Soldier Still at War,* Harcourt, Brace, Jovanovich

Chicago Tribune, *Illinois*

CNN

Court TV

Daily Gazette, Charleston, W. Virginia

Dateline, NBC News

Douglas, John and Mark Olshaker, 1995, *Mind Hunter,* Scribner

Farber, David, 1994, *The Sixties,* Chapel Hill

Feldman, Bob, *Being Left, Years After the 1968 Columbia Revolt Interviews Bernardine Dohrn*

Gitlin, Todd, 1987, *The Sixties, Years of Hope, Days of Rage,* Bantam

Grathwohl, Larry, 1976, *Bringing Down America,* Arlington House

Hayden, Tom, 1988, *Reunion, A Memoir,* Random House

Hearst, Patricia Campbell, Alvin Moscow, 1982, *Every Secret Thing*, Doubleday

Hoffman, Jack, Daniel Simon, 1994, *Run, Run, Run*, Tarcher, Putnam

Hollis, Judi, Ph.D., 1994, *Fat and Furious*, Ballantine Books

Horowitz, David 1997, *Radical Son*, Simon & Schuster

Horowitz, David, Peter Collier, 1989, *Destructive Generation*, Simon & Schuster

Imber-Black, Evan, Ph.D., 1998, *The Secret Life of Families*, Bantam

Jewish Bulletin of Northern California

www.jewishworldreview.com

Jiminez, Janey, as told to Ted Berkman, 1977, *My Prisoner*, Sheed Andrews and McMeel, Inc.

Kelley, Robert, *Transformations, University of California, Santa Barbara, 1909-1979*

Larry King Live, Patty Hearst interviews

Lektric Press

www.lektrik.com/sinc/

Los Angeles Magazine, The Fugitive, Thomas Carney, California

Los Angeles Times, *California*

McLellan, Vin, Paul Avery, 1977, *The Voices of Guns*, G. P. Putnam's Sons

Miller, Sue, 1999, *While I Was Gone*, Ballantine Books

Minnesota Monthly, *Minnesota*

www.myrnaopsahl.com

New York Times, *New York*

Newsweek

Olson, Sara Jane, 1999, *Serving Time, America's Most Wanted Recipes*

Pascal John, Francine Pascal, 1974, *The Strange Case of Patty Hearst*, Signet

Payne, Cril, 1979, *Deep Cover, An FBI Agent Infiltrates the Radical Underground*

Payne, Les, Tim Findley, Carolyn Craven 1976, *Life and Death of the SLA*

Ballantine Books

People magazine

Prime Time Thursday, ABC

Reader's Digest, Bomb Squad

Roth, Philip, 1997, *American Pastoral*, Vintage

Sacramento Bee, *California*

Sacramento Union, *California*

Samenow, Stanton E., Ph. D, 1984, *Inside the Criminal Mind*, Times Books

San Francisco Bay Guardian, *California*

San Francisco Chronicle, *California*

San Francisco Examiner, *California*

San Francisco Gate, *California*

www.saraolsondefense.com

www.Soliah.com

St. Paul Pioneer Press, *Minnesota*

Star Tribune, *Minneapolis, Minnesota*

The Oregonian, *Oregon*

The Recorder/California Law

The Trial of Patty Hearst, Complete Transcripts, 1976, *The Great Fidelity Press*

Thompson, Josiah, 1988, *Gumshoe*, Fawcett

True Believer

Time magazine

Wall Street Journal, *New York*

Walsh, John, 2001, *Public Enemies*, Pocket Books

Acknowledgments

While I was writing this book, its dramatic story was unfolding in the newspapers like scenes from a play. In my wildest imagination, I could not have anticipated the final chapter early on. When Sara Jane Olson's arrest hit the local newspapers, in 1999, a friend said, "Sharon, here is your next book." The seed was planted. I was skeptical about writing about another "woman in trouble," but as with my previous works, I started to collect newspaper articles and court transcripts—just in case. In the beginning, most people I spoke with felt that Sara Jane was being persecuted unfairly. The phrase, "context of the times," came up often. I immersed myself in the history of radical groups of the '60s and '70s, hoping to understand their passions, their reasons for using violence to hasten social change. What would make a person cross that line?

I collected many out-of-print books and was astounded to find out how often the "Soliah" name appeared. I spent hours researching at the Wilson Library at the University of Minnesota, where I pored over *Los Angeles Times* and *San Francisco Chronicle* articles from the seventies. The Soliahs were prominent in those articles as well. More information was available for the asking from police reports and transcripts. And I am so grateful for all the people who went out of their way to help me.

Thank you to FBI agents, Larry Brubaker, Colleen Rowley, and Andrew Black for your information and assistance; Ray DiPrima—DiPrima Investigations, as always for your friendship and your leads; Debbie Fallehy of the Oakland Police Department; Mark Morris and Randy Allen at the *Sacramento Bee;* Tim Berger at the *San Gabriel Valley* newspaper; Lisa Nelson at A/P Wire Photos for your assistance (keep writing); Mitchell Pearlstein; Deborah Rybak at the *Star Tribune* in Minneapolis; Karen Dollinson at the *Barnesville Record Review;* Kyle Christopherson—Assistant Public Information Officer for Los Angeles Superior Court; Joan Magruder—UCSB Director of Media Relations, and the Special Collections Department of the Davidson Library, UCSB; artist Wendy Yoshimura for inviting me into your home; Sandi Gibbons, Public Information Officer at the D.A.'s office in Los Angeles, for your information and your sense of humor; to Eleanor Hunter and Michael Latin—Deputy District Attorneys of the Major Crime Division in Los Angeles, for your hospitality; to Gerald Parker for sharing; and to Jon Opsahl.

For your insightful critiques, mailings, advice, and support: David Kidwell, Nan Wisherd, Martha Marchand, Bill Marchand, Mardene Eichhorn, Mary Logue, Esq. Bob Awsumb, Rita McMahon, Robyn Cook, Sue Gilhoi, Pam Leinberger, Juleen Close, Priscilla Nei, Lynda Henes, Mary LeBow, Karen Majewski, Brian Dec, Terrance Slogar, Priscilla Nei, and Peggy Watson. Thanks to my stimulating book club, Tuesdays with Books; Jack Cole and the Hennepin County Library Foundation Board; Archie Spencer and the Midwest Independent Publisher's Association (MIPA); and Jack Golan for your website, input, and incredible research.

Special thanks to Greg Lang and www.soliah.com. What would I have done without your e-mails? You are a generous man.

Thank you to my editors, Kate Green, and Marybeth Lorbiecki for making me accountable and encouraging me to rise to the occasion; To Paula Schanilec and Kellie Hultgren for your fine-tuning; Megan Junius and Peter Hill at Axon Garside Hill for a great cover; John Kudrle at the Bookmen for your continued support; and Wendy Holdman at Stanton Publication Services for your design work and your professionalism.

To Gene Steven Darby (my favorite brother) for my website www.soliah-sla.com; my husband, Bruce, who read draft after draft without complaining—you have more patience than anyone I've ever met; my children, Amy and Jill and my son-in-law Rob, who always encouraged me. I am a lucky woman.

About the Author

Sharon Darby Hendry divides her time between the Twin Cities and northern Wisconsin. Her first manuscript, *An Element of Truth*, a true story about a woman con artist, was translated into a made-for-TV movie, starred Donna Mills, and aired on CBS in September 1995. Her second book, *Glensheen's Daughter, The Marjorie Congdon Story,* is a regional bestseller.

NC

DISCARD

DEMCO